PROVENCE
THE BEAUTIFUL COOKBOOK

AUTHENTIC RECIPES FROM THE REGIONS OF PROVENCE

Barthelasse Sautéed Chicken (recipe page 122)

AUTHENTIC RECIPES FROM THE REGIONS OF PROVENCE

PROVENCE
THE BEAUTIFUL
COOKBOOK

RECIPES AND FOOD TEXT BY
RICHARD OLNEY

REGIONAL TEXT BY
JACQUES GANTIÉ

FOOD PHOTOGRAPHY BY
PETER JOHNSON

STYLED BY
JANICE BAKER

SCENIC PHOTOGRAPHY BY
MICHAEL FREEMAN

HarperCollinsPublishers

First published in USA 1993
by Collins Publishers San Francisco.
Reprinted in 1993; 1998; 1999

Produced by Weldon Owen Inc.
814 Montgomery Street
San Francisco, CA 94133 USA
Phone (415) 291 0100 Fax (415) 291 8841

Chairman: Kevin Weldon
President: John Owen
General Manager: Stuart Laurence
Co-Editions Director: Derek Barton
Publisher: Jane Fraser
Senior Editor: Anne Dickerson
Editorial Assistant: Jan Hughes
Copy Editor: Sharon Silva
Proofreader: Jonathan Schwartz
Translator: Barbara McGilvray
Production: Stephanie Sherman, Mick Bagnato
Design: Tom Morgan, Blue Design
Production Assistant: Jennifer Petersen
Design Concept: John Bull, The Book Design Company
Photography Editor: Sandra Eisert
Map: Kenn Backhaus
Illustrations: Diana Reiss-Koncar
Index: Frances Bowles
Assistant Food Stylists: Cara Hobday, Liz Nolan,
    Amanda Biffin
Photographic Assistants: Robert White, Miriam Miller

For information address HarperCollins Publishers, Inc.,
10 East 53rd Street, New York, NY 10022.

Library of Congress Cataloging-in-Publication Data:

Provence, the beautiful cookbook : authentic
    recipes from the regions of Provence / recipes
    and food text Richard Olney ; regional text
    Jacques Gantié ; food photography by Peter
    Johnson ; styled by Janice Baker ; scenic
    photography by Michael Freeman.
        p.   cm.
    Includes index.
    ISBN 0-00-255154-3 : $45.00
    1. Cookery, French—Provençal style.
    2. Cookery—France—Provence. 3. Provence
    (France)—Description and travel.
    I. Olney, Richard. II. Grantié, Jacques.
    TX719.2.P75P76   1993
    641.59449—dc20   93–55
                                         CIP
        ISBN 0-06-757598-6 (pbk.)

Printed by Toppan in China

A Weldon Owen Production

*Endpapers: Romanesque statues adorn a facade in Aix en
Provence.*

*Pages 2-3: The sweeping valleys of Alpes-de-Haute-Provence
are some of the most tranquil and least populated regions
of Provence.*

*Right: The Carmargue is the French Wild West: home to
fighting bulls, wild horses and the gardians, French cowboys.*

*Pages 8-9; left to right: Gratin of Mashed Potatoes and
Garlic with Cheese (recipe page 176), Turnip Gratin
(recipe page 201).*

*Pages 12-13: A charming, unpretentious fishing village along
the Riviera, Cassis offers a quiet harbor, excellent seafood
restaurants and celebrated local white wines.*

At Domaine Tempier, Bandol, from left to right: Macédoine of Fruits in Bandol Wine (recipe page 236), Creamy Lemon Custard (recipe page 238)

CONTENTS

A palette of warm, Mediterranean ochers and yellows pervades Provençal art and architecture.

PROVENCE:
CUISINES OF THE SUN

Those who look at Provence in a distant and detached way no doubt find it a single region with no precise definition. Yet this is a profoundly false impression. Provence is not one but many regions, and those who care to explore its depths and discover its secrets, who seek to understand its culinary truths, will speak of "the Provences," in the same way as the historian or the geographer approaches this amazing southeastern corner of France.

The plural, in fact, appropriately defines these lands of the sun, which do not allow themselves to be tamed easily. Nor is it a simple matter to know their flavors. This is a region whose personality is revealed only to those who take the time to pursue it: to those prepared to take their taste as a leisurely stroll, who know that the garden's treasures are not to be devoured but rather looked at, conversed with, gathered with love and then eaten in relaxed enjoyment.

There is no question, then, that there are Provences, plural. The Provence of the high country where the mistral blows, icy and biting at times, after it has swept along the valley of the Rhône, is not the Provence of the dazzling white coves between Marseilles and Cassis. Nor is it that of the peaceful hills of the Var, the ochers of the Esterel or the villages perched high on the Alpes-Maritimes where culinary traditions have their origins among mountains and valleys and where the bright, popular accents of Italian influence are seen.

Of course, the country air is the same, from melodious Vaucluse to the Lubéron, from Digne to Les Baux-de-Provence, from the golden dreams of Saint-Tropez to Nice, Cannes, Menton. To pause at each is like visiting different members of the same family.

And if Provence wants more attention, it has only to extract from beneath its oaks, its walnut and chestnut trees up in the hinterland, around Aups or between Ventoux and the Lubéron, its rich storehouse of truffles, brought here from the Balkans or from the Middle East first by the Romans and later by the Italians of the Renaissance.

In Provence, cooking is an artist's affair. Neither too much shadow nor too much sun. Neither excessive colors nor dominant flavors. In such conditions, with *la joie de vivre* everywhere, the culinary treasures of Provence become eloquent. This character is reflected in thick soups that whet the appetite and yet are the simplest concoctions in the world: served cold at midday—fish soup, tomato soup, crab soup—or in more robust versions in the evening—broad (fava) bean soup, squash soup, green bean soup. Great classics such as *aïoli, bouillabaisse, brandade de morue* (creamed salt cod*), bourride* (fish soup with *aïoli*), a variety of daubes, and *pot-au-feu* echo the same eloquence.

So, too, do *pan bagnat,* in which the classic *niçois* ingredients of tomato, olives, sweet peppers (capsicums), young broad beans and so on are sandwiched between

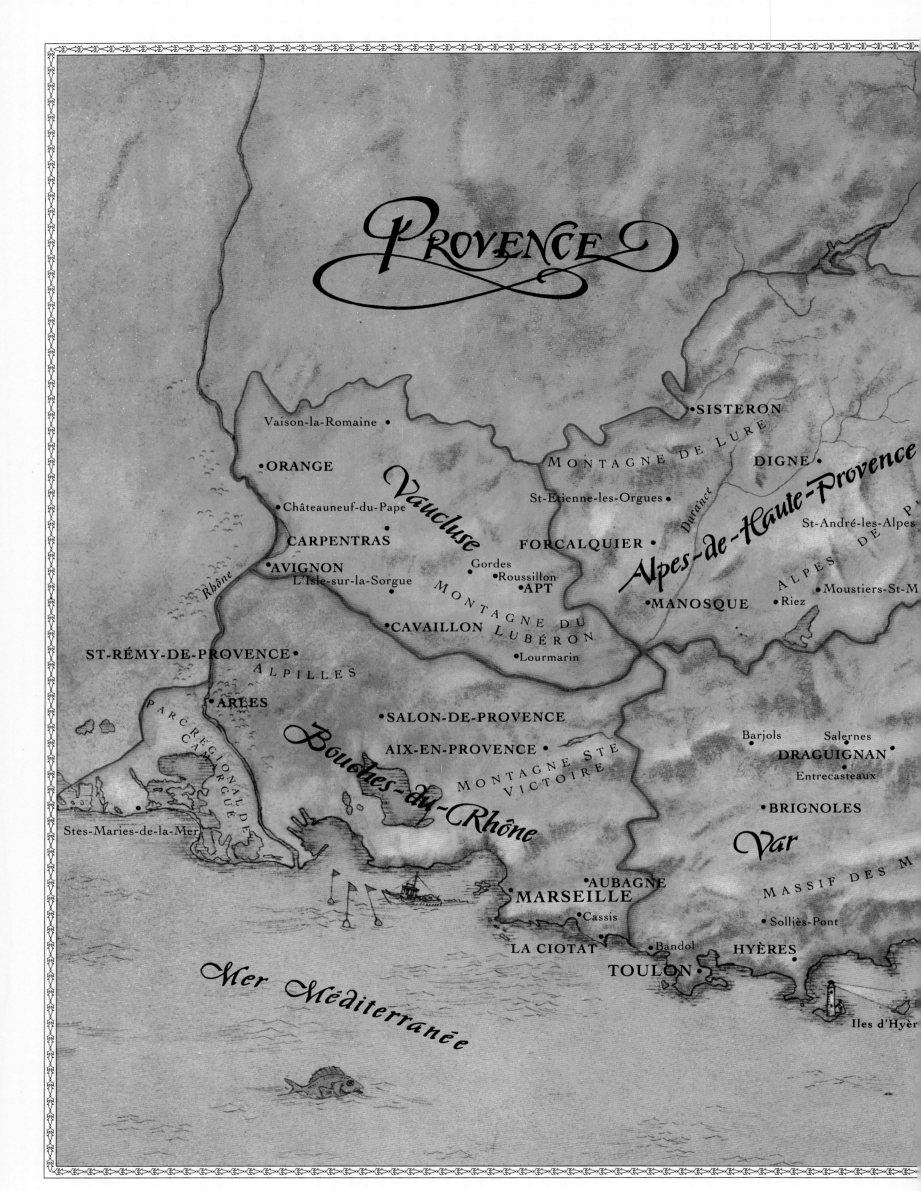

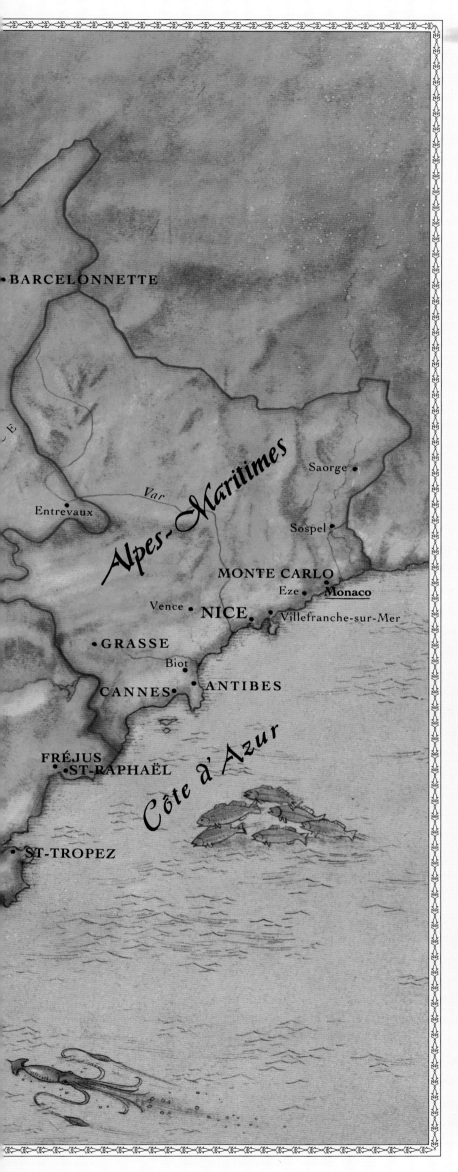

halves of French bread, and with the *casse-croûte,* or snack, known in the *niçois* dialect by its Italian name *merenda,* which is put together from next to nothing—toasted bread rubbed with garlic, *tapénade* or *anchoïade,* or even *panisses,* those *bonnes pâtes* made from chick-pea flour that have given their name to one of Marcel Pagnol's heroes. Although these may sound like foods for the famished, they are in fact the first rays of the cuisine of the sun.

As we approach the end of the century, notable chefs, some of whom work in Provence, have realized the importance of these simple preparations and have turned them into fashionable and delicious "back-to-the-country" food. In days gone by these providential morsels provided a treat for the peasants; today it is well-heeled gourmets who go into raptures over them, with no thought of ever laboring in fields! Without knowing it they are emulating the Countess de Sévigné, who wrote enthusiastically in a letter of 1694: "These partridges fed on thyme and marjoram . . . the white, sweet figs, muscat grapes like edible grains of amber that would certainly make the head swim if one were to eat them indiscriminately. . . . What a life, my dear cousin!"

The Provences have their distinctive moods and personalities, however. Writers and artists who have celebrated the south of France have discovered for us, as only poets can, their differences and hidden truths. Jean Giono, Marcel Pagnol, Alphonse Daudet, Colette, Zola, Matisse, Picasso, Signac, Cocteau, Dufy, Cézanne and Van Gogh were unerring in their words and their colors, and it was no uncertain country they evoked when they took the time to live and create in Aix, Manosque, Arles, Nice or Saint-Tropez.

The balmy weather of the Côte d'Azur attracts street musicians and people watchers to seaside cafés throughout the year.

Outdoor restaurants of Old Nice welcome patrons enjoying the summertime pleasures of the Côte d'Azur.

18

Likewise, the chefs of Provence, and before them the mothers of families who spent hours, or even days preparing soups, terrines, fritters and daubes, have always been able to find the correct proportions, experiment with flavorings and gauge quantities of the products of the sun according to whether they live on a hillside, in the depths of the valley, in a village atop a mountain or in the shelter of a fishing port.

But while places and people have their importance, it is when hunger calls and we sit down at the table that we uncover special idiosyncrasies of these golden lands and what constitutes the common language spoken throughout Provence. It is the language of the joy of cooking, a language that demands the use of *une pointe d'ail*—that is to say, "a touch of garlic"—the minute amount that clings to the tip of the knife.

It also demands that dishes be flavored with an olive oil that comes, if possible, from one of the last remaining independent presses in Maussane, Oppède, the Rouret, Contes, Nyons, Cucuron or another of the sacred places where people still process the olives grown on their own land. Sometimes it will be a light oil for cooking, and by all means a fruity one for salads. Once upon a time the aptly named, although today to some extent forgotten, *olivade* was the commonest of all family celebrations. The peasants marked the festivities by making *aïoli,* or by crushing garlic and anchovies onto chunks of bread steeped in virgin olive oil and toasting them over the fire.

And it demands that the dishes of the sun be enriched, in moderation, of course, with aromatic herbs whose use is limited only by the need not to be so

The church bell tower is the centerpiece of Bargemon, a quaint village perched in the austere countryside of northeastern Var.

The Alpes-Maritimes backcountry is home to timeless hamlets where old traditions endure.

aggressive as to "kill" a dish. Rosemary, basil, bay leaf, fennel, mint, marjoram, thyme and saffron all provide intelligent company when wisely used.

While Provençal cooking enraptures poet and traveler alike, it does not put on airs. Indeed, from the Alps to the Mediterranean it is often dubbed the "poor man's cuisine." This is exactly what gives it strength and imagination. Other regions of France possess more obvious wealth and traditions, and to the eyes of the world are seen as the culinary power brokers and custodians of the science of taste. They will keep you at the table for hours. Here, impetuous winds (the mistral off the water and the *tramontana* from the north), a burning sun, dry earth and the brisk, choppy sea have dictated other, more immediate rituals and knowledge.

Provence, before it became a pacific territory to be conquered only by the tourist, experienced much unhappiness and many invasions in the course of its history. It learned from such excursions to nourish its men and women to live long and to live on little.

In the old days, when knowledge and communication were passed on by word of mouth, families got together to share bread on their return from the fields or the hills, and on various important occasions. One such celebratory gathering centered around the *gros souper,* or "big supper," held on December 24. It called for not only thirteen round bread loaves placed in the center of the table, but also for thirteen desserts—the array a symbol of Christmas in Provence—including raisins, figs, almonds, walnuts, pears, apples and nougats.

A Provençal count wrote the following description of *un gros souper* early in the nineteenth century: "First, the '*raito,*' a kind of hash of cod or eel, different species of fish,

The colorful maze of twisting streets, narrow windows and wrought iron lampposts give the old town quarter of Nice its characteristic charm.

The café is an intrinsic part of Provençal life; here couples enjoy afternoon refreshments while taking in the scenes of Marseilles.

Grasse, known as the perfume capital of France, has had distilleries since the 16th century; here a worker prepares fresh rose petals for the extraction vat.

grilled, and raw artichokes, cardoons, celery and various kinds of vegetables make up the first course. The first tablecloth is removed and then the *calenos* are set down; these consist of cakes, dried fruits, jams, biscuits and sweetmeats. The dessert may be more or less sumptuous according to the family's affluence. But cakes, dried fruits and chestnuts are always present. Nor are the wines and liqueurs forgotten."

Alas, today such venerable culinary customs and day-to-day formalities have largely disappeared. Despite their absence, however, the gourmand inheritance has not been wasted. Indeed, this cuisine has developed into one of the lightest in the world: an art of good living that inspires our daily diet and that a handful of great chefs in the kitchens of the finest restaurants in Provence and on the Côte d'Azur interpret and export in their individual ways. These masters have given a new style and new clothes to the ancient recipes. But their imagination, which characterizes the cuisine of the sun and the gastronomy of the south, has not brought an end to simple ideas. Provence has provided these artists and the rest of us with the foundations of a cultural inheritance.

Alpes-Maritimes

ALPES-MARITIMES

S ome call *niçoise* cooking "cuisine of the poor," or at worst an Italian cuisine and at best an Italo-*niçoise* one. What happens to this sunny, spirited table in the Alpes-Maritimes, where we are no longer quite in Provence and not yet in Piedmont or Lombardy, the area's neighboring Italian regions, that makes people pay such scant regard to its originality and traditions?

The end of the century is fast approaching and it is becoming increasingly difficult to gain recognition and respect for the culinary traditions of the Nice region. It is as if there were a European movement absorbing this delicious idiosyncracy into a more general concept of Provençal cuisine or Mediterranean cuisine, even though today the area clearly functions as a school in the development of French taste and gastronomy.

And yet when we speak of this *département* in far southeastern Provence, of its sea, hills and mountains, these very *niçoises* traditions are the only ones we can rely on: the traditions of a county that was tied to France back in 1860. History's invasions here met plenty of obstacles. The highlands of Nice, Grasse and Menton, made up of mountain passes and valleys (Roya, Tinée, Vésubie, Var) were coveted, in succession, by the Greeks, the Romans, the Genoese, the Savoyards, the Piedmontese, and the Sardinians. These invaders did not try to put down lasting roots in this mountainous and hostile country, where mules followed the "salt route" between the fifteenth and the nineteenth centuries, transporting the precious commodity along the

Previous pages: The medieval village of Peillon captures the rosy glow of a Mediterranean sunset. Left: A part of France only since 1860, the old section of Nice retains its distinctly Italian character.

25

peaks that connected Nice with Tende, passing through the villages of Lucéram, Sospel, Lantosque and Saorge.

This hilly country is somewhat secluded, but it lights up as soon as one begins climbing around the many villages that cling to its peaks or to the sides of *baous* (the Provençal term for *rocks*): Bonson, Saint-Jeannet, Peillon, Gattières, Gourdon, Cabris, Saorge, Marie, Sainte-Agnès, Utelle. In fact it was here, where carefully tended plots cling to rocky cliffs, that kitchen-garden cuisine originated: a family-based and fiercely independent style of cooking that has laid down its flavors over the centuries.

It is a cuisine of contrasts, spontaneous and subtle, much like the land itself, which moves into a rapid ascent while still in view of the sea and boldly plays at mountains. In these gallant hills in days gone by, the women of the house transformed the family plots into countless bastions of the products of the sun.

Family kitchen gardens were, in effect, closed, sacred places that established the reputation of this so-called poor cuisine. All that came out of them in those early days were a few goat's milk products; the only fat was contributed by the solitary pig that many families possessed up to the beginning of the present century. Yet it was a complex and aromatic cuisine, rich in its own way, and above all a cuisine of patience.

The mountain area begins very close to Nice. In these tiny hilltop heavens we find, not far from the olive—the king of Provence trees—and the fig, the legendary plants that nourish the Mediterranean: vegetables, the region's chief treasures.

The vegetables too are "poor." There is the onion, the heart of the *pissaladière,* a tart garnished with anchovies and black olives. Chick-peas are used to make the famous *socca,* a large, flat cake cooked (in olive oil, naturally) in a hot wood-fired oven, and still served today, cut into

The quiet life is enjoyed by the locals in Alpes-Maritimes, the less populous, vast back-garden of the French Riviera.

golden slices, on the streets that surround the vegetable markets of picturesque Nice and Menton.

Then there are the more sun-drenched vegetables, such as corn, served as polenta if you wish, or tomatoes, which first appeared here in the mid-fifteenth century. And one must not forget broad (fava) beans (the young ones, *févettes,* consumed raw); the renowned zucchini (courgette), the pale green Cinderella of the kitchen garden that is indispensable to a ratatouille (eaten just warm, of course) or prepared as a gratin or fritters; or the sweet pepper (capsicum); artichoke; fennel or eggplant (aubergine). And finally there is Swiss chard (silverbeet), most notably used in a sweet tart scented with orange flower water or brandy called *tourta de blea,* one of the most famous desserts in the county of Nice.

Those who seek to rediscover the tastes and traditions of earlier times love the miracle products that illuminate a particular cuisine. In the Alpes-Maritimes these roles are filled by the inevitable, ever-present garlic (in the old days it was a custom in Nice for people to throw whole cloves into the fire on the Festival of Saint Jean, to guard against bad luck); fennel, sage, rosemary, thyme and the famous *balico* ("basil"), pounded in a mortar with garlic, Parmesan and olive oil to make *pistou.* Even the salad here asserts its individuality, in a lively mixture of escarole, lettuce, curly endive (chicory), arugula (rocket) and other greens called *mesclun.*

Of course Italy is close by, and the *niçois* region also embraces influences from Piedmont and the Ligurian coast. Ravioli, *gnocchi, capellini,* and *tortellini* are part of the local culinary history, as evidenced by the giant ravioli banquet prepared for the Stacada, a historic festival organized every four years in Breil-sur-Roya north of Menton. Ravioli, however, are almost an everyday dish. They are, in fact, the ubiquitous *raïlolas* seen at country feasts in the *niçois* highlands, although these days one can no longer guarantee that they are *cousus main,* that is, handmade.

As has been explained, the history of the county of Nice is not a closed one. An illustration of this is the presence of stockfish, or *estocaficada,* the most surprising of all popular dishes. Its strong smell is its best defense against democratization. And yet it comes from afar. It is the cod of the Atlantic peoples, the haddock of the Scandinavians.

In the nineteenth century, Mediterranean navigators took their olive oil in barrels to Norway, and, so they would not have to come home with empty boats, accepted in exchange cases of smoke-dried haddock, which the Scandinavians called stick fish. The French sailors might just as well have called it money, for once they reached the port at Nice or Villefranche, they used the stockfish to pay their *camalous,* the dockers who unloaded the cargo. Then it was up to local cooks to soak this foreign fish for over a week and restore it to life and a kind of unobtrusive charm with red sweet peppers (capsicums), garlic, onions, tomatoes, potatoes and the small black olives—*piccholines*—so typical of the Nice region. The *niçois* writer Louis Nucera evokes this culinary devotion thus: "The grandmother is camped by her stove. For a week this conspiracy has kept her laboring here, for that is how long the stockfish has been soaking in constant changes of water . . . saucepans, stew pot, sauté pan and steamer surround the cook. All these play a role in the preparation and separate cooking processes." And so the famous Nice *ragoût* was born, a classic dish for Friday, traditionally a meatless day, and one whose memory is still rigorously

Originally named for the cane surrounding its marshes, Cannes, now famous for its international film festival, is dubbed the French Beverly Hills.

protected in Nice by an association of purists set up in 1905 called *L'estocaficada.*

This then is a Provençal cuisine, certainly, but one that sits on the fringe of other cuisines. The cuisine *du pays nissart,* as it is called, is so closely linked to the work of the grandmothers of earlier times that a former mayor of Nice, Jacques Médecin, decided one day to pay homage to them. He wrote *The Cuisine of the County of Nice,* which is still used as a reference for its 300 recipes. In it are tastes and words that only truly sing when they are expressed in the *niçois* dialect: *lou pietch* (stuffed veal), and the *bagna cauda* (a fondue of Piedmont origin) over which, again in the words of Louis Nucera, "the grandmother keeps watch; at the merest hint of steam she would feel herself disgraced." Then there are *porchetta,* stuffed suckling pig, admittedly of central Italian origin; *trule,* a sausage made with herbs; *merda de can, gnocchi* rolled by hand, filled with chard and strewn with Parmesan; and, finally, the all-too-rare *poutine,* minute baby fish that can only legally be caught between Antibes and Menton during a forty-five-day period from February to April, thanks to an imperial charter dating back to the time of Sardinian rule before 1860.

So it is not the Nice of the Promenade des Anglais, the casinos or the town houses of the middle-class suburb of Cimiez that speaks to the culinary heart. It is instead the town painted in Italian colors, the cottage industries, and the narrow streets of Old Nice. It is not so far removed after all from the town Raoul Dufy painted, at times just a simple outline seen through a window between a row of palms and the seashore.

Finally, the people of Nice do not have to go far to survey their vine plantings or to find the right accompani-

ment, if required, for their popular dishes. The Bellet vines on the hills next to the Var plain belong to a pocket-sized winery of roughly 150 acres (about sixty hectares) that recently celebrated its fiftieth year, although its vines go back more than five centuries. It is a vineyard so precious that at the time of the French Revolution, when all the village names containing reference to religion had to be changed, the inhabitants of Saint-Roman (of Bellet) chose the name of Bacchus! The vine growers here between Château de Crémat and Château de Bellet, with their subtle reds and wonderfully fine whites, continue to resist the concrete that is steadily creeping up from the valleys.

And if we are talking about the real Provence, we must go up to Villars sur Var in the hills, where the microscopic realm of M. Sassi, Clos Saint-Joseph, officially attached to the Côtes de Provence, is conducting its own resistance, with less than eight acres (three hectares)!

The abundance of local blessings almost forbids the suggestion the *niçoise* cuisine is a cuisine of the poor. Nonetheless it is true that these days the authentic eating places, restaurants offering genuine *niçoise* cuisine, can almost be counted on the fingers of one hand.

But even if the guardians of the temple are disappearing one by one, we still have the memory of this cuisine, and on a larger scale this time. The Alpes-Maritimes have the first Museum of Culinary Art, between Nice and Saint-Paul-de-Vence at Villeneuve-Loubet. The famous Auguste Escoffier Museum is named for one of the most innovative French chefs of the late nineteenth and early twentieth century— the creator of peach Melba—who was born here in 1846 and went on to conquer Paris, Monte Carlo, Lucerne, Rome and London (first at the Savoy and later at the Carlton).

SOUPS AND
STARTERS

Mixed spices create a splash of color and texture in an open market in Moustiers-Ste-Marie.

SOUPS AND STARTERS

In Provence traditions are tenacious. Although the midday meal is now called *déjeuner* instead of *dîner*, in the villages and in family life it is still the main meal of the day. For those whose days are composed of long hours of physical labor—farmers, vineyardists, masons—a morning break at 8:30, called *le casse-croûte matinal*, is usual; it consists of charcuterie, cheese, bread and red wine, often supplemented by cold flat omelets, *pan bagnat* or another easily transportable local specialty.

Except for special occasions, supper is a light meal, usually soup followed by cheese and a fruit. When the soup is an unthickened broth, it is poured over semidry slices of bread, called *croûtes,* or "crusts," which may have been first anointed with olive oil. Many soups—indeed, some of the best—are simple combinations of finely cut-up vegetables or shredded greens boiled in water or broth and poured over crusts. Recipes for soups often finish with the phrase *Trempez votre soupe,* which might be translated "Soak your sop," and which means "pour the soup over slices of bread placed in a soup tureen," a reminder that originally *soupe* was the piece of bread over which one poured a hot liquid.

Provençal cooking is home cooking. The inventions of professional cooks "in the Provençal mode" never ring true. Stocks, *demi-glace* and sauce bases are unknown to the Provençal housewife or to the men who gather in country cabins to roast hunted birds or to boil a *bouillabaisse* over an open fire. When it is available, leftover *pot-au-feu* broth is the base for many soups and it enrichens daubes, braised vegetables or rice. For this reason, *pot-au-feu* is presented at the beginning of the soup section. The term, *pot-au-feu,* applies both to the pot and to the food prepared in it. A traditional *pot-au-feu* is a large, deep earthenware pot with slightly bulging sides and a slightly rounded bottom. Sizes vary, but an average pot holds ten quarts (10 l), is ten inches (25 cm) deep and measures nine inches (23 cm) in diameter at the brim. Any large, heavy, deep pot can replace it; enameled ironware *pot-au-feu* pots are manufactured.

When the kitchen contains no meat broth, the Provençal cook does not wring his or her hands in despair. Instead, water, wine or vegetable cooking liquid is substituted; chick-pea cooking liquid is especially admired. Plain water is better than that tainted by bouillon cubes.

Chick-peas, hardly eaten elsewhere in France, are adored in Provence, but in the entire repertory of Provençal cuisine only two "recipes" occur. Chick-peas are prepared as a salad, normally a first course but many willingly transform a chick-pea salad into a whole meal, preceding it with olives and *saucisson,* radishes or seasonal crudités. Leftover chick-peas are puréed with their cooking liquid to make a wonderful soup, accompanied with a dish of little croutons fried in olive oil.

The Provençal table is an intimate reflection of the seasons, of the native passion for raw things, be they from the sea, the uncultivated hillsides or the kitchen garden, and for freshly cooked vegetables, accompanied by olive

Previous pages, left to right: Marinated Fennel (recipe page 34), Stuffed Tomatoes and Zucchini (recipe page 62)

oil and lemon or vinegar. This is never more evident than in the luncheon starters, replete with tastes and textures that cannot be translated into recipes.

From September through April, a selection of sea urchins, *vioulets,* mussels, a half dozen different clamlike bivalves (*praires, coques, palourdes, clovisses, vernis, dattes de mer,* as well as clams, transplanted from the western Atlantic) and several varieties of oysters, all alive, frequently opens a meal. The small, purple-quilled Mediterranean sea urchins, whose saffron-red corals also transform scrambled eggs, fish soups and fish sauces, are the sweetest and most delicate of all urchins. *Vioulets,* primitive, amorphously shaped creatures that fix themselves to the seabed, go by the particularly appropriate Latin name microcosmus. It describes the incredible deep seascape of plant and animal life adhering to the *vioulets'* wrinkled, leathery exteriors. When cut open, these rough cases expose a heart of tender, yellow flesh with an exquisite lemony sea flavor. They are worshipped on the coast between Marseilles and Toulon and practically unknown elsewhere.

The Provençal gardener plants broad (fava) beans each year in October with the dream of being able to eat raw baby *fèves,* or *fèvettes,* for the new year. The ground nearly always freezes and the first *fèves* do not appear until March. At the raw-eating stage, the pods, warm green, velvety and firm to the touch, are about six inches (15 cm) long and the beans are the size of a little fingernail. A platter heaped high with unshelled broad beans is placed at table and everyone goes to work, shelling. They are eaten *à la croque-au-sel,* each bean first dipped in salt (it is sometimes necessary to moisten it on the tip of the tongue to make the salt cling), and often accompanied with slices of raw ham (prosciutto) from the Alpes-de-Haute-Provence (*jambon de montagne*) or from Bayonne, Corsica or Parma. Rustic bread (*pain au levain*) and cold, unsalted, unpasteurized butter complete the perfection.

Tender, chokeless artichokes appear in November, disappear with the first freezes and come back in February to remain throughout the spring. They are called *poivrade* and are served raw, with pepper mill, salt, vinegar and olive oil at table. Each person prepares a vinaigrette, in the hollow of a tilted plate, in which to dip, first the leaves, then the quartered heart.

Cultivated green asparagus from the Vaucluse (northern France prefers white, Provence prefers green) are around from the end of February until the end of May; they are perfect in March and April. The best of all come from Nice, and are never seen outside of the Alpes-Maritimes. They are only about six inches (15 cm) long, with dark purple tips and an intense flavor with an edge of the sea. Asparagus stalks are peeled, tied in bundles, boiled in salted water until the stalks are barely tender, and served hot or warm, folded in a napkin. The Provençaux have heard of hollandaise but do not consider the possibility of eating asparagus without olive oil. Cruets of oil and vinegar are at table. Individual asparagus plates have a well to one side in which to prepare a vinaigrette, or a normal dinner plate is tilted, the far side propped on a knife or fork, as for the raw artichokes. Asparagus is eaten with one's fingers: dip and bite, dip and bite; it is a ritual celebration.

April is the month of wild asparagus. At the same time that the hillsides turn violet with the blossom of wild thyme, fragile shoots, never more than an eighth of an inch (3 mm) thick, spring from the bases of unsightly, prickly wild asparagus plants. They are collected when eight to ten inches (20–25 cm) long and, in the kitchen, are snapped at the point where the tip turns tender. The tips are rapidly sautéed in olive oil and beaten into eggs to make a *drooly* or *baveuse* (rolled omelet). The flavor is the wild essence of asparagus, the center of the omelet is the voluptuous sauce.

Sweet, orange-red–fleshed melons from Cavaillon, in the Vaucluse, and Hyères, in the Var, begin their summer career the end of May. They are eaten with salt and pepper and, as in Italy, accompanied by slices of raw ham, sliced less thinly than across the border. In the fall, fresh figs escort the ham.

In late June and early July, green almonds appear at the lunch table. They look like green apricots, their still-tender shells, beneath the green, future black husk, easily cut through with a knife; the whitish skin of the nut itself is peeled off to reveal a milk-white, tender-crisp almond of wonderful delicacy. Coarsely chopped green almonds are also added to omelets, salads and myriad desserts.

Tomatoes are in their glory in July and August. A tomato salad can be anything. It is often scattered with black olives, anchovy fillets, sweet onion rings, fresh basil leaves, served in combination with a cucumber salad, or it may be simply fanned-out tomato slices, sprinkled with salt, pepper, olive oil and a few drops of vinegar. In whatever form, it is one of the openers of nearly every summer luncheon.

The only rule seriously respected in Provence is that tomatoes be freshly picked and very firm, with a green blush at the stem ends still visible. Completely ripened tomatoes are reserved for cooking. Throughout the summer, small, tender green beans, topped, tailed, rapidly boiled and served hot with olive oil and lemon sections, provide a delicious luncheon opener. Cauliflower florets, broccoli (stems peeled and sliced), spinach and Swiss chard (silverbeet) are served in the same way.

Garlic reigns as the most essential ingredient in Provençal cooking.

Sweet Pepper Salad

SALADE DE PIMENTS DOUX
Sweet Pepper Salad

*Large red, yellow or green sweet bell peppers, grilled, peeled and
seeded, are a precious addition to any of the salads invented anew
each day in Provence. Choose evenly formed peppers; twisted or
crumpled shapes are difficult to peel. This salad can be enriched
with a latticework of anchovy fillets and a scattering of black olives.*

2 lb (1 kg) large bell peppers (capsicums)
1 clove garlic
large pinch of coarse salt
freshly ground pepper
1 tablespoon Provençal herb vinegar (see glossary)
¼ cup (2 fl oz/60 ml) olive oil
1 sweet white onion, thinly sliced into rings, or 5 or 6
    young green shallots (see glossary) or green (spring)
    onions, sliced
fresh basil sprigs, including leaves and flower buds

◉ Prepare a fire in a charcoal grill or preheat a broiler (griller)
or electric grill. If using a broiler or electric grill, arrange the
peppers on a baking sheet. (Line the baking sheet with aluminum foil to make clean-up easy.) Place the peppers on the grill
rack or under a broiler and grill, turning several times, until the
skins are blistered and irregularly charred on all sides, 20–30
minutes. Place the grilled peppers on a plate and enclose the
plate in a plastic bag with the open end folded beneath the
plate. Let stand for 30 minutes; the steam will loosen the skins.
Working over a bowl to collect any juices, pinch the skins to
loosen them from the core and pull them off. Discard the core,
tear each pepper into 3 or 4 sections and slip off the clinging
seeds with your fingers. Pass all the juices through a small sieve
to remove the seeds. Set aside.
◉ Arrange the pepper sections, peeled sides up and side by side
touching, on a platter. In a mortar pound together the garlic,
salt and pepper to taste to form a paste. Stir in the vinegar, the
reserved pepper juices and, finally, the olive oil.
◉ Spoon the sauce evenly over the peppers and scatter the
onion rings over the surface. Tear the basil leaves into fragments and crumble the flower buds. Scatter over the top.

SERVES 4

ALPES·DE·HAUTE·PROVENCE

PÂTES AUX HERBES

Herb Pasta

An alpine bouquet of green things, wild and cultivated, this pasta is never twice the same, for it depends upon what is available at the moment. Young dandelions, purslane and any other wild salad greens are good elements. In spring when the young shoots are tender, a discreet amount of winter savory is good. Basil and cultivated marjoram flower buds and leaves, lemon balm (melissa), arugula (rocket), hyssop, parsley, sorrel, celery leaves and green (spring) onions can be filled out with spinach or Swiss chard (silverbeet).

large pinch of coarse salt
4–5 oz (125–150 g) mixed fresh herbs and salad greens, chopped (see recipe introduction)
about 3 cups (12 oz/375 g) all-purpose (plain) flour
2 eggs
3–4 tablespoons (4 fl oz/125 ml) tepid water
1 tablespoon olive oil
Parmesan cheese and grater, unsalted butter and pepper mill for serving

◎ In a mortar pound together the salt and herbs and greens to form a paste. Put 2 cups (8 oz/250 g) of the flour into a mixing bowl and make a well in the center. Add the contents of the mortar and the eggs to the well and stir with a fork, moving outward to absorb the flour progressively and adding, if necessary, a bit of warm water or more flour to form a soft but coherent, sticky dough.

◎ Thickly flour a work surface and turn the dough out onto it. Knead repeatedly: turn it in the flour, push with the heel of your hand to stretch it, fold it, turn it in the flour, give it a quarter turn, push it again and so forth—push, fold, flour, turn. The greens progressively release their liquid, absorbing more flour. When the dough is silken and no longer sticky but still supple (it must be soft enough to be easily rolled out by hand), form it into a ball, cover it with a towel and leave to rest for 1 hour.

◎ Scrape the work surface clean, flour it again and roll out the dough about ⅛ in (3 mm) thick, turning it over (flip it or roll it up on the rolling pin) on the floured surface two or three times as you work. Cut it into strips about 1½ in (4 cm) wide and cut across the strips into squares.

◎ Bring a large pot filled with salted water to a boil. Add the oil. Toss the squares loosely in your hands to rid them of excess flour and drop them in the boiling water. When the water returns to a boil, adjust the heat to maintain a gentle boil and cook, stirring regularly with a wooden fork, until tender, about 6 minutes.

◎ Drain and serve in warmed soup plates. Offer cheese, butter and pepper at the table.

SERVES 4

Herb Pasta

MARINADE DE FENOUIL
Marinated Fennel

*Split celery hearts, trimmed; whole or quartered young artichokes
(see glossary); sections of the white parts of leeks; cauliflower florets
or cultivated mushrooms (quartered if large) can be prepared,
separately or in combination, in the same manner as the fennel.
Peeled, seeded, and chopped tomatoes and plumped currants or
raisins may be added with a pinch of sugar and a dash of cayenne.*

2 lb (1 kg) fennel bulbs
bouquet garni (see glossary)
½ lb (250 g) pickling onions
4 cloves garlic, crushed
pinch of fennel seeds
pinch of coriander seeds
½ teaspoon peppercorns, coarsely crushed
salt
5–6 tablespoons (3 fl oz/80 ml) olive oil
juice of 1 lemon
½ cup (4 fl oz/125 ml) dry white wine

◙ Remove the outer stalks of the fennel bulbs. Slice off the
remaining tough stalk ends at an angle; reserve any feathery,
green leaves. Split the bulbs into quarters lengthwise.
◙ Place the bouquet garni in a flameproof earthenware casserole (preferably) or in a saucepan. Arrange the fennel quarters,
onions and garlic in the pan, wasting no space. Scatter over the
dry seasonings. Pour over the oil, lemon juice, white wine and
enough water just to immerse the contents. Bring to a boil,
cover and cook at a gentle boil until the fennel is tender but still
firm, about 25 minutes.
◙ Discard the bouquet garni and pour the contents of the pan
into a terrine or deep serving dish. Let cool and serve at room
temperature or cover and chill before serving. Chop the
reserved fennel leaves and scatter over the top before serving.

SERVES 4 *Photograph pages 28–29*

SALADE FRANCILLON À LA TAPÉNADE
Mussel and Potato Salad with Tapénade

*The cooked potatoes must be peeled and sliced while they are still
hot, in order to absorb the flavor of the mussels' cooking liquid.
Protect your hands from burns by cradling the potatoes in a folded
towel as you handle them.*

2 lb (1 kg) mussels, opened with white wine over heat
   (see glossary)
1 lb (500 g) small, firm yellow-fleshed potatoes
3 or 4 young green shallots (see glossary) or green (spring)
   onions, thinly sliced
FOR THE VINAIGRETTE:
1 tablespoon Provençal herb vinegar (see glossary)
salt and freshly ground pepper
3 tablespoons *tapénade* (recipe follows)
¼ cup (2 fl oz/60 ml) olive oil

◙ Prepare the mussels as directed, reserving the cooking liquid
in a bowl and placing the shelled mussel meats in a salad bowl.
Meanwhile, place the potatoes in a saucepan filled with salted
water, bring to a boil and boil until just done, about 30 minutes.
Drain and peel while hot. As soon as each potato is peeled, slice
it into the bowl containing the mussels' cooking liquid.

◙ When the potatoes are cool, drain them (the mussels' liquid
can be reserved for soup) and join them to the mussels. Then
add the shallots or green onions.
◙ To prepare the vinaigrette, in a small bowl stir together the
vinegar and salt and pepper to taste. Then stir in the *tapénade*
and, finally, the olive oil. Pour the vinaigrette over the salad
ingredients, toss and serve.

SERVES 4

TAPÉNADE
Caper and Black Olive Spread

Tapeno is Provençal for "capers." Reboul, author of La cuisinière
provençale, *writes that tapénade is a creation of his friend,
Meynier, chef at La Maison Dorée in Marseilles during the last
century (others claim that it was known to the ancient Greeks).
In addition to the ingredients listed below, Meynier's recipe contains
marinated tuna, English mustard and Cognac; it contains no garlic.
Serve tapénade at room temperature spread onto individual croutons,
or mashed with hard-cooked egg yolks to stuff hard-cooked egg
whites, or mounded in small, seeded tomatoes, and so on. It is also
a delicious accompaniment to roast lamb.*

1⅔ cups (½ lb/250 g) Greek-style black olives, pitted
½ cup (3½ oz/100 g) capers, rinsed and well drained
3 salted anchovies, rinsed and filleted (see glossary)
pinch of Provençal mixed dried herbs (see glossary)
pinch of coarse salt
freshly ground pepper
2 cloves garlic
4–5 tablespoons (2–3 fl oz/60–90 ml) olive oil

◙ Combine the olives, capers and anchovies in a food processor fitted with the metal blade and purée. In a mortar pound
together the herbs, salt, a generous grind of pepper and the
garlic to form a paste. Add the olive mixture and work together, turning the pestle and adding olive oil, a little at a time,
until the mixture is the consistency of a thin paste.

SERVES 6

TROUCHA
Swiss Chard or Spinach Omelet

*Most omelets in Provence are flat and the eggs play a secondary
role, binding together the main ingredients. The Niçois believe this
omelet, la troucha, to be uniquely theirs. In Nice it is made with
Swiss chard greens. Frédéric Mistral, the Provençal poet, placed
troucha in the Vaucluse, where it is made with spinach. The
Marseillais and the Toulonnais willingly mix spinach and chard,
often adding a few chopped sorrel leaves and a couple of chopped
anchovy fillets.*

5–6 tablespoons (3 fl oz/90 ml) olive oil
1 clove garlic, finely chopped
1 lb (500 g) Swiss chard (silverbeet) greens or spinach,
   parboiled, squeezed dry and chopped (see glossary)
salt and freshly ground pepper
4 eggs
1 tablespoon unsalted butter, chilled and diced

◙ Warm 2 tablespoons of the olive oil in a frying pan over
medium heat. Add the garlic and, when it begins to sizzle, add
the chopped greens and salt and pepper to taste. Toss or stir
with a wooden spoon for 2–3 minutes. Remove from the heat.
◙ Combine the eggs, salt and pepper to taste and butter in a

On the bar of Le Caveau de la Tour de l'Isle, L'Isle-sur-la-Sorgue, clockwise from left: Swiss Chard or Spinach Omelet, Mussel and Potato Salad with Tapénade, Tapénade Stuffed Eggs

mixing bowl. Break up the eggs with a fork, whisking only enough to mix the whites and yolks. Add the greens, stirring and beating with the fork at the same time to disperse the heat throughout the mass of eggs.

▨ Select an omelet pan measuring 11 in (28 cm) at the top and 8 in (20 cm) at the bottom. Warm 3 tablespoons olive oil in the pan over high heat, rotating the pan to coat the sides with oil. Pour in the egg mixture and stir, or swirl, the mixture with the back of the fork without touching the bottom or sides of the pan. Smooth the surface with the fork, cover the pan and lower the heat for a minute or so.

▨ When the omelet begins to set, unmold it from the pan by first jerking the pan back and forth to loosen the omelet and then turning it out onto a lid. Add another tablespoon olive oil to the pan, return the omelet browned side up and turn the heat up for about 20 seconds to finish the cooking. Alternatively, finish the omelet without turning it out by slipping it under a hot broiler, removing it when it is no longer liquid at the center but not quite firmly set. Slide onto a serving platter and serve, hot or tepid, cut into wedges.

SERVES 4

35

PROVENCE

SOUPE AU PISTOU
Provençal Vegetable and Basil Soup

This soup migrated from Genoa to Provence during the last quarter of the 19th century. The pounded garlic and basil mixture, called pistou ("pestle") has not changed, but a century ago the soup itself was comprised of only potatoes, beans, tomatoes and pasta. It contained practically no liquid, and recipes warned the reader of the danger of its sticking and burning.

Many cooks find it easier to mix the pistou into the soup before serving it at table, but the beauty of a handsome mortar in the center of the table and the pleasure of seasoning one's soup to taste are then lost. If the guests season their soup to taste, twice as much pistou will be required than for a soup seasoned in the kitchen.

2½ qt (2.5 l) water
1 piece red- or yellow-fleshed winter squash, about 1 lb
    (500 g), peeled, seeded and cut into ½-in (12-cm) cubes
1 lb (500 g) fresh white (*coco*) shell beans or half cranberry
    and half white shell beans, shelled (see glossary)
large bouquet garni (see glossary)
salt
1 lb (500 g) potatoes, peeled, quartered lengthwise, and
    thickly sliced crosswise
2 sweet white onions, thinly sliced
2 leeks, including the tender green parts, thinly sliced
3 tomatoes, peeled, seeded and coarsely chopped
½ lb (250 g) carrots, peeled, split lengthwise and thickly sliced
5 oz (150 g) green beans, trimmed and cut into ½-in
    (12-mm) lengths
2 small zucchini (courgettes), coarsely diced
large handful of short macaroni or broken spaghetti

FOR THE *PISTOU:*

large pinch of coarse salt
freshly ground pepper
4 large cloves firm, crisp garlic
large handful of fresh basil leaves and flower buds
about 2 oz (60 g) Parmesan cheese
about ¾ cup (6 fl oz/180 ml) olive oil

🔲 Pour the water into a large saucepan and add the squash, shell beans, bouquet garni and salt to taste. Bring to a boil,

Mixed Salad with Garlic Croutons

reduce the heat to medium-low, cover and cook at a gentle boil for 20–30 minutes. Add the potatoes, onions, leeks, tomatoes and carrots, return to a boil, cover and cook at a gentle boil for about 30 minutes longer. Add the green beans, zucchini and pasta and cook for about 15 minutes longer (note that in a soup the pasta should not be al dente).

🔲 While the soup is cooking, prepare the *pistou*. Place the salt, pepper to taste, garlic and basil in a mortar and pound with a wooden pestle until everything is reduced to a liquid paste. Grate in some of the cheese, then pound and turn the mixture until it is a stiff paste. Dribble in some of the olive oil, turning the paste all the while until it becomes liquid again. Add more cheese, then more oil and so forth, until you are satisfied with the quantity. Precise measures are of no importance. Scrape the pestle clean with a tablespoon and place the mortar and spoon at the table.

🔲 Remove and discard the bouquet garni from the soup pot and place the pot on the table. Ladle out generous servings of the soup and let each guest season his or her own with *pistou* to taste—normally, a scant tablespoon of *pistou* to each full soup plate. Reheat the soup before a second service.

SERVES 6

On a terrace in Lourmarin, Provençal Vegetable and Basil Soup

MESCLUN AUX CHAPONS
Mixed Salad with Garlic Croutons

Mesclun means "mixture." A Niçois mesclun *is basically a mixture of young dandelion leaves, wild and cultivated arugula (rocket) and any number of fragile, just-sprouted, untransplanted lettuces. To these may be added fragments of chervil and watercress, purslane, "wild" chicory (a bitter, elongated green leaf that in Provence is also cultivated) and radicchio (red chicory); basil and chopped hyssop are welcome additions. Throughout Provence* mesclun *is priced in the markets by the hecto, which is equal to 100 grams, or roughly 3½ ounces—an honest portion for two people. Use whatever you can find and don't worry about missing elements.*

The best bread for the croutons is a large, firm-crumbed sourdough loaf that is several days old. The slices should be grilled over dying embers, or otherwise, until the surfaces are dry and crisp but hardly colored.

The salad greens should be absolutely dry; many of the leaves are too small or too fragile to support the rough treatment of a salad basket. Instead they must be picked out of the rinsing water by handfuls, shaken vigorously, spread out on a towel, rolled up and, then rolled up again, tightly, in the opposite direction.

salt
freshly ground pepper
1 tablespoon Provençal herb vinegar (see glossary)
5 tablespoons (3 fl oz/80 ml) olive oil
5 or 6 young green shallots (see glossary) or green (spring) onions, thinly sliced
½ lb (250 g) *mesclun* (see recipe introduction)
2 large slices semidry bread, about ¾ in (2 cm) thick, lightly grilled, rubbed on both sides with garlic and cut into cubes
2 hard-cooked eggs, shelled and coarsely chopped

◈ In the bottom of the salad bowl, combine salt and pepper to taste. Add the vinegar, stir, then add the olive oil and stir again. Stir in the shallots, then cross the salad utensils over the dressing to minimize contact between the vinaigrette and greens.
◈ Pile the *mesclun* on the vinaigrette, scatter over the garlicky croutons and the chopped eggs and present at table. Toss at the last moment, with splayed fingers for the most perfect toss, or repeatedly with the salad service, turning, lifting and tossing.

SERVES 4

TOURTE DE BLETTES À LA NIÇOISE
Swiss Chard Pie

Provençal pastry dough (see anchovy-and-onion tart on
    page 49)
2 lb (1 kg) Swiss chard (silverbeet) greens, parboiled,
    squeezed dry and chopped (see glossary)
2 eggs
½ cup (2 oz/50 g) freshly grated Parmesan cheese
salt and freshly ground pepper
1 tablespoon olive oil

☒ Prepare the pastry dough and chill for about 1 hour. Preheat
an oven to 350°F (180°C).
☒ In a mixing bowl combine the chard, eggs, cheese and salt
and pepper to taste. Using your hands, mix thoroughly.
☒ Lightly oil a round baking sheet 10 in (25 cm) in diameter.
Divide the pastry in half. Roll out half of dough and line the
baking sheet as directed in anchovy-and-onion tart (recipe
page 49), allowing the edges to overhang slightly. Mound the
chard filling in the center and spread it to the edges. Roll out the
remaining pastry and transfer it to the top of the pie. Trim the
edges, if necessary, before pinching the top and bottom pastries together and rolling them up on the edge of the dish to form
a rim. Crimp with a floured thumb or the back of the tines of
a fork. Using the tips of pointed scissors held at an angle, snip
the pastry's surface 4 or 5 times to create steam vents. Brush the
surface and the rim of the pastry lightly with the olive oil.
☒ Place in the oven and bake until golden, about 30 minutes.

SERVES 4

CRESPÈU AUX COURGETTES
Zucchini Omelet

Throughout Provence flat omelets are commonly called crespèu
*(Provençal culinary scholar René Jouveau claims this designation
should, rightfully, be reserved for flat bacon or potato omelets).
When available, a handful of peeled, tender green almonds,
coarsely chopped, are a lovely addition to the omelet.*

about ¾ lb (375 g) small, firm zucchini (courgettes)
salt
5–6 tablespoons (3 fl oz/90 ml) olive oil
3 eggs
freshly ground pepper
large pinch of fresh flower buds and tender leaves of sweet
    marjoram, finely chopped
1 tablespoon unsalted butter, chilled and diced
¼ cup (1 oz/30 g) freshly grated Parmesan cheese

☒ Preheat a broiler (griller). Remove the stem and flower ends
of the zucchini. Depending upon their size, cut them crosswise in thirds; if they are large split them in half lengthwise
first. Pass them through the medium blade of a *mouli-julienne*
or a food processor fitted with the shredding disk. Layer the
shredded zucchini in a mixing bowl, sprinkling each layer
generously with salt, and leave for 30 minutes. Then pick up
the mass and squeeze repeatedly between both hands to rid
it of its water.
☒ Warm 2 tablespoons of the olive oil in a frying pan over high
heat. Add the zucchini and toss often, stirring and breaking it
up with a wooden spoon when necessary, for 2–3 minutes.
Remove from the heat.

☒ Combine the eggs, pepper to taste, marjoram and butter in
a bowl and break up with a fork, whisking only enough to mix
the whites and yolks. Add the sautéed zucchini, stirring and
beating with the fork at the same time to disperse the heat
throughout the mass of eggs.
☒ Select an omelet pan measuring 11 in (28 cm) at the top and 8 in

Top to bottom: Zucchini Omelet, Swiss Chard Pie

(20 cm) at the bottom. Warm the remaining 3 tablespoons olive oil in the pan, rotating the pan to coat the sides. Pour in the zucchini mixture and stir, or swirl, the mixture with the back of the fork without touching the bottom or sides of the pan. Smooth the surface with the fork, cover the pan and lower the heat for a minute or so. Sprinkle with the cheese, taking care that none touches the sides of the pan (lest it stick) and push the pan beneath the hot broiler until the cheese is melted and the center is no longer liquid but not quite firm. Slip the omelet onto a round platter and serve, hot or tepid, cut into wedges.

SERVES 4

SALADE D'ENCORNATS

Squid Salad

Small squid, if sautéed very rapidly, are meltingly tender and delicate. If overcooked, they toughen and must, then, be braised for a relatively long period to become tender again.

2 tablespoons olive oil
2 lb (1 kg) small squid, body pouches 4–6 in (10–15 cm)
    long, cleaned and body pouches cut crosswise into rings
    ½ in (12 mm) wide (see glossary)
salt and freshly ground pepper

FOR THE VINAIGRETTE:

2 garden-ripe tomatoes, peeled, seeded and cut into large dices
fine salt
pinch of coarse salt
freshly ground pepper
1 small clove garlic

1 tablespoon Provençal herb vinegar (see glossary)
the reduced squid cooking liquid
1 tablespoon chopped fresh flat-leaf (Italian) parsley
¼ cup (2 fl oz/60 ml) olive oil

▣ Heat the olive oil in a large frying pan over high heat. Add the squid rings and tentacles and salt and pepper to taste. Toss and stir for no more than 1 minute, or until the squid have released an abundant amount of liquid and the flesh has firmed up, losing its translucent cast and turning opaque. Using a slotted spoon, transfer the squid to a salad bowl. Reduce the cooking liquid over high heat to 1–2 tablespoons of light syrup. Pour into a bowl and reserve.

▣ To prepare the vinaigrette, sprinkle the tomato pieces with fine salt and place them on an overturned drum sieve or a wire rack to drain for 30 minutes. Chop them, quite finely, but not to a purée. In a mortar pound together the coarse salt, freshly ground pepper to taste and garlic to form a paste. Slowly stir in the vinegar, reduced squid liquid, tomatoes, parsley and, finally, olive oil. Pour over the squid, toss and serve.

SERVES 6

1 fresh thyme sprig
large pinch of fennel seeds
10–12 peppercorns
10–12 coriander seeds
2 cups (16 fl oz/500 ml) dry, acidulous white wine such as
    Sauvignon or Muscadet

◼ Rub the sardines gently under running water to scale them. Cut off the heads. Slit the abdomens, gut them and, using fingertips and a knife tip, pry the fillets free from the central bone, pinching it off at the tail. Leave the fillets attached at the tail and the length of the back. Rinse the sardines and pat them dry between layers of paper towels. Lay the sardines out, skin side down. Sprinkle lightly with salt, then roll each up from head to tail and pierce it with a wooden toothpick to hold the roll in place. Arrange the *paupiettes* on a tray or large platter, sprinkle well with salt on all sides and let stand for 3 hours.
◼ Combine all the ingredients for the marinade in a saucepan. Bring to a boil, reduce the heat, cover and cook at a gentle boil for 10 minutes. Remove from the heat and let cool.
◼ Sponge the *paupiettes* dry with paper towels and arrange them, side by side, in a terrine or deep, straight-sided dish. Discard the celery stalk, bay leaf and thyme sprig and pour the cold marinade over the sardines. Cover and refrigerate for a couple of days before serving.

SERVES 6

PROVENCE

SOUPE AUX MOULES
Mussel Soup

This recipe uses mussels that have been opened in a fragrant mix of wine and herbs.

2 lb (1 kg) mussels, opened with white wine over heat, shelled
    and immersed in a little of the cooking liquid (see glossary)
4 tablespoons (2 fl oz/60 ml) olive oil
1 sweet onion, finely chopped
1 leek, including the tender green parts, thinly sliced
3 garden-ripe tomatoes, peeled, seeded and coarsely chopped
large pinch of saffron threads or a knife tip (⅛–¼ teaspoon)
    of powdered saffron
2 or 3 short lengths wild fennel or a large pinch of fennel
    seeds pounded to a powder in a mortar
the mussels' decanted cooking liquid plus enough water to
    measure 4 cups (32 fl oz/1 l)
salt
4 egg yolks
freshly ground pepper
4 semidry slices bread, rubbed with a garlic clove

◼ Prepare the mussels as directed.
◼ Warm 2 tablespoons of the olive oil in a heavy saucepan over low heat. Add the onion and leek and cook gently until softened but not colored, 10–15 minutes. Add the tomatoes, saffron and fennel, raise the heat and stir for a few minutes. Add the mussels' cooking liquid–water mixture and cook at a gentle boil until the flavors are well blended, about 20 minutes. Taste for salt and remove from the heat.
◼ In a small bowl mix the egg yolks with the remaining olive oil and grind in pepper to taste. Drain the mussels and add the liquid to the egg mixture. Stir the egg mixture into the broth with a wooden spoon, return the saucepan to low heat and continue stirring until the broth barely coats the spoon, about 8–10 minutes; it must not boil. Remove and discard the fennel stalks and stir in the mussels just to heat through.
◼ Place a garlic-rubbed bread slice in each soup plate and ladle the soup into the bowls.

SERVES 4

Clockwise from top: Provençal Fish Soup (recipe page 42), Squid Salad, Marinated Sardine Paupiettes, Mussel Soup

BOUCHES·DU·RHÔNE

PAUPIETTES DE SARDINES EN MARINADE
Marinated Sardine Paupiettes

Fish merchants in Provence put out signs advertising sardines de l'aube ("dawn sardines"), which means they were netted that morning. Very fresh sardines are bright eyed, stiff and arched, with steely blue glints.

2 lb (1 kg) fresh sardines
salt
FOR THE MARINADE:

1 carrot, peeled and thinly sliced
1 onion, thinly sliced
2 cloves garlic, crushed
1 small celery stalk with leaves
1 bay leaf

Aïgo Bouido
Garlic Broth

Aïgo bouido (or boulido) means "boiled water." This broth has given its name to the popular folk saying Aïgo bouido sauvo la vido—"It saves your life." It is particularly recommended as a palliative to gastronomic or bacchic excesses. After straining the broth, eggs are sometimes poached in it. Or the hot broth can be whisked into 2 or 3 beaten egg yolks, with or without the addition of grated cheese. A branch of fennel can replace the sage, and some cooks add a strip of dried orange peel.

6 cups (48 fl oz/1.5 l) water
salt
2 bay leaves
1 small fresh sage sprig
10–12 cloves garlic
4–5 tablespoons (2–3 fl oz/60–80 ml) olive oil
8 thin slices semidry bread
¾ cup (3 oz/100 g) freshly grated Gruyère or Parmesan cheese

▦ In a saucepan over high heat, combine the water, salt to taste, bay, sage, garlic and 2 tablespoons of the olive oil. When the water boils, reduce the heat, cover with the lid ajar and simmer for 15 minutes. Discard the herbs and pass the broth and the garlic through a sieve.

▦ Place 2 bread slices in each soup plate. Sprinkle the remaining 2–3 tablespoons olive oil and the cheese evenly over the slices. Reheat the broth and pour it over the bread.

SERVES 4

Soupe de Vermicelle aux Tomates
Tomato Soup with Angel's Hair Pasta

In France the commercial pasta known elsewhere as angel's hair or capelli d'angelo is called vermicelle. Any small soup pasta can be substituted for it in this soup, however. If you prefer to purée the soup before adding the pasta, the tomatoes need not be peeled. When this soup is made without the pasta, it is poured over bread slices that have first been anointed with olive oil and then sprinkled with cheese; in Toulon, this soup is garnished with little fried sausages and called rate-rate.

3 tablespoons olive oil
1 onion, finely chopped
1 lb (500 g) garden-ripe tomatoes, peeled and coarsely chopped
1 clove garlic, crushed
1 bay leaf
salt
4 cups (32 fl oz/1 l) water or vegetable broth such as chick-pea, lentil, white bean, leek, or potato, boiling
large handful of angel's hair pasta
freshly ground pepper

▦ Warm the olive oil in a flameproof earthenware casserole or heavy saucepan over low heat. Add the onion and cook gently until softened and lightly colored, about 10 minutes. Add the tomatoes, garlic and bay and season to taste with salt; the amount of salt will depend upon whether you are using water or broth. Raise the heat and cook, stirring, for a couple of minutes. Pour in the boiling water or broth and boil lightly for 4–5 minutes.

▦ Add the pasta and cook for 10 minutes longer. Season to taste with pepper and serve.

SERVES 4

Soupe de Poissons
Provençal Fish Soup

A good Provençal fish soup is infused with an exquisite essence of the sea. On the Mediterranean coast, the soup must include a large selection of rockfish fry, varying from less than 1 inch (2.5 cm) to more than 2–3 inches (5–7 cm) in length, and miniature versions of all the fish traditionally used in a bouillabaisse (see recipe on page 59).

FOR THE PASTA:
about 1½ cups (6 oz/180 g) bread (hard) flour
large pinch of salt
¼ teaspoon powdered saffron
1 egg
1 tablespoon olive oil

FOR THE SOUP:
¼ cup (2 fl oz/60 ml) olive oil
½ lb (250 g) onions, chopped
½ lb (250 g) leeks, including the tender green parts, thinly sliced
5 or 6 cloves garlic, crushed
3 lb (1.5 kg) Mediterranean soup fish or small, gutted rockfish plus heads and carcasses from sliced or filleted white-fleshed fish such as cod, snapper and whiting, gills discarded
1 thick slice conger eel, about ½ lb (250 g), cut into small pieces
1 monkfish (anglerfish) head, chopped, or 1 thick slice monkfish, flesh and backbone cut into small pieces
small handful of coarse sea salt
1 or 2 cayenne peppers or other hot (chili) peppers
2 large sprigs fresh thyme
2 bay leaves
3 or 4 fennel stalks, each about 6 in (15 cm) long or a large pinch of fennel seeds
1 lb (500 g) garden-ripe tomatoes, coarsely chopped, or 1 can (15 oz/400 g) Italian chopped tomatoes with juice
2 cups (16 fl oz/500 ml) white wine
8 cups (64 fl oz/2 l) water, boiling
1 lb (500 g) small, lively crabs such as blue swimmers or sand crabs
large pinch of saffron threads or ½ teaspoon powdered saffron
salt

▦ First, prepare the pasta dough. While it is resting, put the soup on to cook, and while it is cooking, roll out and cut the pasta.

▦ For the pasta, put ¾ cup (3 oz/90 g) of the flour, the salt and saffron into a mixing bowl. Stir with a fork, then make a well in the center. Add the egg and olive oil to the well. Using the fork, stir from the center outward to incorporate as much flour as possible. Next, mash and work the mixture until it begins to pull together, sprinkling over a little additional flour as necessary to create a fairly soft, supple dough.

▦ Flour a work surface and turn the dough out onto it. Knead with your knuckles, continuously folding the dough and sprinkling it with more flour if it is sticky, until it is a smooth, consistent texture. Form it into a ball, cover with a folded towel and let rest for 1 hour.

▦ If you are using a hand-crank pasta machine, cut the dough in half and, using the heel of your hand, press one half on a floured surface to flatten it as much as possible. Turn it over and press again, then pass it slowly through the machine's rollers set at the maximum (kneading) width. Flour the dough again on both sides, fold the ends inward to meet and fold again to make four thicknesses. Flatten again with the heel of your hand and pass it again through the rollers set at the maximum width. Fold in half and pass again, if necessary (the fewer times it is passed, the better it will be; pasta that is folded and passed repeatedly through the machine loses its attractive rustic texture and fresh egg flavor). Without folding the dough, pass it through the rollers two or three times more, diminishing the

Left to right: Tomato Soup with Angel's Hair Pasta, Garlic Broth

thickness each time and finishing at the next to last "notch," or thickness. Hang the dough sheet over a broomstick suspended between two chairbacks until it is dry but still supple to the touch, about 30 minutes. Repeat with the other dough portion. Cut the dough sheets crosswise into 2-in (5-cm) lengths and pass each piece through the *tagliatelli* (the narrowest) cutter on the pasta machine. Sprinkle the cut pasta with flour and toss the pasta loosely with spread fingers to prevent it from sticking together before cooking.

◼ To roll out the pasta by hand, flatten it with the heel of your hand on a floured work surface, sprinkle flour over and roll it out, as thinly as possible, with a rolling pin, turning it over from time to time and sprinkling with flour when necessary to prevent sticking. Hang it over a broomstick to dry for 30 minutes, then return it to the floured work surface. Flour the surface of the pasta, roll it up loosely from one side to the center and then from the other side to the center. Using a large knife, cut the rolled pasta crosswise into ¼ -in (6-mm) widths. Slip the knife blade, backside to the center, beneath the cut pasta and lift up to unroll it. With the side of your hand, lift the sections of cut pasta from the knife, spread them out lengthwise and cut across into approximately 2-in (5-cm) lengths. Sprinkle with flour and toss to prevent the pasta from sticking together.

◼ To prepare the soup, warm the olive oil in a large, heavy (8–10 qt/8–10 l) saucepan or stockpot over medium heat. Add the onions, leeks and garlic and stir for 4–5 minutes until softened; do not permit them to color. Throw in all of the fish, the salt, cayenne peppers and all the herbs. Cook for 10 minutes or so, stirring and crushing the contents with a wooden spoon. Add the tomatoes and continue to stir until the tomatoes break up and begin to boil, about 5 minutes. Add the wine, raise the heat, and stir until the contents come to a full boil. Pour in the boiling water and stir to amalgamate the contents. Throw in the crabs and adjust the heat to maintain a gentle boil. Cover with the lid slightly ajar and cook for a few minutes. Remove from the heat.

◼ Three or four at a time, transfer the crabs to a mortar and crush and pound them with a wooden pestle until they are reduced to a coarse, broken-up purée. Spoon them back into the pot and pound the others. When all the crabs have been crushed, wash out the mortar with a ladle of broth and pour it back into the pot. Return the pot to the heat and continue to cook the soup gently until all the flavors have been drawn out by the liquid, about 40 minutes.

◼ Remove the pot to a work surface. Pass 2 or 3 ladlefuls of the soup through a sieve placed over a large bowl, pushing and pressing with the pestle to extract all the liquid and flavor. Discard the dry paste of shells and debris from the sieve and begin again, picking out and discarding the herbs as they turn up. When all the soup has been passed, clean out the soup pot and rinse the sieve, taking care to remove any tiny bones that may be caught in the mesh. Place the sieve over the pot and pour all of the liquid through it again; shake the sieve gently but do not stir the contents. Discard the fine purée that collects in the sieve. Add the saffron to the soup pot and reheat.

◼ While the soup is reheating, fill a saucepan with water, add salt to taste and bring to a boil. Add the noodles and cook until tender, no more than 2 minutes, then drain and add to the soup. Ladle into heated soup plates and serve.

SERVES 6–8   *Photograph pages 40–41*

BOUCHES·DU·RHÔNE / VAR

SOUPE DE FAVOUILLES

Crab Soup

Favouille *is the Provençal name for the little Mediterranean green shore crab whose shell is only about 2–3 in (5–7 cm) wide. The same crab is found in Venice, where it is cultivated for eating, like the soft-shell blue crabs in America, at the time of molting. The distinctive peppery taste of the* favouille *is considered indispens-* able to the complex flavor of a soupe de poissons *(recipe on page 42) or a* bouillabaisse *(recipe on page 59).*

3 tablespoons olive oil
1 large, sweet white onion, sliced
½ lb (250 g) leeks, including the tender green parts, thickly sliced
5 or 6 cloves garlic, crushed
about 2 dozen small, lively crabs such as blue swimmers or sand crabs
2–3 tablespoons marc de Provence (see glossary) or Cognac
½ cup (4 fl oz/125 ml) dry white wine

1 lb (500 g) garden-ripe tomatoes, coarsely chopped
large bouquet garni, including a fennel stalk (see glossary)
salt
a few grains cayenne pepper
6 cups (48 fl oz/1.5 l) water, boiling
large pinch of saffron threads
2 or 3 slices semidry bread, lightly toasted, rubbed on both
    sides with garlic and cut into cubes

◉ In a large, heavy sauté pan over medium heat, warm the olive oil. Add the onion, leeks and garlic and stir for 4–5 minutes until softened; do not permit them to color. Throw in the crabs and stir until they have begun to turn red on all sides. Add the brandy and, a minute later, the white wine and tomatoes. Bring to a rapid boil, stirring all the while. Add the bouquet garni, salt to taste and cayenne and cook, stirring, until the tomatoes have begun to disintegrate and the crabs are completely red, about 5 minutes. Remove from the heat.

◉ Three or four at a time, transfer the crabs to a mortar and crush and pound them with a wooden pestle until they are all reduced to a coarse, broken-up purée. Spoon them back into the pan and pound the others.

◉ Transfer the contents of the sauté pan to a saucepan (to avoid excess reduction) and add the boiling water. Bring to a boil, cover with the lid ajar and cook at a gentle boil for about 15 minutes. Remove and discard the bouquet garni.

◉ Pass 2 or 3 ladlefuls of the soup through a fine-mesh sieve placed over a large bowl, pushing and pressing with the pestle to extract all the liquid and flavor. Discard the dry paste of shells and debris and begin again. Repeat until all of the soup has been forced through the sieve. Add the saffron to the broth, reheat it and serve accompanied with a dish of garlic croutons.

SERVES 4

PROVENCE

POT-AU-FEU À LA PROVENÇALE

Provençal Pot-au-Feu

A Provençal pot-au-feu is distinguished by the presence, in addition to the usual beef cuts, of a lamb shank (béquet), which lends complexity to the flavor and softness to the texture of the broth. The famous gastronome Austin de Croze, writing in 1928, claims that it is obligatory to accompany a Provençal pot-au-feu with a warm chick-pea salad. He is often quoted but rarely respected.

1 pig's foot (trotter)
3 lb (1.5 kg) boned beef shank (shin), in a single piece
1½ lb (750 g) beef short ribs
1 lamb shank (shin) on the bone, about 1½ lb (750 g)
1 large beef marrow bone, about 1½–2 lb (750 g–1 kg), tied
    in cheesecloth (muslin)
½ cup (4 fl oz/125 ml) dry white wine
handful of coarse salt
1 large onion stuck with 2 whole cloves
1 whole head garlic
large bouquet garni (see glossary)
1 lb (500 g) young, tender carrots, peeled
1 lb (500 g) small, crisp turnips, peeled
2 lb (1 kg) leeks
6 slices semidry bread
coarse sea salt, capers and gray, unrefined black olives, if
    available, for serving

◉ Place the pig's foot in a saucepan, add cold water to cover and bring to a full boil. Drain, rinse under cold water, drain again and set aside.

◉ Using kitchen twine, tie the beef shank and short ribs together in a compact package. In a traditional earthenware

pot-au-feu or a deep, heavy saucepan with a capacity of about 10 qt (10 l), arrange all of the meats, including the pig's foot, so that no space is wasted but they are not packed tightly. Pour in cold water to cover the meat by about 2 in (5 cm) and place the pot over low to medium heat, protected from the direct flame by a flame-tamer. Bring slowly to a boil; this should require nearly 1 hour. As gray scum rises to the surface, skim it off continually. When the water begins to boil, add the wine and continue to skim.

◉ Add the salt, clove-studded onion, head of garlic and bouquet garni. Continue to skim until the liquid approaches a boil again. Cover with a lid slightly ajar and adjust the heat, repeatedly if necessary, so that a bare simmer is maintained. Cook for 2 hours. Check the pot from time to time; the liquid should never boil.

◉ After 2 hours add the carrots and the turnips and continue to simmer. Meanwhile, remove the dark green tops from the leeks and slit the upper leaf part; wash well and tie the leeks into a bundle. When the carrots and turnips have been cooking for 30 minutes, add the leeks and cook for 30 minutes longer.

◉ The *pot-au-feu* should be ready about 3 hours after it was first brought to a boil. Pierce the beef shank with a trussing needle or sharp skewer to see if the shank is tender (it requires the longest cooking of all the meats).

◉ Skim the excess fat from the surface of the broth. Discard the onion, head of garlic and bouquet garni, and put the pig's foot aside to be added to a salad another day. Remove the marrow bone from its wrapping and slip the marrow out onto a plate. Spread the marrow on the bread slices and place 1 slice in each soup plate.

◉ Serve the broth directly from the pot, leaving the meats and vegetables in the broth to keep them hot. Snip the strings from the meats and carve them, cutting only as much as you think may be eaten. The remainder will be easier to slice thinly for a *mironton* (recipe on page 152) when cold. Arrange the cut meats on a platter. Snip the string from the leeks and arrange the leeks and all the other vegetables around the meats. Pour some broth into a small pitcher or bowl and place on the table for those who wish to moisten their meats. Offer the sea salt, capers and olives at the table as well. When the meal is finished, remove the meat from the broth, wrap well and refrigerate.

SERVES 6

Provençal Pot-au-Feu

HOURTÊTE
Kitchen Garden Soup

Hourtête, which means "little garden," is no doubt as old as Provence; the recipe was first published in Le cuisinier Durand, *the earliest Provençal cookbook and still one of the best. The author, Charles Durand, was born in 1766; his career was mainly divided between Nîmes and Marseilles and spanned the Ancien Régime, the Revolution, the Napoleonic era and the reigns of Louis XVIII, Charles X and Louis-Philippe.*

6 cups (48 fl oz/1.5 l) water or broth
salt, if using water
5 oz (150 g) spinach leaves, stemmed, tightly rolled up and finely sliced
5 oz (150 g) Swiss chard (silverbeet) greens, tightly rolled up and finely sliced
5 oz (150 g) sorrel leaves, stemmed, tightly rolled up and finely sliced
small handful of celery leaves, chopped
small handful of fresh chervil sprigs, chopped
1 clove garlic
1 sweet white onion, thinly sliced
4 egg yolks
freshly ground pepper
thin slices semidry baguette
3–4 tablespoons (2 fl oz/60 ml) olive oil

▦ In a saucepan over high heat, add salt, if desired, and bring the water or broth to a boil. Add the spinach, chard, sorrel, celery, chervil, garlic and onion and boil gently for about 15 minutes.

▦ In a small bowl, break up the egg yolks with a fork and grind over pepper to taste. While stirring constantly, add a small ladleful of the hot soup. Remove the saucepan from the heat and let stand for a couple of minutes. Using a wooden spoon, stir in the egg mixture. Return the saucepan to low heat and continue to stir until the soup just begins to coat the spoon thinly, 8–10 minutes; it must not boil.

▦ Place the bread in a soup tureen or divide among individual soup plates and dribble with the olive oil. Ladle the soup over the bread and serve.

SERVES 4

OMELET AUX TOMATES
Tomato Omelet

5 tablespoons (3 fl oz/80 ml) olive oil, or as needed
1 sweet white onion, halved and thinly sliced
¼ lb (125 g) Italian sweet peppers or other sweet peppers (capsicums), cut in half lengthwise, seeded, deribbed and thinly sliced crosswise
2 cloves garlic, crushed
2 garden-ripe tomatoes, peeled, seeded and coarsely chopped
salt
cayenne pepper
5 eggs
freshly ground black pepper

▦ Warm 2 tablespoons of the olive oil in a wide, heavy frying pan over low heat. Add the onion and peppers and cook, stirring occasionally with a wooden spoon, until soft but not colored, about 15 minutes. Raise the heat and add the garlic,

tomatoes, salt to taste and a discreet dash of cayenne. Toss the contents of the pan repeatedly until the tomatoes begin to break up and boil, about 5 minutes. Turn the heat to low and simmer for about 15 minutes, stirring from time to time. Raise the heat to high once again and toss to evaporate any remaining liquid. Empty the tomatoes onto a plate and leave until completely cooled.

▦ In a mixing bowl combine the eggs and a pinch of salt. Grind over some black pepper and break up the eggs with a fork, whisking enough only to mix the whites and the yolks. Stir in the cooled tomato mixture.

▦ Select an omelet pan measuring 11 in (28 cm) at the top and 8 in (20 cm) at the bottom. Warm 3 tablespoons olive oil in the pan over high heat, rotating the pan to coat the sides with oil. Pour in the egg mixture and stir, or swirl, the mixture with the back of the fork without touching the bottom or sides of the pan. Gradually working around the circumference of the omelet, lift the edges with the fork tip, tilting the pan each time to permit the liquid egg on the surface to run beneath the underside.

▦ When the omelet begins to set, unmold it from the pan by first jerking the pan back and forth to loosen the omelet and then turning it out onto a lid. Add another tablespoon olive oil to the pan, return the omelet browned side up and turn the heat up for about 20 seconds to finish the cooking. Alternatively, finish the omelet without turning it out by slipping it under a hot broiler, removing it when it is no longer liquid at the center but not quite firmly set. Slide onto a serving platter and serve, hot or tepid, cut into wedges.

SERVES 4

OEUFS À LA TRIPE
Eggs in Onion Sauce

2 tablespoons unsalted butter
1 lb (500 g) sweet white onions, thinly sliced
salt
1 tablespoon all-purpose (plain) flour
1 cup (8 fl oz/250 ml) milk
freshly ground pepper
whole nutmeg
⅛ teaspoon powdered saffron dissolved in 1 tablespoon boiling water
6 hard-cooked eggs, shelled and quartered
chopped fresh flat-leaf (Italian) parsley for garnish

▦ Melt the butter in a heavy saucepan or sauté pan over low heat. Add the onions and salt to taste, cover and cook, stirring often with a wooden spoon until the onions are very soft but not colored, at least 30 minutes.

▦ Sprinkle the flour over the onions, stir around, and slowly add the milk, stirring all the while. Raise the heat to medium-high and continue stirring until a boil is reached. Reduce the heat to low and cook gently for another 30 minutes, stirring often.

▦ Grind over some pepper and scrape in a hint of nutmeg. Stir in the dissolved saffron and add the eggs, stirring carefully to avoid breaking them up. Heat through.

▦ Turn the mixture into a preheated serving dish and sprinkle with parsley.

SERVES 4

In a Lourmarin garden, clockwise from top: Kitchen Garden Soup, Tomato Omelet, Eggs in Onion Sauce

BOUCHES·DU·RHÔNE

SOUPE TÔT FAITE

Fast Soup

Also called soupe vite facho *and a refreshing change from the usual long-cooked potato-and-leek soup. Here, the vegetables are finely cut and boiled only briefly.*

1½ lb (750 g) potatoes
6 cups (48 fl oz/1.5 l) water
salt
1 lb (500 g) leeks, including the tender green parts, thinly sliced
4 slices semidry bread

2–3 tablespoons olive oil
freshly ground pepper

◙ Peel the potatoes, cut in half lengthwise and then slice each half into 3 or 4 lengthwise slices. Now thinly cut the slices crosswise. Set aside.
◙ In a saucepan over high heat, combine the water, salt to taste, potatoes and leeks. Bring to a boil and boil until the potato slivers are easily crushed against the side of the saucepan with a wooden spoon, about 20 minutes.
◙ Place 1 bread slice in each soup plate. Sprinkle with olive oil to taste and then grind pepper over the top. Ladle the soup over the bread and serve.

SERVES 4

Fast Soup

48

Anchovy and Onion Tart

PISSALADIÈRE
Anchovy and Onion Tart

Pissaladière *takes its name from* pissalat, *a traditional Niçois preparation of fish fry, salted and placed under a weight for a week before being sieved into a purée to be used as a seasoning (the same preparation, in the Bouches-du-Rhône, is called* melet). *Today salt anchovies nearly always replace the* pissalat. *Cooks in Provence often buy bread dough from the baker to roll out for their* pissaladières. *Some knead a bit of olive oil into it first; others prefer to use a butter-and-flour short crust or a Provençal olive-oil pastry dough. The best onions for a* pissaladière *are large, freshly dug, sweet white onions, which have a high water content.*

FOR THE PROVENÇAL PASTRY DOUGH:

2 cups (8 oz/250 g) all-purpose (plain) flour
large pinch of salt
1 egg
¼ cup (2 fl oz/60 ml) olive oil
¼ cup (2 fl oz/60 ml) lukewarm water
additional flour for rolling out dough

5 tablespoons (3 fl oz/80 ml) olive oil
3 lb (1.5 kg) sweet white onions, thinly sliced
3 or 4 cloves garlic
salt
1 bay leaf
1 fresh thyme sprig
8 salt anchovies, rinsed, filleted and mashed (see glossary)
¾ cup (4 oz/125 g) black olives
freshly ground pepper

To prepare the dough, place the flour and salt together in a mixing bowl and stir together with a fork. Add the egg, olive oil and water. Mix first with the fork and then knead in the bowl with your knuckles until you have a soft, consistent dough. Form into a ball and leave in the bowl. Cover with a folded towel and let stand at kitchen temperature for about 1 hour before rolling out.

Warm 3 tablespoons of the olive oil in a flameproof earthenware casserole or a heavy sauté pan over very low heat. Add the onions, garlic, salt to taste and herbs. Cover and cook over the lowest possible heat for about 1 hour, stirring occasionally with a wooden spoon. The onions must not color. If the cooking vessel is right and the heat low enough, they will be absolutely white and purée-soft after an hour of cooking. Remove from the heat and remove and discard the bay leaf and thyme sprig. Stir in the anchovies.

Preheat an oven to 350°F (180°C). Lightly oil a large, round or rectangular heavy baking sheet. Flour a work surface and place the dough on it. Flatten the dough with your hand, then sprinkle it with more flour. Roll it out thinly to the approximate size and shape of the baking sheet. Drape the pastry around the rolling pin and transfer it to the sheet. Press it gently onto the bottom and sides of the sheet. Roll the edges under to form a rim. Crimp all around the edge with the side of your thumb, repeatedly dipping it in flour so it is not sticky. Prick the surface of the pastry here and there with the tines of a fork, then spread the onion mixture over the pastry. Push the olives into it, one by one, half buried and regularly distributed. Brush the rim of the pastry with a little of the remaining 2 tablespoons of olive oil, then sprinkle a bit more over the surface of the onions.

Place in the oven and bake until the rim of the pastry is golden and crisp, about 30 minutes. Remove from the oven and grind over some pepper.

SERVES 6

CAVIAR D'AUBERGINE

Eggplant Spread

The spread is best served warm, as an hors d'oeuvre accompanied with warm toasts and chilled white or rosé wine.

3 elongated eggplants (aubergines), about 1½ lb (750 g) total
   weight
2 cloves garlic
pinch of coarse salt
2 salt anchovies, rinsed and filleted (see glossary)
freshly ground pepper
fine salt

4–5 tablespoons (2–3 fl oz/60–90 ml) olive oil

◉ Preheat an oven to 350°F (180°C).
◉ Prick the eggplants several times and place them in a shallow baking dish. Bake until the flesh is very soft when pierced with a knife tip, about 45 minutes. Remove from the oven and, when cool enough to handle, split the eggplants in half. Using a spoon scrape the flesh onto a plate. Discard the skins and mash the flesh to a coarse purée with a fork.
◉ In a mortar pound together the garlic and coarse salt to form a paste. Add the anchovies, grind in pepper to taste and pound again. Empty the contents of the plate into the mortar and turn with the pestle, slowly adding the olive oil until the mixture is a loose, spreadable consistency. Add fine salt to taste.

SERVES 4

bouquet garni (see glossary)
3 tablespoons olive oil
1 onion, thinly sliced
1 leek, including the tender green parts, thinly sliced
1 carrot, peeled and diced
2 cloves garlic, crushed
½ lb (250 g) Swiss chard (silverbeet) greens, shredded
salt
freshly ground pepper

◈ Place the lentils in a bowl, add cold water to cover and let stand for 2–3 hours.
◈ Drain the lentils and place in a flameproof earthenware casserole or an enamelware pot. Add water to cover, bring to a boil and boil for 5 minutes. Drain, return the lentils to the pot and pour in the boiling water.
◈ Add the bouquet garni, cover and simmer over low heat while you prepare the rest of the soup.
◈ In a saucepan over low heat, warm the olive oil. Add the onion, leek and carrot and cook gently until softened, about 15 minutes. Add the garlic, chard and salt to taste. Raise the heat and cook until the chard softens and its juices evaporate, about 5 minutes. Add the contents of the saucepan to the lentils and continue to simmer until the lentils are tender, about 1 hour. Season with salt, grind in some pepper and serve.

SERVES 6

ALPES·MARITIMES

POTAGE PRINTANIER

Spring Soup

Broad beans for soup should be more mature than those eaten raw, with each bean about the size of a thumbnail. The flesh should be a clear green and the beans should not have begun to turn starchy. At this stage, the peel on each bean is slightly tough and bitter and must be removed, but the flesh beneath should be tender and not hard to the touch. Petite green peas can be substituted or added.

8 cups (64 fl oz/2 l) water
salt
3 young, tender artichokes, trimmed, halved lengthwise,
    chokes removed if necessary and thinly sliced (see glossary)
10 oz (300 g) new potatoes, peeled and diced
½ lb (250 g) Swiss chard (silverbeet) greens, tightly rolled up
    and finely sliced
5 oz (150 g) young green shallots (see glossary) or green
    (spring) onions, sliced or chopped
2 or 3 fresh winter savory sprigs, tied together
2 lb (1 kg) young broad (fava) beans, shelled and each bean
    peeled
2 eggs
2 tablespoons olive oil
freshly ground pepper
Parmesan cheese for serving

◈ Pour the water into a large saucepan, add salt to taste and bring to a boil. Add the artichokes, potatoes, chard, shallots or onions and savory. Cover with the lid slightly ajar and cook at a gentle boil for about 15 minutes. Add the broad beans and cook until they are meltingly tender but still intact, about 10 minutes.
◈ Remove and discard the savory bouquet. In a small bowl combine the eggs and olive oil. Grind in pepper to taste and beat with a fork until blended. Stir in a small ladleful of the broth. Remove the pan from the heat and stir in the egg mixture. Serve at once, with a wedge of Parmesan and a grater on the side.

SERVES 6

Top to bottom: Spring Soup, Lentil Soup, Eggplant Spread

ALPES·MARITIMES

SOUPE DE LENTILLES À LA NIÇOISE

Lentil Soup

Tiny, speckled lentils, called lentilles vertes *or* lentilles du Puy, *are the best. They must be carefully sorted over by pouring small quantities at a time onto a plate from which they are shifted to a bowl. It is rare not to discover one or two tiny bits of gravel—very unpleasant to bite into if overlooked.*

1 cup (6 ½ oz/200 g) lentils, preferably *lentilles vertes* (see glossary)
8 cups (48 fl oz/2 l) water, boiling

GAYETTES/CAILLETTES À LA VAUCLUSIENNE
Vaucluse Pork Crépinettes

The name of this dish is thought to derive from the Provençal word gaio, *meaning "pork sweetbreads," which were, no doubt, once included in its composition along with the heart, spleen and lungs of the pig. It is nearly always served at room temperature.*

¼ lb (125 g) each pork liver, poultry livers and salt pork (green bacon), finely chopped or passed through the medium blade of a meat grinder
½ lb (250 g) sausage meat (see glossary)
1 lb (500 g) spinach, parboiled, squeezed dry and chopped (see glossary)
1 onion, finely chopped and sautéed in 1 tablespoon olive oil until soft but not colored
persillade made with 2 cloves garlic (see glossary)
large pinch of Provençal mixed dried herbs (see glossary)
salt, freshly ground pepper and ground allspice
2 eggs
about 2 oz (60 g) caul, soaked briefly in tepid water with a dash of wine vinegar and drained (see glossary)
fresh sage leaves or small sprigs
about ½ cup (4 fl oz/125 ml) water

◙ In a large bowl combine all the ingredients except the caul, sage and water, adding salt, pepper and allspice to taste. Using your hands, mix thoroughly, squeezing the mixture repeatedly between your fingers.
◙ Preheat an oven to 400°F (200°C). Stretch the caul out on a work surface and cut it into 5-in (13-cm) squares. Moisten your hands in water and form balls of the meat mixture the size of a small orange. Wrap each ball in a square of caul and flatten the ball slightly with the palm of your hand. Turn it over so the pleat is on the bottom and press a sprig or leaf of sage on top.
◙ Pour the water into the bottom of a shallow baking dish. Arrange the balls, side by side and touching but not crowded, in the dish. Place in the oven and bake until the surfaces are nicely colored and the caul is transformed into a beautiful golden brown lace, about 30 minutes. Serve at room temperature.

SERVES 4

BEIGNETS
Fritters

Mixed fritters are always more amusing than a single element. Other vegetable possibilities are little green (spring) onions, thin slices of zucchini (courgette) and eggplant (aubergine), zucchini or other squash flowers, parboiled green beans or cauliflower florets and precooked salsify. Live mussels, removed from their shells at the last minute, and raw, peeled shrimp make lovely fritters.

FOR THE BATTER:

1 cup (4 oz/125 g) all-purpose (plain) flour
salt and freshly ground pepper
2 eggs, separated
1 tablespoon olive oil
¾ cup (6 fl oz/180 ml) warm beer

2 or 3 small squid, cleaned (see glossary)
3 oz (100 g) fresh cultivated mushrooms, whole if small and quartered if larger

6 small or 4 medium young, tender artichokes, trimmed, quartered if small or cut into eighths if medium and chokes removed if necessary (see glossary)
1 tablespoon finely chopped mixed fresh herbs such as parsley, chives, and tarragon or hyssop or marjoram
juice of ½ lemon
1 tablespoon olive oil
salt and freshly ground pepper
about 8 cups (64 fl oz/2 l) corn oil or peanut oil
8 young, tender sorrel leaves, stems snipped close to leaf
handful of tiny bouquets of fresh flat-leaf (Italian) parsley leaves
2 cups (16 fl oz/500 ml) tomato sauce, heated (see glossary)

◙ In a mixing bowl whisk together the flour, salt and pepper to taste, egg yolks, oil and beer, moving from the center of bowl outward and whisking only long enough to produce a smooth batter. Cover with a plate and rest for 2 hours at room temperature. Just before using, in a

Left to right: Vaucluse Pork Crépinettes, Fritters

separate bowl whisk the egg whites until they hold limp peaks and fold them gently into the batter.

◙ Pull the wings off the squid pouches. Cut the upper part of the pouches into rings about ⅓ in (1 cm) wide and split the pouch tips in two. Using paper towels sponge the squid pieces dry, including the tentacles. Assemble them in a bowl with the mushrooms and the artichokes. Sprinkle the herbs, lemon juice, olive oil and salt and pepper to taste over the top, toss and marinate at room temperature for about 30 minutes. Toss 2 or 3 times.

◙ Following the directions for deep-frying in the glossary, heat the corn or peanut oil in a large pan. Add a few pieces of the squid, mushrooms and artichokes to the batter, turning them around so that all are perfectly coated. Hold the bowl next to the vessel of hot oil and, using a fork, lift each batter-coated piece, pausing above the bowl for a couple of seconds to allow excess batter to fall off. Then slip it into the oil from just above the surface. Do not crowd the fritters in the hot oil. After a couple of minutes, when the floating fritters are golden at the edges, turn each over in the oil, nudging it from underneath with a rounded knife tip or similar instrument. Unless you are working with an electric fryer with a built-in thermostat, you may want to turn the heat up or down from time to time. When the fritters are beautifully colored on both sides—after 3–4 minutes—lift and drain them as directed.

◙ When all of the marinated elements are fried, pick up the sorrel leaves, one at a time by the stem end, dip each into the batter and then slip it into the oil and fry until golden. Remove and drain as for the other ingredients. When all of the sorrel has been removed from the fryer, drop the parsley leaves into the oil and stand back; there will be an explosive crackling for 1–2 seconds and they are done. Remove the parsley to paper towels. Scatter the parsley over the fritters and serve with the tomato sauce on the side.

SERVES 4

OMELETTE BAVEUSE AUX ASPERGES

Asparagus Omelet

Rolled omelets in Provence are reserved for special garnishes—wild-asparagus tips, truffles, sea urchin corals, mussels, sea anemones—all of which are especially succulent bathed in the saucelike interior of an omelette baveuse. *Visually beautiful omelets can be prepared any size, but a perfect rolled omelet, sufficiently moist inside, is difficult to prepare with more than 4 or 5 eggs. If serving more than two people, it is wiser to make two or more omelets—each requires about one minute's preparation from the time the eggs are poured into the pan to the time they are rolled onto the platter. The following recipe is designed for readers who have no access to wild asparagus. Asparagus, prepared in the same way, are also delicious incorporated into scrambled eggs.*

½ lb (250 g) asparagus
4–5 tablespoons (2–3 fl oz/60–80 ml) olive oil
4 eggs
1 tablespoon unsalted butter, chilled and diced
salt and freshly ground pepper

◙ Cut off any tough asparagus stalk ends and peel each stalk to the point at which the skin becomes tender. Slice each spear, on the bias, into slivers varying in thickness from ¼ in (6 mm) at the tender tip end to ⅛ in (3 mm) at the stalk end. Bring a saucepan filled with salted water to a boil. Plunge the slivers into the boiling water and, as soon as the water returns to a boil, drain them.

◙ Warm 1 tablespoon of the olive oil in a sauté pan over high heat. Add the asparagus slivers and sauté for a few seconds. Remove from the heat.

◙ In a mixing bowl combine the eggs, butter and salt and pepper to taste. Break up the eggs with a fork, whisking enough only to mix the whites and yolks. Add the asparagus, stirring and beating with the fork at the same time to disperse the heat immediately throughout the mass of eggs.

◙ Select an omelet pan measuring 11 in (28 cm) at the top and 8 in (20 cm) at the bottom. Warm 2 tablespoons olive oil in the pan over high heat, rotating the pan to coat the sides with oil. Pour in the egg mixture and stir, or swirl, the mixture with the back of the fork without touching the bottom or sides of the pan. Gradually working around the circumference of the omelet, lift the edges with the fork tip, tilting the pan each time to permit the liquid egg on the surface to run beneath the underside.

◙ When the omelet begins to set, begin rolling the omelet at the handle side of the pan, lifting the edge with the side of the fork and folding it over. Fold again, pull the pan toward yourself, tilting it sharply to cradle the omelet at the far side, over the heat. Press the outer edge of the omelet against the rolled mass with the fork tines and hold the pan, still at an angle, over the heat for a few seconds to color the underside. Roll the omelet out onto a warmed platter, seam side down and golden side up, by partially inverting the pan.

SERVES 2

Asparagus Omelet

In the park of the Château de Lourmarin, Scrambled Eggs with Tomatoes and Basil

BROUILLADE AUX TOMATES

Scrambled Eggs with Tomatoes and Basil

2 tablespoons olive oil
1 clove garlic, finely chopped
1½ lb (750 g) garden-ripe tomatoes, peeled, seeded and
   coarsely chopped
salt
1 bay leaf
10 eggs
¼ cup (2 oz/60 g) unsalted butter, chilled and diced
freshly ground pepper
handful of fresh basil leaves, torn into fragments at the last
   minute

◼ Warm the olive oil in a flameproof earthenware casserole over low heat. Add the garlic and, before it begins to color, add the tomatoes, salt to taste and bay leaf. Raise the heat slightly until the tomatoes are heated through and bubbling, then lower it and cook, uncovered, stirring occasionally with a wooden spoon, until all the liquid evaporates, about 10–15 minutes. Remove from the heat and remove and discard the bay leaf.
◼ In a mixing bowl, combine the eggs, a pinch of salt, butter and freshly ground pepper to taste. Break up the eggs with a fork, whisking only enough to mix the whites and yolks. Place the pan holding the tomatoes over medium-high heat and pour in the eggs. Stir constantly, scraping the sides and bottom of the pan with the wooden spoon, until the mixture begins to form a thick cream.
◼ Remove from the heat, add the basil and continue stirring as the eggs continue to absorb heat from the pan. Serve directly from the pan.

SERVES 4

Ratatouille

RATATOUILLE

Ratatouille is especially interesting to prepare in large quantity at the height of summer when all of the vegetables are at their best and usually in great abundance. It is a refreshing cold summer luncheon starter and the flavors meld and improve after a couple of days. Serve it hot with grilled or roast lamb, pork, veal or poultry, or mix it into scrambled eggs.

about 1 cup (8 fl oz/250 ml) olive oil
2 lb (1 kg) onions, coarsely cut
2 lb (1 kg) firm, glossy, elongated eggplants (aubergines), thickly sliced and then cut into large cubes
2 lb (1 kg) red, yellow and green sweet peppers (capsicums), halved lengthwise, seeded, deribbed and cut into squares
2 lb (1 kg) garden-ripe tomatoes, peeled, seeded, and coarsely cut
1 head garlic, cloves separated and peeled
handful of coarse sea salt

large bouquet garni, including 3 bay leaves and several fresh
  thyme sprigs (see glossary)
2 lb (1 kg) small, firm zucchini (courgettes), quartered
  lengthwise and thickly sliced crosswise
freshly ground pepper
fresh basil leaves

◙ Warm half of the olive oil in an 8–10-qt (8–10-l) stockpot
over low heat. Add the onions and cook gently until softened
but not colored, about 10 minutes. Stir occasionally with a
wooden spoon as you begin to cut up and progressively add all
the other vegetables, with the exception of the zucchini. Add
the salt and stir gently, scraping the bottom of the pot, until the
vegetables begin to release their liquid. Raise the heat to
medium and bring the liquid to a boil. From the time the onions
were added to the pot to the moment the boil is reached, 45
minutes to 1 hour should elapse.
◙ Bury the bouquet garni beneath the vegetables, reduce the
heat to maintain a light, bubbling simmer and cover with the
lid slightly ajar. After about 30 minutes, add the zucchini,
forcing it beneath the liquid's surface with the back of the
wooden spoon. Simmer for another 45 minutes to 1 hour, or
until all of the vegetables are meltingly tender.
◙ The vegetables must now be drained and their juices
reduced. The most practical way to do this is to place a large
colander with legs inside a large (12 in/30 cm in diameter),
heavy sauté pan. Pour the contents of the pot (slowly and away
from yourself, to avoid splattering) into the colander. Let drain
for a couple of minutes, then prop the colander over the empty
stockpot to continue draining.
◙ Place the juices over high heat, bring to a boil, and then
reduce the heat to maintain a gentle boil. Place a platter beside
the stockpot and, from time to time, move the colander to the
platter to empty newly drained juices from the pot into the
reducing liquid. About 1 hour will be required for the juices to
reduce to a deep, mahogany-colored syrup with a foamy boil.
Toward the end of the reduction, survey the pan constantly,
stirring often, and remove it from the heat the moment the
foamy boil begins to subside into a staccato bubble.
◙ Return the vegetables to their cooking pot, remove the
bouquet garni and pour in the reduced juices, scraping the pot
clean. Gently stir the vegetables until all are evenly coated with
the reduced juices. Turn them into a large dish to cool.
◙ Grind over some pepper and stir several spoonfuls of the
remaining olive oil into the cooled vegetables. Unless the dish
is meant to be consumed at a single sitting, spoon only as much
as you think necessary for the meal into a smaller serving dish
before adding a few more drops of olive oil to the surface. Tear
basil leaves into fragments and scatter them over the top.
Tightly cover the remainder and refrigerate.

SERVES 10–12

BROUILLADE AUX TRUFFES
Scrambled Eggs with Truffles

*The northernmost section of the Vaucluse consists of a small enclave
within the department of the Drôme. Here, the villages of Valréas
and Richerenches are important truffle centers. The black truffle
season begins around the first of December, the truffles are best in
January and February and, then, the season is over. Eggs are a
perfect vehicle for the truffles' magic perfume. The eggs are cooked
in a* bain-marie, *a heavy saucepan placed on a low tripod in a
larger saucepan that is filled with water to about the level of the
eggs in the smaller pan. To gauge the amount of water necessary,
assemble the pans and the tripod in advance, pour water into
the larger pan until it reaches the correct level and then
remove the smaller pan.*

1 clove garlic, cut in half
3 oz (100 g) black truffles, brushed and sliced
⅓ cup (3 oz/100 g) unsalted butter, chilled and diced
10 eggs
salt
freshly ground pepper

◙ Rub the inside surfaces of a mixing bowl with the cut surface
of a half clove of garlic. Add the truffles and half the butter.
Break in the eggs, cover the bowl with a plate and leave for 30
minutes for scents and flavors to intermingle.
◙ Assemble the *bain-marie* as described in the recipe introduction and remove the small pan. Bring the water in the larger pan
to a boil and lower the heat so the water is hot but distinctly
beneath a boil. Rub a wooden spoon with the remaining half
clove of garlic. Sprinkle salt and pepper to taste over the eggs
and beat very briefly with a fork. Pour the egg mixture into the
smaller saucepan, wiping the bowl clean, and place the pan on
the tripod in the hot water. Stir the eggs with the garlic-rubbed
spoon, adjusting the heat when necessary to prevent the water
from boiling. At first, nothing seems to happen, but when,
finally, the eggs begin to thicken, it happens very rapidly. Stir
more rapidly at this point, removing the pan for a moment
from the water if you fear losing control. As the eggs begin to
turn into a thick, but easily pourable cream, remove the pan
from the water, add the remaining butter and continue stirring
for a few minutes. The amount of time necessary to cook the
eggs will vary, depending upon the cooking vessel. The longer
they take, the better their texture, however.
◙ Serve directly from the saucepan onto a warm—but not
hot—plate.

SERVES 4

Scrambled Eggs with Truffles

ALPES·MARITIMES

RAÏOLA
Ravioli

In Provence ravioli are made from daube, leftover or prepared especially for that purpose the previous day. The meat should be removed from its braising liquid while still warm. The reheated braising liquid is the sauce, and old women are known to guard jealously the "secret" of their ravioli sauces. Benoit Mascarelli, author of La table en Provence *(1946), writes, "We have seen old Niçois weep at the mere sound of the lovely name 'Raïola'!" In Nice ravioli stuffing typically contains chard (silverbeet) greens, and often a poached and puréed lamb's brain lends suavity.*

double recipe pasta dough made without saffron (see
    Provençal fish soup on page 42)

FOR THE STUFFING:

1 tablespoon olive oil
1 onion, finely chopped
¼ lb (125 g) Swiss chard (silverbeet) greens or spinach,
    parboiled, squeezed dry and finely chopped (see glossary)
½ cup (1 oz/30 g) fresh bread crumbs
2–3 tablespoons daube braising juices, chilled to jellied state
    (see Provençal daube on page 122)
½ lb (250 g) braised beef from daube, chilled, finely chopped
¼ cup (1 oz/30 g) freshly grated Parmesan cheese
1 egg
freshly ground pepper
whole nutmeg
salt

about 2 cups (16 fl oz/500 ml) daube braising juices
few drops olive oil
½ cup (2 oz/60 g) freshly grated Parmesan cheese

◾ Prepare the ravioli several hours in advance so that, at the last minute, you only have to boil them and put on the braising juices to simmer. First prepare the pasta dough and let it rest for about 1 hour.

◾ To make the stuffing, warm the olive oil in a flameproof earthenware casserole or a heavy sauté pan over low heat. Add the onion and cook over low heat until softened but not colored, about 15 minutes. Add the greens and cook, stirring with a wooden spoon, for several minutes. Add the bread crumbs and a chunk of jellied daube braising liquid and simmer, stirring, until no

Top to bottom: Spinach Dumplings, Ravioli

liquid remains, about 5 minutes. Remove from the heat and stir in the chopped meat. Add the cheese, egg, grind over some pepper and, using the blade of a paring knife, scrape in a bit of nutmeg. Mix thoroughly and taste for salt. (In the past this stuffing was pounded to a purée and passed through a sieve. If you prefer a fine purée, you can assemble the stuffing up to this point and pass it briefly in a food processor fitted with the metal blade).

◾ Divide the pasta dough in half. On a floured work surface, roll out 1 dough portion as thinly as possible into a rectangle. Roll out the second portion into a rectangle of approximately the same size. On one, arrange teaspoonfuls of the stuffing, spacing them at 1-in (2.5-cm) intervals on all sides. Using a pastry brush dipped in water, moisten the areas between the rows of stuffing. Transfer the second rectangle to rest on top of the first and, using a stick ¼ in (6 mm) wide, press firmly between the rows to seal the dough sheets together. Using a pastry cutting wheel or a knife, cut along the middle of the sealed rows to separate the ravioli. Place them, side by side and not touching, on floured towels until ready to be cooked.

◾ Heat the braising juices in a saucepan and maintain at a simmer. Bring a saucepan filled with salted water to a boil and add the olive oil. Plunge the ravioli into the boiling water and boil until tender, 6–7 minutes. Pour a ladleful of hot braising juices into a warmed deep serving dish or oven dish and, using a spider or a large, flat slotted spoon, remove the ravioli, a few at a time, each time reposing the spoon on a folded towel to drain them before slipping them into the dish. Ladle additional braising juices over each layer of ravioli and sprinkle with some of the cheese. Cover the dish and hold in a warm place for 3–4 minutes before serving in warmed soup plates.

SERVES 4

ALPES·DE·HAUTE·PROVENCE

CAILLETTES GAVOTTES
Spinach Dumplings

½ lb (250 g) *brousse* (see glossary) or ricotta cheese
1 lb (500 g) spinach, parboiled, squeezed dry and chopped
    (see glossary)
salt and freshly ground pepper
persillade made with 1 clove garlic (see glossary)
2 eggs
about 2 cups (8 oz/250 g) all-purpose (plain) flour
2 cups (16 fl oz/500 ml) tomato sauce, heated (see glossary)
½ cup (2 oz/60 g) freshly grated Parmesan cheese
¼ cup (2 oz/60 g) unsalted butter

◾ In a mixing bowl and using a fork, mash together the *brousse*, spinach, *persillade,* eggs and salt and pepper to taste. Slowly add 1 cup (4 oz/125 g) of the flour, first stirring and then mixing and kneading with your hands until the mixture is firm but still supple, adding more flour as needed to achieve correct consistency. Cover with a towel and leave to relax for 1 hour.

◾ Thickly flour a work surface. Using the palms of your hands, roll pieces of the mixture on the surface into thick, elongated logs about 1 in (2.5 cm) in diameter. Cut each log into 2½-in (6-cm) lengths to form the dumplings. Roll the dumplings in the flour again, flouring the cut ends.

◾ Preheat an oven to 450°F (230°C). Bring a large pot filled with salted water to a boil. Drop in the dumplings. When the water returns to a boil, adjust the heat to maintain a gentle boil and cook for 15–20 minutes. Using a spider or a large slotted spoon, remove the dumplings to a platter. Layer half the dumplings in a gratin dish of a size just to contain them. Ladle half of the tomato sauce over the top, sprinkle with half of the cheese, and scatter over shavings of the butter. Repeat the layers.

◾ Place in the oven and bake until the sauce begins to bubble and the cheese melts, 6–7 minutes.

SERVES 4

One-Eyed Bouillabaisse

BOUILLABAISSE BORGNE

One-Eyed Bouillabaisse

For a bouillabaisse d'épinards or épinards à la marseillaise, omit the tomatoes and the dried orange peel. Add 2 lb (1 kg) spinach, parboiled, squeezed dry and chopped (see glossary), to the saucepan with the onion and leeks and cook as directed before combining with the other ingredients. For a bouillabaisse de petits pois, omit the tomatoes and the dried orange peel and add 2 lb (1 kg) small green peas, shelled, with the potatoes.

4–5 tablespoons (2–3 fl oz/60–80 ml) olive oil
½ lb (250 g) leeks, white and tender green parts, thinly sliced
1 sweet white onion, thinly sliced
4 cloves garlic
2 or 3 garden-ripe tomatoes, peeled, seeded and coarsely chopped
salt and cayenne pepper
large pinch of saffron threads
large bouquet garni, including a fennel stalk and a strip of dried orange peel (see glossary)
6 cups (48 fl oz/1.5 l) water, boiling

1 lb (500 g) potatoes, peeled, sliced ¼ in (6 mm) thick and rinsed
4 eggs
4 thin slices semidry bread, rubbed with a garlic clove

◼ Warm 3 tablespoons of the olive oil in a flameproof earthenware casserole or a heavy saucepan over low heat. Add the leeks and onion and cook, stirring occasionally, until softened but not colored, 10–15 minutes. Add the garlic, tomatoes, salt to taste, a suspicion of cayenne and the saffron. Raise the heat and cook for 5 minutes longer, shaking the pan and stirring the contents.

◼ Add the bouquet garni, the boiling water and potatoes. Return to a boil, adjust the heat to maintain a gentle boil, cover and cook until the potatoes are easily crushed against the side of the pan, 25–30 minutes. Remove from the heat.

◼ One at a time, break the eggs into a saucer and slip each egg into the soup so it floats on top. Cover the pan and leave the eggs to poach until the whites are opaque, 2–3 minutes.

◼ Place a bread slice in each soup plate. Dribble a little of the remaining olive oil over each slice. Using a slotted spoon remove a poached egg to each bread slice, then ladle the potatoes and broth directly from the cooking vessel into the bowls.

SERVES 4

In Roussillon, from top to bottom: Chick-pea Salad, Niçois Salad

SALADE DE POIS CHICHES
Chick-pea Salad

Chick-peas are sensitive to hard water with a high calcium content. In the country, rainwater can be collected in pails in the open, away from trees and rooftops. In cities, the best solution is to use a neutral bottled mineral water; the most commonly used brand in Provence is Volvic. Chick-peas may require from 1½–3 hours or more cooking time, depending upon whether they are from this year's harvest or older and on the quality of the water. It is the custom to prepare more than are needed for the salad to make certain that some remain for a soup.

3¾ cups (1½ lbs/750 g) dried chick-peas
about 4 qt (4 l) neutral mineral water
1 large carrot, peeled and cut into thirds
1 onion stuck with 2 whole cloves
1 fresh thyme sprig
1 bay leaf
salt

FOR THE TABLE:

1 sweet white onion, finely chopped, or a handful of young
    green shallots (see glossary) or green (spring) onions,
    finely sliced
3 or 4 cloves garlic, finely chopped
bouquet of fresh flat-leaf (Italian) parsley, finely chopped
cruets of olive oil and vinegar
salt and pepper mill

▨ Place the chick-peas in a bowl and pour over 1 bottle (1 qt/1 l) of slightly warmed mineral water. Let stand overnight.

▨ Drain the chick-peas, put them into a flameproof earthenware casserole or an enameled ironware pan and pour in a bottle of cold mineral water. Bring to a boil, cover and cook at a gentle boil for about 30 minutes. Meanwhile, bring the remaining mineral water to a boil.

▨ Drain the peas and return them to the cooking vessel. Add the carrot, onion, herbs, salt to taste and enough boiling mineral water to immerse the peas by about 1½ in (4 cm). Bring back to a boil, adjust the heat to cook at a gentle simmer, cover and cook until tender—intact but easily crushed. If, while cooking, the water level seems low, add more boiling mineral water. If the chick-peas become tender more quickly than expected, remove from the heat and reheat just before serving.

▨ Remove and discard the carrot, onion and herbs. Serve the chick-peas hot, directly from the cooking vessel, using a spider or a slotted spoon. The table condiments—chopped onion, garlic and parsley—may be arranged in neat piles on a single plate or served in individual dishes. Each person seasons to taste with the condiments, olive oil, vinegar, salt and pepper. If the olive oil is freshly pressed, thick and cloudy, it is a great moment; if not, it is still wonderful. The explosion of perfume as the olive oil contacts the hot chick-peas is intoxicating.

SERVES 8

SALADE NIÇOISE
Niçois Salad

One of the principles of a salade niçoise is that it contain no cooked vegetables. A handful of shelled young broad (fava) beans or trimmed and thinly sliced baby artichokes (see glossary), tossed in lemon juice and drained, may be added. Pan bagnat is salade niçoise enclosed in a bread roll, left to soak for a while and eaten as a sandwich. In this case the tomatoes, eggs and anchovy fillets should be chopped and the olives pitted.

1 small cucumber
1 clove garlic, cut in half lengthwise
salt
3 barely ripened tomatoes, cored and cut into wedges
2 Italian green sweet peppers or other sweet peppers
    (capsicums), seeded, deribbed and thinly sliced crosswise
3 or 4 young green shallots (see glossary) or green (spring)
    onions, including the tender green parts, thinly sliced
2 hard-cooked eggs, shelled and quartered lengthwise
4 or 5 salt anchovies, rinsed and filleted (see glossary)
handful of black olives
handful of fresh basil leaves
freshly ground pepper
5–6 tablespoons (3 oz/90 ml) olive oil

◙ Peel the cucumber and cut it in half lengthwise. Scoop out the seeds, then cut crosswise into thin slices. Layer the slices in a bowl, sprinkling each layer with salt. Let stand for 30 minutes, then squeeze out excess liquid and sponge the slices dry.
◙ A wide, shallow dish permits the most attractive presentation. Rub the dish all over with the cut surfaces of garlic. Scatter the cucumber, tomatoes, peppers, shallots, eggs, anchovy fillets and olives casually but artfully into the dish. Tear the basil leaves into fragments and scatter over the surface. Present the dish at table. Sprinkle on salt and grind over pepper to taste. Pour the olive oil in a fine stream back and forth over the surface. Toss and serve.

SERVES 4

RISSOLES
Deep-fried Savory Pastries

Rissoles are deep-fried ravioli, one of the many inspired ways of giving new life and a fresh look to leftovers. They can be made from any pastry or pasta dough, and the variety of possible stuffings is limited only by one's imagination. Instead of forming them into square ravioli, they are often cut into circles, stuffed, moistened around the edges, folded and sealed, by pressing with fingertips, into half-moons.

2 tablespoons olive oil
1 onion, finely chopped
¼ lb (125 g) fresh cultivated mushrooms, finely chopped
salt and freshly ground pepper
whole nutmeg
small pinch of Provençal mixed dried herbs (see glossary)
persillade made with 1 clove garlic (see glossary)
about 1 teaspoon fresh lemon juice
½ lb (250 g) leftover roast chicken, boned, skinned and
    finely chopped
3 tablespoons *tapénade* (recipe on page 34)
3 egg yolks
double recipe pasta dough made without saffron (see Provençal
    fish soup on page 42)

corn oil or peanut oil for deep-frying
2 cups (16 fl oz/500 ml) tomato sauce, heated (see glossary)

◙ Warm the olive oil in a heavy frying pan over low heat. Add the onion and cook over the low heat until soft but not colored, about 10 minutes. Add the mushrooms and raise the heat to high. Season to taste with salt and pepper and scrape in a suspicion of nutmeg. Add the herbs and toss or stir with a wooden spoon until the liquid from the mushrooms evaporates and the mixture is nearly dry. Add the *persillade* and stir around until you can smell the characteristic odor of frying garlic and parsley. Add a few drops of lemon juice, stir and remove from the heat.
◙ In a mixing bowl, stir together the mushroom mixture and chicken and leave to cool a bit. Add the *tapénade* and egg yolks and beat with the wooden spoon to mix well. Cover and chill the mixture to firm it up.
◙ While the filling is chilling, prepare the pasta dough and let it rest for about 1 hour.
◙ On a floured work surface, roll out 1 dough portion as thinly as possible into a rectangle. Roll out the second portion into a rectangle of approximately the same size. On one rectangle, arrange 2 teaspoonful mounds of the chicken mixture, spacing them 2 in (5 cm) apart on all sides. Using a pastry brush dipped in water, moisten the areas between the rows of stuffing. Transfer the second rectangle to rest on top of the first. Using your fingertips or the side of your hand, press firmly between the rows to seal the dough sheets together. Using a pastry cutting wheel or a knife, cut along the middle of the rows into 2-in (5-cm) squares. You can hold them for a while, spread out on floured towels, or fry them immediately.
◙ Following the directions for deep-frying in the glossary, heat the oil in a large pan. Slip a few of the pasta squares into the hot oil. Do not crowd the pan. Fry them, turning them over in the oil, until crisp and golden, about 5 minutes. Drain and keep warm as directed. Repeat with the rest of the squares.
◙ Serve the *rissoles* hot, accompanied with the tomato sauce.

SERVES 4

Deep-fried Savory Pastries

ANCHOÏADE
Anchovy Spread

An anchoïade, *or* anchoyade—*or, in Marseilles, a* quichet—*was, in the past, a ritual performance. It was described by 19th-century Marseillais chef Caillat as the* hors d'oeuvre de rigueur *for every country lunch (*déjeuner champêtre*). Each person had slices of semidry bread and small pieces of fresh bread. Anchovy fillets were bathed in a plate of olive oil and laid on the dry bread, while the pieces of fresh bread were repeatedly dipped in the olive oil, pressed, sponged and rubbed on the anchovy fillets, then eaten. Finally, when the semidry crust was impregnated with disintegrated anchovy and olive oil, it was grilled over embers and eaten. In Nice,* sauce provençale froide, *or anchovy aïoli, is called* anchoïade.

½ cup (4 fl oz/125 ml) olive oil
1 teaspoon Provençal herb vinegar (see glossary)
10–12 salt anchovies, rinsed and filleted (see glossary)
freshly ground pepper
1 semidry baguette, cut crosswise into quarters, then split in half lengthwise and surfaces dried in the sun or in a slow oven
3 or 4 cloves garlic

▨ Warm the olive oil, vinegar and anchovies in a flameproof earthenware casserole or heavy sauté pan over the lowest possible heat. The anchovies should not cook, but will melt in contact with the warmth. Grind in pepper to taste and stir to mix. Rub the dried cut surfaces of bread with the garlic cloves and spread them with the oil-anchovy mixture. Leave for 1 hour or so until the bread is thoroughly saturated.
▨ Meanwhile, prepare a fire in a charcoal grill or preheat a broiler (griller). Place the bread slices on a grill rack over dying embers or under the broiler (griller) and grill first on the crust side and then on the anchovy spread side. Serve hot.

SERVES 4

BAGNA CAUDA
Raw Vegetables with Hot Anchovy Sauce

Crudités—*raw vegetables—are among the commonest of spring and summer Provençal lunch openers. Often they are simply served with cruets of olive oil and vinegar and salt and pepper. Or they may be accompanied by* aïoli *(see glossary),* pistou *(recipe on page 36) or* tapénade *(recipe on page 34).* Bagna cauda *is an import from Piedmont, by way of Nice, now embraced by all of Provence. A Piedmont* bagna cauda *contains much more butter and, often, chopped or sliced white truffles.*

SUGGESTED VEGETABLES:

Italian sweet peppers or other sweet peppers (capsicums), split lengthwise into quarters
Belgian endive (chicory/witloof), split lengthwise into quarters
celery hearts, split lengthwise into quarters
fennel bulb hearts, split lengthwise into quarters, or sliced radicchio (red chicory) leaves
small romaine (cos) leaves
young green shallots (see glossary) or green (spring) onions
radishes with leaves attached
cauliflower florets
crisp young cucumbers with undeveloped seeds, peeled and split lengthwise into quarters
carrots, peeled and split lengthwise into quarters
tender, young artichokes, tough outer leaves removed

4 firm, crisp cloves garlic
pinch of coarse salt
¾ cup (6 fl oz/180 ml) olive oil
2 tablespoons unsalted butter
12 salt anchovies, rinsed, filleted and chopped (see glossary)
bread for serving

▨ Arrange a selection of the suggested vegetables on attractive platters.
▨ In a mortar pound together the garlic and salt to form a paste. Place the paste in a small, flameproof earthenware casserole or enameled ironware casserole over low heat. Add the olive oil, butter and anchovies and stir with a wooden spoon until all the ingredients are melted together to form a sauce.
▨ At the table, place the pan over a spirit lamp or on a hot plate at low heat. Surround it with the platters of vegetables. Guests should take care to stir the sauce with each vegetable piece they dip into it and to hold a piece of bread nearby to collect dribbles when transporting the vegetable from the sauce to their mouths.

SERVES 4

PETITS FARCIS
Stuffed Tomatoes and Zucchini

Leftover braised or roasted meat is often used to prepare these stuffed vegetables. They are no less good as a starter when prepared without meat and are, then, also an appropriate garnish for grilled or roasted meats. As recently as 25 years ago, in the village streets of Provence on a Sunday morning one could see children carrying large trays of stuffed tomatoes and zucchini to the baker to be put into the ovens when the last batch of bread came out. Today, most households have ovens and few bakers still burn wood fires.

4 tomatoes, about 5 oz (150 g) each
salt
4 zucchini (courgettes), about 5 oz (150 g) each
6 tablespoons (3 fl oz/90 ml) olive oil
1 onion, finely chopped
¼ lb (125 g) sausage meat (see glossary)
¼ lb (125 g) boneless lean lamb, finely chopped
freshly ground pepper
pinch of Provençal mixed dried herbs (see glossary)
persillade made with 1 clove garlic (see glossary)
1 cup (2 oz/50 g) fresh bread crumbs
¼ cup (1 oz/30 g) freshly grated Parmesan cheese
1 or 2 eggs
dried bread crumbs

▨ Preheat an oven to 350°F (180°C).
▨ Cut a slice from the top of each tomato. Using a teaspoon, scoop out the flesh from the center of the tomato; discard the seeds and liquid but reserve the flesh. Salt the inside of each tomato and place the tomatoes, upside down, on a wire rack to drain.
▨ Remove the stem end and a sliver from the flower end of each zucchini. Cut each zucchini in half lengthwise and empty the halves with a melon baller, taking care not to cut too close to the walls. Reserve the flesh. Fill a large pot with water and bring to a boil. Slip the emptied zucchini halves into the pot and boil until the flesh is slightly softened but not cooked, 6–7 minutes. Remove them carefully with a slotted utensil, placing them, cut surface down, on a towel to drain.
▨ Chop the reserved zucchini and tomato flesh. Heat 2 tablespoons of the olive oil in a frying pan over low heat. Add the onion and cook until soft but not colored, about 10 minutes. Add the chopped zucchini and tomato and salt to taste and cook, stirring and tossing, for about 15 minutes, or until very soft and reduced, but not browned.
▨ Turn the cooked vegetables out into a mixing bowl. Add the meats, pepper to taste, herbs, *persillade,* fresh bread crumbs and

Top to bottom: Raw Vegetables with Hot
Anchovy Sauce, Anchovy Spread

Parmesan; mix thoroughly. Add 1 egg and a spoonful or so of the olive oil and mix with your hands. If the stuffing seems too dry, mix in another egg. Taste for salt.

✪ Arrange the tomato and zucchini shells in a shallow baking dish of a size to just hold them without touching (or, if easier, bake them in separate dishes). Sprinkle each with a little salt and then dribble with a thread of olive oil. Using a teaspoon, distribute the stuffing evenly among the vegetables, pressing

gently with the back of the spoon to force it into place. Sprinkle the surfaces with dried bread crumbs and then dribble a thread of olive oil back and forth. Pour a little water into the bottom of the dish. Place in the oven and bake until the surface of the stuffing is golden and the vegetables are somewhat wrinkled and shrunken. Serve hot, warm or at room temperature.

SERVES 4   *Photograph pages 28–29*

BALLOTTES À LA NIÇOISE
Niçois Croquettes

This is a typical home-kitchen, all-purpose stuffing. Any leftover roast or braised meat or poultry can be used or the leftovers can be replaced by sausage meat (see glossary), ground lamb or beef or a combination. Semidry bread crumbs, soaked in milk and squeezed dry, often replace the potatoes. The little balls can simply be floured, without being breaded, and fried, or they can be poached, drained, spread in a gratin dish, sprinkled with grated cheese, covered with tomato sauce and passed for 10 minutes in a hot oven. These croquettes can also be fried in a frying pan in olive oil to a depth of about ¼ in (6 mm), shaking the pan gently to turn them around and over.

2 potatoes, about 6 oz (185 g), peeled
½ lb (250 g) leftover *pot-au-feu*, finely chopped (recipe on page 45)
persillade made with 1 clove garlic (see glossary)
3 or 4 young green shallots (see glossary) or green (spring) onions, finely chopped

salt and freshly ground pepper
3 or 4 eggs
all-purpose (plain) flour
dried bread crumbs
vegetable oil for deep–frying
2 cups (16 fl oz/500 ml) tomato sauce, heated (see glossary)

◼ Place the potatoes in a saucepan filled with salted water, bring to a boil and boil until just done, about 30 minutes. Drain, transfer to a plate and, using a fork, mash while still hot. Combine the mashed potatoes in a bowl with the meat, *persillade*, shallots, salt and pepper to taste and one of the eggs. Using your hands, mix thoroughly. If the mixture seems very stiff, add another egg.

◼ Sprinkle a tray or large platter with flour. Beat 2 eggs in a soup plate. Open several thicknesses of newspaper on a work surface and sprinkle thickly with bread crumbs. With moist hands, form the meat mixture into balls the size of large walnuts, placing them in a single layer on the flour as they are formed. Sprinkle more flour over the tops and roll the balls around, shaking or rotating the tray or platter, until well floured on both sides. Put several at a time into the eggs, rotate, rolling them around again, until they are well coated with the egg. Using a teaspoon, remove them, one by one, to the crumbs. Sprinkle more crumbs over the tops and roll them around with your hands in the crumbs. Leave them in the crumbs, sprinkled with more crumbs, to dry for 1 hour or so.

◼ Following the directions for deep-frying in the glossary, heat the oil in a large pan. Toss the balls in your hands to shake them free of loose crumbs and them slip them into the hot oil. Do not crowd the pan. Fry them, turning them over in the oil, until crisp and golden, about 4–5 minutes. Drain and keep warm as directed. Repeat with the remaining balls.

◼ Serve the croquettes hot, accompanied with tomato sauce.

SERVES 4

Niçois Croquettes

TERRINE DE GIBIER À PLUME
Game Bird Terrine

Wild duck, pheasant, partridge and woodcock are all wonderful elements in a game terrine, as are European wild rabbits or American cottontails. Farmed mallard ducks can be very good. Be sure the birds include the hearts, livers and gizzards. Use whatever is available, supplementing it, if necessary, with domestic duck or rabbit. Truffles are always a welcome addition.

2 game birds, or more if they are small, cut into pieces (see recipe introduction for suggestions)

FOR THE BROTH:

1 onion, coarsely chopped
1 carrot, sliced
1 bay leaf
1 fresh thyme sprig
broken-up bird carcasses
salt

5 oz (150 g) poultry livers
1 lb (500 g) sausage meat (see glossary)
¼ lb (125 g) pork back fat, chilled and cut into ¼-in (6-mm) dice
¼ lb (125 g) shank (shin) end of raw ham such as prosciutto, finely chopped
1 onion, finely chopped and cooked in 1 tablespoon olive oil until soft but not colored
large pinch of coarse salt
2 cloves garlic
1 cup (2 oz/60 g) fresh bread crumbs
large pinch of Provençal mixed dried herbs (see glossary)
¼ cup (2 fl oz/60 ml) marc de Provence (see glossary) or Cognac

At La Tourtine vineyard, Domaine Tempier, Game Bird Terrine

3 eggs
salt, freshly ground pepper and ground allspice
thin sheets of fresh pork back fat
boiling water as needed

◎ Remove the flesh from the pieces of game bird, set aside with the hearts, livers and gizzards. Discard the skins. Chop or break up any awkwardly shaped pieces of carcass.

◎ To prepare the broth, place the onion, carrot, bay and thyme in the bottom of a saucepan and arrange the carcass pieces on top. Cover generously with cold water and bring to a boil. Skim off any scum and froth and add salt to taste. Adjust the heat to maintain a simmer, cover with a lid slightly ajar and simmer for 2 hours. Strain, return to the saucepan and boil gently until reduced to about ½ cup (4 fl oz/125 ml); skim off any fat. Set aside.

◎ Cut the birds' breast meat into ¼-in (6-mm) dice. Chop the remaining flesh coarsely and place in a food processor fitted with the metal blade. Add the hearts, the fleshy lobes of the gizzards, the livers and the extra poultry livers. Process to a smooth purée.

◎ Combine all the meats and the cooked onion in a large mixing bowl. In a mortar pound together the coarse salt and garlic to form a paste. Add and mix in the bread crumbs, then add the reduced broth and stir to form a paste. Add the contents of the mortar to the mixing bowl, along with the herbs, brandy, eggs and salt, pepper and allspice to taste. Using your hands mix thoroughly.

◎ Preheat an oven to 325°F (165°C). Line a terrine, or more, depending upon size, with sheets of pork fat, pressing them firmly against the sides and bottom of the terrine(s). Pack the mixture, large spoonfuls at a time, into the terrine(s), pressing into place so as to leave no air pockets. Press a sheet of fat over the surface(s) and cover the terrine(s) with a lid or with aluminum foil.

◎ Place the terrine(s) in a large pan in the oven and pour in boiling water to reach halfway up the sides of the terrine(s). Place in the oven and bake small terrines (4 cups/16 fl oz/1 l) for about 1 hour and larger ones, depending upon their size, for up to 2 hours. They are done when the juices run clear, or when a trussing needle, thrust into the heart of the terrine, comes out quite warm to the touch.

◎ A terrine must be cooled under a weight to render the body compact for neat slicing. The weight should not exceed 1 ½– 2 lb (750 g–1 kg). Place the terrine(s) on a tray, lest any juices overflow. Remove the lid(s), place a sheet of foil over the surface(s) and then stiff cardboard cut to the inside dimensions of the terrine(s). Place the weight, or weights, on top—tinned goods are practical for this purpose. When cooled, cover and refrigerate the terrine(s). The flavor will improve with 2 or 3 days ripening. If a terrine is to be kept, uncut, for more than a few days, melted lard should be poured over the surface to seal it. A partially consumed terrine should be protected from contact with air by a sheet of plastic wrap pressed to the cut surface.

SERVES 10

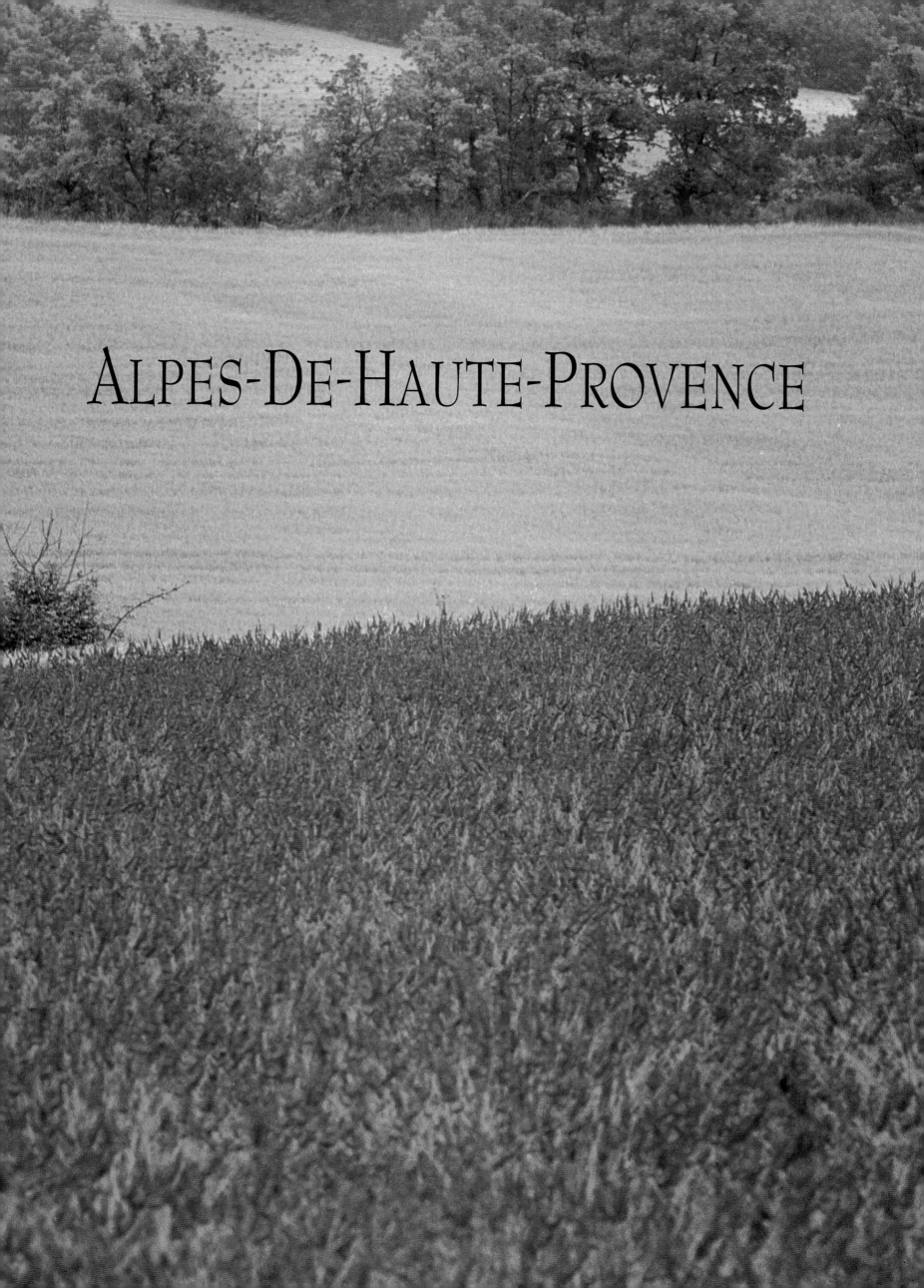

ALPES-DE-HAUTE-PROVENCE

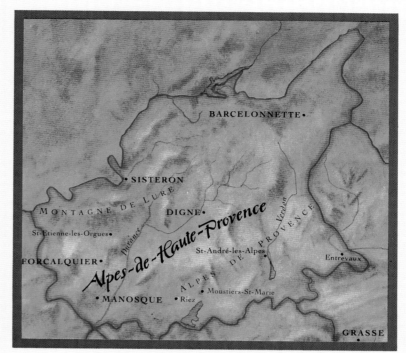

ALPES-DE-HAUTE-PROVENCE

The people of the Alpes-de-Haute-Provence live at the crossroads. These are the hinterlands, a Provence far from the Mediterranean, a sprawling area that stretches from the Italian border to the Montagne de Lure and the Vaucluse Mountains and encompasses the Mercantour National Park and the Verdon region. It is balanced between two lakes, Serre-Ponçon and Sainte-Croix, and is crossed by the Durance, a river once tumultuous and exuberant, which provided the route for invaders and for flocks moving to new pastures. Frédéric Mistral called it "one of the three evils of Provence."

This *département,* laced with hills and valleys, is the least tamed and most solitary of the region, its culinary customs seem a little more uncivilized than those in other parts of Provence.

The valleys of the Ubaye, the Bléone, the Jabron and the Durance, all the stories of the plateaus of Valensole and Forcalquier and Albion lead to uncharted territory. The first person to penetrate it was Jean Giono, writer of the stars, the man from Manosque, lord of Contadour, a hamlet of the Commune of Redortiers to the north of Banon. It was to Contadour, late one summer in 1935, that he led an expedition of citizens enamored of open spaces and frugal living. The author of *Regain* and *Collines* portrayed better than anyone else has done the rough, secretive, tormented peasants who inhabited a cold land beneath the purest of skies.

Previous pages: Still one of the most remote regions in Provence, the peaceful valleys of Alpes-de-Haute-Provence glow with blooming lavender in the summer. Left: Grand Canyon du Verdon, one of France's natural wonders, spans 12½ miles (21 km) in length and is 5,000 feet (1,500 m) deep.

The locals of Entrevaux find a quiet place in the shade and catch up on the day's events.

The way of life of the people in these parts still reflects Giono's Provence. Nor is it so very different from the one portrayed in another literary genre by Pierre Magnan, prominent author of local detective novels, who was born in Manosque and whose main character answers to the charming name Superintendent Laviolette. She, too, symbolizes a land of light where astronomers and all those who search for the stars come flocking. No doubt this explains, although only in part, why winter evenings by the fire with friends seem longer here than in other places.

In this special region, the thread that leads out of the labyrinth is the Durance. The river (which locals refer to as *la rivière* rather than *le fleuve,* thus more readily representing it as a female character) serves in its own way to bring together the culinary customs of the area, simply because the people have always moved along its banks, from the Dauphiné to the Rhône region. Another great writer from the south, Avignon-born Henri Bosco recalls the beneficial properties of the water of the Durance: " . . . water that makes the chick-pea, tomato, celery, asparagus, eggplant (aubergine) and bean grow as they grew in the Garden of Eden; water that will cook you a leek in ten minutes, water you don't just drink, you sip it and savor it; water without which all these or-

Here they make the golden *crespèu,* the omelet of the sun; they butcher the pig; they bake leg of lamb in the oven with potatoes; and around Barcelonnette, they eat a soup made with eggless pasta shells known as *crouzets.* In earlier days fish, which remain the magic of the Durance, even came back up the river, in boats, of course, and cooks prepared the anchovies, sardines and cod in spicy tomato sauces.

That said, the Alpes-de-Haute-Provence is nevertheless first and foremost a region of wild herbs that go into making magic soups, of little scrubland birds and of spelt, the poor man's corn that was highly valued in medieval times and is today making a return, this time to the most sophisticated tables. Although many foods are being rediscovered that are outside the reach of tourists, travelers will, no doubt, remember the cheese from Banon, wrapped in its chestnut leaf steeped in brandy and left to ferment, or covered in dried savory leaves and immersed in marc. Of course they will certainly also recall scrambled eggs with truffles, albeit not always served with due respect in the restaurants of the great far south. And they will remember the lamb, but only on the condition that it be the wonderful lamb from the Sisteron region, delicious at Easter and used in particular to prepare *le gigot aux olives,* leg of lamb roasted with olives, or *les côtelettes grillées à la braise,* tender lamb cutlets grilled over charcoal.

For color, finally, we have lavender, known as blue gold. There is indeed a Provence of lavender. The plant flourishes in summer on the high plateaus around Albion, the Montagne de Lure and Valensole, and plunges down to the hills of Grasse in the Alpes-Maritimes and the ocher Maures Mountains in the Var, on its way to join the Mediterranean.

Each year on August 15 a festival is held in Digne-les-Bains to celebrate lavender. The honored plant has had its share of misfortune, though; it is forced to share its empire with a hybrid, *lavandin.* The latter first appeared in the thirties, and now it is threatened by highly profitable artificial oils and essences.

The blue of the plateaus is a symbol of the inland paradise of the Alpes-de-Haute-Provence, a paradise that constitutes an obligatory route among pinnacles and orchards, an azure land where the legends, like the cooking, simmer for a long, long time among the stones of the country houses.

Much of the 20,000 acres of lavender harvested annually in Provence is reserved for the essence used in perfume and cosmetics, while the rest is dried to make sachets.

chards, kitchen gardens and the gardens full of apricot, peach, cherry and plum trees would be nothing but a desert of stones and rosehips."

In the end we must listen to the writers who throughout their lives have remained attached to their native soil. Paul Arène was another man of the Durance, born in Sisteron. He called himself Jean des Figues because he swore he was born at the foot of a fig tree, and rechristened his hometown Canteperdrix, because at that time (in the nineteenth century) it was still one of the last kingdoms of that delicate game bird, the *bartavelle* or "rock partridge."

Between the hills and the plains, however, cooking habits change. In the north and at high altitudes, cooks favor walnut oil, and in the old days lard and pork fat were used.

Restaurant seafood displays lure diners along the Côte d'Azur.

FISH AND SHELLFISH

A Provençal fishmonger's display of the catch brought in at dawn to the village fishing ports is a wondrous thing, for its fresh beauty if not for its abundance. In fact, only single—or very few—specimens of the most noble varieties may be present: *loup de mer* (Mediterranean sea bass), *daurade royale* (gilt-head bream), *sar, denti, pageot* (other Mediterranean breams), *pagre* (red porgy, the only Mediterranean bream to have crossed the Atlantic) and *chapon de mer* (large red rascasse or scorpionfish) are likely to be in attendance. The latter, because of the firmness of its flesh, its thick, short, round body and its large head, which forms a single cavity along with that of the body, is the most wonderful of all fish for stuffing and baking. It need not be sewn up; it sits neatly on its belly and arrives at the table looking very grand. There may also be *mostelle* (also called *mustelle* or *moustelle* and, in English, fork beard, whose silken flesh probably has no equivalent outside of the Mediterranean); *murène* (moray eel); and little *rougets de roche* (red mullets), which require three or four for each serving and may be limited to only a dozen or two for sale. Usually there is also a pile of fish labeled *bouillabaisse* that can furnish no more than two or three clients. Whatever its composition, this pile always includes beautiful, spiky *rascasses,* both red and black; multicolored, striped splashed and speckled *rouquiers* and *lucrèces* (both wrasses); and *vives* (weavers) and often *rascasses blanches* (star gazers). *Grondin* (gurnard), *St.-Pierre* (John Dory), *congre* (conger eel), *baudroie* (monkfish or anglerfish) and the scuttling, furious *favouilles,* or green shore crabs, (called, for that reason, *enragées*) are sold separately to complete the *bouillabaisse.*

Sometimes a freshly caught thirty-inch (75-cm) *loup de mer* appears. It is rarely displayed for more than a few minutes before a proud client takes off with the prize at

This poissonnerie in the Alpes-de-Haute-Provence has fresh fish trucked in from the coast daily.

Previous pages, clockwise from top left: Provençal Crayfish (recipe page 99), Stuffed Squid (recipe page 88), Sautéed Shrimp (recipe page 88).

The fish mongers usually have a pile of fresh fish labeled bouillabaisse; *this mixture provides the key ingredients to the celebrated fish stew.*

come loose from the carapaces. They are done at this point and should be removed before drying out.

Fish nomenclature in America is a slippery thing. Depending on the locality, a single fish may be known by a number of different names or different fish may be known by the same name. This is more troublesome for the scholar than for the cook, since the fish that move in this confusion can all receive the same treatments in the kitchen. America's answer to the *loup de mer* is the striped bass. The Mediterranean breams find their equivalents in America's porgies (red porgy, scup, pinfish, sheepshead). Red snapper, red drum, black sea bass, kingfish, weakfish, spot and many others can receive the same treatments, usually baked or grilled, as the breams; they may also be used in the famous fish stews of Provence. The thick-lipped wrasses always present in a *bouillabaisse* are represented in America by the tautog (blackfish, chub) and the cunner. Any of the fish known as ocean perch, rockfish or redfish are good choices for the fish stews, as is grouper, when available. Sea robin represents the gurnards.

The fish market is a daily event on Quai des Belges in the old port of Marseilles.

breath-taking cost. (At the other extreme of the price scale, it is possible to feed four with stiff, arched, brightly glinting sardines, freshly netted, for very little money.) The *loup,* fresh from the sea, intact, unscaled and grilled over incandescent wood embers—about forty minutes for a six pound (3-kg) fish that will serve six people— embodies all of the poetry and the beauty of Provence and the Mediterranean. As it grills, the scales and the skin weld together, forming a charred, protective sheath, detached from the flesh. The fish is presented at the table in its blackened armor. The sheath is cut along the back, next to the fin bones, the length of the abdomen and at the tail and at the head. It is then lifted off like a lid to reveal miraculously white flesh sparkling in its own juices. It is seasoned by the sea. Salt and pepper cannot improve it and lemon will dull its clear sweetness.

Other large fish may be poached, grilled or baked whole and presented at the table to admiration and great expectation among the guests. In Provence, the fish most often presented in this way are sea bass, the various breams (porgies) and gray mullet. In America, among the many possibilities, red snapper, black sea bass and tautog should certainly be added to the list.

Also to be savored unseasoned (unscaled and ungutted—the scales are scraped off at table and the liver and other innards form the sauce) are the little *rougets de roche,* grilled for no more than a couple of minutes on each side, and one-pound (500-g) langoustes, or spiny lobsters, each an individual portion. The langoustes are grilled whole for about fourteen minutes and split in two at the moment of serving. When first put on the grill, they want to curl up their tails, but after a couple of turns the tails can be spread out. After a minute or two the legs begin to

BOUCHES·DU·RHÔNE

THON AUX ARTICHAUTS À LA MARSEILLAISE

Tuna with Artichokes

This is one of the many Marseillaise *variations on the theme of* bouillabaisse. *It is sometimes accompanied by* aïoli *(see glossary) or* rouille *(see* bouillabaisse *on page 108).*

1½ lb (750 g) tuna steak, skinned

FOR THE MARINADE:

freshly ground pepper
⅛ teaspoon powdered saffron
1 bay leaf
2 or 3 fresh thyme sprigs
3 cloves garlic
3 tablespoons olive oil

5 tablespoons (3 oz/80 ml) olive oil
3 young, tender artichokes, trimmed, halved lengthwise,
   chokes removed if necessary and sliced (see glossary)
salt
1 large onion, finely chopped
2 large tomatoes, peeled, seeded and coarsely chopped
3 oz (100 g) sorrel, stemmed and chopped
3 cups (24 fl oz/750 ml) water, boiling

8 slices baguette, partially dried in a warm oven and then
   rubbed with a garlic clove

◙ The natural structure of a tuna steak divides it neatly into quarters with a cross-shaped bone at the center. Quarter the steak, discard the bones and cut each quarter in half. Put the tuna pieces into a large bowl. For the marinade, grind some pepper over the tuna, then sprinkle with saffron. Add the bay leaf, thyme sprigs and garlic and pour the olive oil. Using your hands, toss all the ingredients together until the tuna pieces are evenly colored with saffron and coated with oil. Leave to marinate at room temperature for 1 hour.
◙ Warm 2 tablespoons of the olive oil in a large sauté pan. Add the artichokes, sprinkle with salt to taste and sauté over high heat until lightly colored, about 5 minutes. Set aside.
◙ Warm the remaining 3 tablespoons olive oil in a large sauce-pan. Add the onion and cook gently until softened but not colored, about 10 minutes. Raise the heat and add the tomatoes and sorrel. Using a wooden spoon stir regularly until they begin to break up, about 10 minutes. Then add the reserved artichokes and the tuna and all of its marinade, wiping the bowl clean. Stir around for a minute, pour in the boiling water and add salt to taste. Boil gently until the fish is tender, about 15 minutes.
◙ Using a large skimming spoon, transfer the tuna and artichoke slices (and anything that comes with them) to a heated platter. Place 1 or 2 slices garlic-rubbed bread in each soup plate and ladle some broth over them. Serve the tuna and artichokes at the same time, or after the broth has been consumed, accompanied with more broth.

SERVES 4

Tuna with Artichokes

Crayfish in Court Bouillon

ÉCREVISSES À LA NAGE

Crayfish in Court Bouillon

This recipe should be shared with friends who don't mind eating with their fingers.

FOR THE COURT BOUILLON:

2 cups (16 fl oz/500 ml) water
2 cups (16 fl oz/500 ml) dry white wine
1 carrot, peeled and thinly sliced
1 onion, thinly sliced
3 cloves garlic, crushed
1 bay leaf

several fresh thyme sprigs
bouquet of flat-leaf (Italian) parsley stems and leaves
salt
4 dozen crayfish

◈ Combine all of the ingredients for the court bouillon in a large saucepan. Bring to a boil and cover with a lid ajar. Cook at a gentle boil for 30 minutes. Add the crayfish, stir them around, cover and cook, stirring a couple of times if all of the crayfish are not completely immersed, until the shellfish are tender, 8–10 minutes.

◈ Serve immediately, either from the saucepan or poured into a large bowl. Or, if you prefer, leave the crayfish to cool until tepid or at room temperature before serving.

SERVES 4

ALPES·MARITIMES

ESTOCAFICADA
Stockfish Niçois

Estocaficada is as sacred to the Niçois as is bouillabaisse to the Marseillais. Stockfish is salt cod that is dried until it is stiff as a board. It must be sawn into pieces and requires at least 4–5 days soaking with repeated changes of water before it can be put to cook. In Nice, the cleansed and salted cod guts are sold separately and need only be soaked overnight before being used. If you are unable to find stockfish intestines, don't despair; a dimension may be lost but the dish will still be wonderful. Finally, if you cannot find stockfish, salt cod may be used, with a radical reduction in cooking time, and the result will be good, if less than sublime.

½ cup (4 fl oz/125 ml) olive oil, plus olive oil for serving
1 large onion, finely chopped
½ lb (250 g) leeks, including the tender green parts,
    thinly sliced
2 large sweet red peppers (capsicums), seeded, deribbed
    and cut into long, narrow strips
4 cloves garlic, chopped
2 lb (1 kg) stockfish, soaked (see recipe introduction),
    skinned, picked over to remove bones and coarsely
    shredded or cut up
3 oz (100 g) stockfish intestines, soaked overnight
    and chopped
½ cup (4 fl oz/125 ml) marc de Provence (see glossary)
    or Cognac
4 lb (2 kg) tomatoes, peeled, seeded and coarsely chopped
large bouquet garni (see glossary)
2 lb (1 kg) new potatoes, peeled and quartered
1 cup (5 oz/150 g) black olives
persillade made with 1 clove garlic (see glossary)
3 salt anchovies, rinsed, filleted and mashed to a purée
    (see glossary)

▦ Warm the ½ cup (4 fl oz/125 ml) olive oil in a large, heavy sauté pan over medium-low heat. Add the onion, leeks and peppers and cook, stirring rapidly with a wooden spoon, until softened and beginning to color, about 20 minutes. Add the garlic, stockfish and intestines and stir with a wooden spoon for 1 minute. Pour in the brandy and stir in well. Empty the contents of the pan into a large, flameproof earthenware casserole or enameled ironware pan.

▦ Return the sauté pan to high heat, add the tomatoes and stir until they begin to boil. Empty the sauté pan into the casserole, stir the contents and tuck in the bouquet garni. Bring slowly to a boil, cover with the lid slightly ajar and simmer for 2 hours.

▦ Place the potatoes in a saucepan and add salted water to cover. Bring to a boil and boil until barely tender, about 20 minutes. Drain the potatoes and add them to the stew along with the olives.

▦ Then, 20 minutes later, stir in the *persillade* and anchovies. Simmer for 5 minutes longer and serve, accompanied with olive oil at table.

SERVES 6

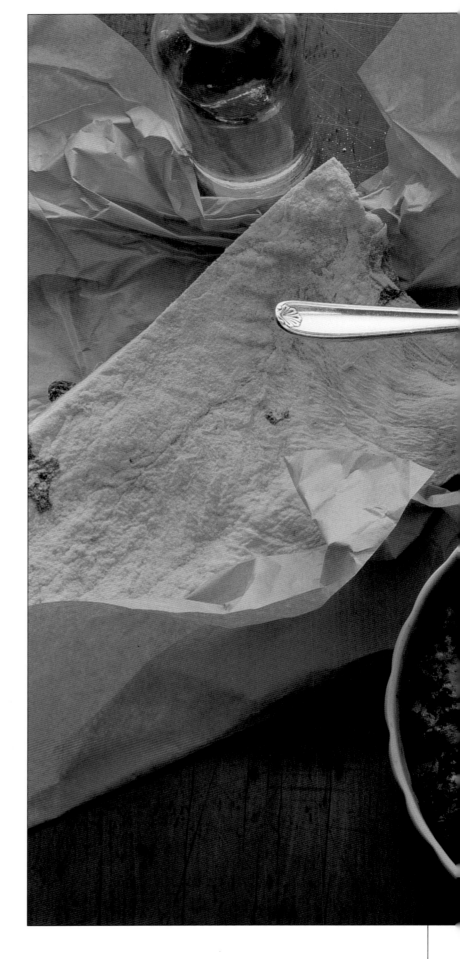

VAUCLUSE

TIAN DE CARPENTRAS
Gratin of Salt Cod with Mixed Greens

For Frédéric Mistral, the Provençal bard, the tian de Carpentras is the real tian, the "gratin of gratins." Parboiled chopped purslane and finely shredded sorrel leaves can add a touch of mystery.

3 eggs
½ cup (2 oz/60 g) freshly grated Parmesan cheese
½ cup (4 fl oz/125 ml) plus 3 tablespoons olive oil
2 cups (16 fl oz/500 ml) milk
salt and freshly ground pepper
whole nutmeg
½ lb (250 g) spinach, parboiled, squeezed dry and chopped
    (see glossary)
½ lb (250 g) Swiss chard (silverbeet) greens, parboiled,
    squeezed dry and chopped (see glossary)

Top to bottom: Stockfish Niçois, Gratin of Salt Cod with Mixed Greens

persillade made with 3 or 4 cloves garlic (see glossary)
1 lb (500 g) salt cod, poached and flaked (see glossary)
4 hard-cooked eggs, shelled and cut in half lengthwise
8 salt anchovies, rinsed and filleted (see glossary)
coarse dried bread crumbs

◙ Preheat an oven to 350°F (180°C). In a mixing bowl whisk the eggs briefly, then whisk in the cheese, the ½ cup (4 fl oz/ 125 ml) olive oil and milk. Season to taste with salt and pepper and scrape in a little nutmeg. Add the chopped greens, *persillade* and cod and, using a wooden spoon, stir well.

◙ Rub a 6-cup (48-fl oz/1.5-l) gratin dish with olive oil and spread the cod mixture in it. Embed the egg halves cut side up, in the mixture, to create a surface design. Press crossed anchovy fillets over each egg half. Sprinkle on bread crumbs generously, then dribble on the 3 tablespoons olive oil in a thread, forming a crisscross pattern.

◙ Place in the oven and bake until no depression remains at the center and the surface is nicely colored, 35–40 minutes. Serve immediately.

SERVES 4

MAQUEREAUX À LA MARINADE CHAUDE

Mackerel in Hot Marinade

This is often served as a starter, but preceded by a simple salad and followed by cheese, it provides a satisfying lunch. Accompanied with a young red wine such as Bandol served quite cool, the mackerel is very much at home.

2 lb (1 kg) small mackerels, cleaned and heads removed
salt and freshly ground pepper
6 tablespoons (3 fl oz/90 ml) olive oil

mixing bowl. Sprinkle with salt, grind over some pepper and add 1 tablespoon of the olive oil. Toss with your hands to coat the fish evenly with the oil and seasoning. Arrange the fish in a gratin dish and put it into the oven for 10 minutes.

❊ Meanwhile, put the remaining oil, the chili peppers, bay leaves and garlic in a saucepan. Place it over high heat and, when the garlic begins to sputter and turn golden, add the vinegar.

❊ Remove from the heat and pour the contents of the saucepan over the hot mackerel. Serve at once.

SERVES 6

VAR

CAPILOTADE À LA FAÇON DE SIGNES
Salt Cod in Caper Sauce

The principle of a capilotade *is the same as that of salt cod in red wine (recipe on page 82)—to simmer fried salt cod briefly in a sauce. Tomato sauce, with or without the addition of black olives, chopped anchovy fillets or* persillade, *often replaces these sauces in dishes called* à la provençale, à la niçoise *or* camarguaise. *The addition of* vin cuit, *a sweet dessert wine made from dark grapes, to a* capilotade *originates in the village of Signes, inland from Toulon and Bandol.*

FOR THE SAUCE:

3 tablespoons olive oil
1 onion, finely chopped
1 leek, including the tender green parts, thinly sliced
¼ cup (2 fl oz/60 ml) Provençal herb vinegar (see glossary)
3 tablespoons all-purpose (plain) flour
3 cups (24 fl oz/750 ml) water
persillade made with 2 cloves garlic (see glossary)
bouquet garni (see glossary)
⅔ cup (3 oz/100 g) capers, rinsed and drained
½ cup (4 fl oz/125 ml) *vin cuit* or Port

1½ lb (750 g) salt cod, soaked and cut into 4 equal pieces (see glossary)
all-purpose (plain) flour
¼ cup (2 fl oz/60 ml) olive oil
freshly ground pepper

❊ To prepare the sauce, warm the olive oil in a heavy saucepan over low heat. Add the onion and leek, cover and sweat until they are softened and simmering in their own juices, about 10 minutes. Uncover, raise the heat and stir with a wooden spoon until the liquid evaporates and the onion and leek begin to turn color and stick to the pan, about 1 or 2 minutes. Add the vinegar and stir until it completely evaporates, 1–2 minutes. Sprinkle the flour evenly over the top and stir for 1 minute. Add the water, slowly at first, stirring all the while. Add the *persillade* and the bouquet garni and bring to a boil. Adjust the heat to a very gentle boil and cook for about 40 minutes, stirring occasionally.

❊ Add the capers and the *vin cuit* and keep at a gentle boil until the sauce has reduced to the right consistency and the taste of alcohol has disappeared, another 10–15 minutes.

❊ Meanwhile, coat the cod pieces with flour, shaking off any excess flour. Heat the olive oil in a frying pan over medium-high heat. Add the fish and fry, turning once, until lightly colored, a couple of minutes on each side. Remove the fish pieces to paper towels to drain.

❊ Place the cod pieces in a flameproof serving dish and grind over some pepper. Pour the sauce over the fish and place over medium heat. Simmer for 10 minutes and serve.

SERVES 4

Along the harbor in Cassis, from top to bottom: Salt Cod in Caper Sauce, Mackerel in Hot Marinade

2 dried cayenne chili peppers or other dried chili peppers
2 bay leaves
6 cloves garlic, crushed in their peels
3 tablespoons Provençal herb vinegar (see glossary)

❊ Preheat an oven to 450°F (230°C). If the mackerel are no longer than 6 in (15 cm), leave them whole. If they are longer than that, cut into 2-in (5-cm) lengths. Put the fish into a

BOUCHES·DU·RHÔNE/VAR

MORUE EN RAYTE
Salt Cod in Red Wine Sauce

Morue en rayte is a traditional Christmas Eve dish in the Var. It is claimed that the sauce was introduced into Provence by the Phocaean sailors who founded Marseilles in 600 B.C., but it has probably only been around since tomatoes came into popular usage in the 19th century.

FOR THE SAUCE:

3 tablespoons olive oil
2 large onions, coarsely chopped
3 tablespoons all-purpose (plain) flour
3 cups (24 fl oz/750 ml) young, tannic red wine
2 cups (16 fl oz/500 ml) water
1 lb (500 g) tomatoes, coarsely chopped
large pinch of fennel seeds
large bouquet garni (see glossary)
salt
¾ cup (4 oz/125 g) black olives
2 tablespoons capers, rinsed

1½ lb (750 g) salt cod, soaked and cut into 4 equal pieces
    (see glossary)
all-purpose (plain) flour
¼ cup (2 fl oz/60 ml) olive oil
1 tablespoon chopped flat-leaf (Italian) parsley

☒ To prepare the sauce, warm the olive oil in a heavy sauce-pan over low heat. Add the onions and cook until softened

but not colored, about 10 minutes. Sprinkle evenly with the flour, stir with a wooden spoon, raise the heat and add the wine, slowly at first, stirring all the while. Add the water, tomatoes, fennel seeds and bouquet garni. Salt lightly and bring to a boil, stirring. Adjust the heat to a simmer or very gentle boil and cook, uncovered, until the sauce is reduced by approximately two thirds, a couple of hours or more.

☒ Discard the bouquet garni. Pass the sauce through a fine-mesh sieve into a bowl, pressing it with a wooden pestle to extract all the liquid. Return it to the saucepan, add the olives and capers and taste for salt. Simmer gently while preparing the fish.

☒ Coat the pieces of cod with flour, shaking off any excess flour. Heat the olive oil in a frying pan over medium-high heat. Add the fish and fry, turning once, until lightly colored, a couple of minutes on each side. Remove the fish pieces to paper towels to drain.

☒ Ladle some of the sauce into a flameproof earthenware casserole or other heavy pot and place the fried fish pieces on top. Pour over the remaining sauce. Warm to a simmer over medium heat and simmer gently for 10 minutes. Sprinkle with the parsley and serve.

SERVES 4

Salt Cod in Red Wine Sauce

BOUCHES·DU·RHÔNE

MORUE À LA BÉNÉDICTINE
Brandade with Potatoes

Brandade is poached salt cod, beaten over low heat with progressive additions of hot olive oil and hot milk until a supple and consistent purée is formed. Puréed garlic is usually added and, less often today, chopped truffles. According to anecdotal history, morue à la bénédictine is so named because a monastery near Marseilles, having only a small quantity of prepared brandade in the kitchen, received, unexpectedly, the visit of monks from a neighboring monastery. The genial cook boiled up a vast quantity of potatoes and incorporated them into the brandade; the guests were ravished and carried away the recipe.

1 lb (500 g) potatoes, peeled
1½ lb (750 g) salt cod, soaked (see glossary)
persillade made with 2 cloves garlic (see glossary)
freshly ground pepper
1 cup (8 fl oz/250 ml) milk, heated
½ cup (4 fl oz/125 ml) olive oil, plus olive oil for top
dried bread crumbs

☒ Place the potatoes in a saucepan. Add water to cover and bring to a boil. Cook until tender when pierced, about 30 minutes.

☒ Meanwhile, poach the cod as directed in the glossary. While it is still hot, flake the flesh, picking out any small bones, and purée it in a food processor fitted with the metal blade or pound it in a mortar.

☒ Preheat an oven to 400°F (200°C). Drain the potatoes and place in a bowl. Mash them and then add the puréed cod and *persillade*. Grind over some pepper. Using a wooden spoon, stir in the hot milk and olive oil, small quantities at a time and alternately, beating when the mixture becomes loose enough. When all of the liquid has been added, the mixture should be very supple but not quite pourable.

☒ Rub a 6-cup (48-fl oz/1.5-l) gratin dish with olive oil. Spread the potato-cod mixture in it and smooth the surface. Sprinkle the crumbs over the top and then dribble over a thread of olive oil. Place in the oven and bake until the surface is colored, 10–15 minutes. Serve hot.

SERVES 4

Top to bottom: Brandade with Potatoes, Salt Cod and Leeks

LA QUINQUEBINE CAMARGUAISE

Salt Cod and Leeks

Adapted from Vieilles recettes de cuisine provençale *by Chanot-Bullier, this preparation can, if one likes, be transformed into a gratin with the addition of bread crumbs and a thread of olive oil.*

3 tablespoons olive oil
2 lb (1 kg) leeks, including the tender green parts, thinly
    sliced
½ cup (4 fl oz/125 ml) water, boiling
salt
2 tablespoons all-purpose (plain) flour
2 cups (16 fl oz/500 ml) milk
persillade made with 2 cloves garlic (see glossary)
2 salt anchovies, rinsed, filleted and chopped (see glossary)
1½ lb (750 g) salt cod, poached and flaked (see glossary)
freshly ground pepper
whole nutmeg
¾ cup (3 oz/100 g) freshly grated Gruyère or
    Parmesan cheese

◈ Warm the olive oil in a heavy sauté pan over medium-low heat. Add the leeks and cook, stirring with a wooden spoon, until they are softened and begin to color, about 20 minutes. Add the water, salt very lightly and simmer until the water evaporates completely and the leeks begin to stick to the pan, 8–10 minutes. Sprinkle the flour evenly over the top, stir well and add the milk slowly, stirring all the while. Stir in the *persillade* and simmer gently for 15 minutes.

◈ Stir in the anchovies and the cod and simmer for 10 minutes. Grind over some pepper and scrape over a bit of nutmeg. Stir in the grated cheese and taste for salt. Simmer for a couple of minutes longer and serve directly from the sauté pan.

SERVES 4

RAIE À LA PROVENÇALE

Provençal Skate

*Because of their eccentric shape, two small skate wings will fill
a large frying pan. For this reason, they must be cooked in relays
or in two large pans.*

4 small skate wings, about 7 oz (220 g) each, or large wings
   skinned and cut into sections (see skate in caper sauce on
   page 88)
salt and freshly ground pepper
all-purpose (plain) flour
¼ cup (2 fl oz/60 ml) olive oil

FOR THE SAUCE:

small pinch of coarse salt
freshly ground pepper
1 clove garlic
3 salt anchovies, rinsed and filleted (see glossary)
1 tablespoon chopped fresh flat-leaf (Italian) parsley
2 cups (16 fl oz/500 ml) tomato sauce (see glossary)

❀ Preheat an oven to 450°F (230°C). Season the skate wings
with salt and pepper and coat them with flour, shaking off
any excess flour.

❀ In a frying pan over medium-high heat, warm the olive oil.
Add the skate wings to the hot oil and fry for about 4 minutes on each side, adjusting the heat when necessary to
achieve a light, golden surface. The wings are ready when a
sharp skewer or trussing needle meets with little resistance
at the thickest parts. Transfer to a gratin dish large enough to
hold the wings in a single layer.

❀ To prepare the sauce, in a mortar pound together the salt,
pepper to taste, garlic, anchovies and parsley to form a paste.
In a saucepan, bring the tomato sauce to a boil and stir in the
paste from the mortar. Pour the sauce over the skate.

❀ Place in the oven and bake until the sauce is bubbling,
8–10 minutes. Serve immediately.

SERVES 4

2 bay leaves
pinch of Provençal mixed dried herbs (see glossary)
5 oz (150 g) sorrel leaves, stemmed, tightly rolled up
    and thinly sliced
salt
2 lemons, peeled, thinly sliced and seeded
½ cup (4 fl oz/125 ml) dry white wine

◉ Using a sharp-pointed paring knife, pierce the surface of the tuna steak in 8 places between the rings of flesh. Slip an anchovy fillet into each slit.

◉ Preheat an oven to 325°F (165°C). Rub the bottom of a casserole whose circumference is only slightly larger than that of the tuna steak with 1 teaspoon of the olive oil. Line it with half of the lettuce leaves and place half of the tomato slices on top. Scatter over half the carrots and onion slices, 1 bay leaf and a small pinch of the dried herbs. Press half the shredded sorrel on top, sprinkle with salt and 1 tablespoon of the olive oil. Place half the lemon slices on top and then the tuna steak. Top with the remaining lemon slices, then the remaining tomatoes, carrots and onions. Sprinkle with the remaining dried herbs, add the remaining bay leaf and press the remaining sorrel over the top. Sprinkle with salt and dribble over the remaining olive oil. Sprinkle with the white wine and cover with the remaining lettuce leaves.

◉ Cover, place in the oven and bake until the flavors are melded, about 1 hour and 10 minutes. Lift off and discard the surface lettuce leaves before serving.

SERVES 4

SOLE À LA MARINIÈRE, MOUTARDE DES PÊCHEURS

Fisherman's Sole with Fisherman's Sauce

Marius Morard, a 19th-century Marseillais chef, recounts his discussions with an old fisherman, who tells him, "In Marseilles, all fishermen are cooks, but we don't make such a fuss about it as you professionals. Here's the way we prepare a sole. We call it la solo dei pescadou *(fishermen's sole). We wash it and clean it in sea water . . ."*

FOR THE SAUCE:

pinch of coarse salt
freshly ground pepper
2 cloves garlic
2 hard-cooked egg yolks
1 tablespoon tarragon mustard
½ cup (4 fl oz/125 ml) olive oil

salt
2 soles, 8–10 oz (250–300 g) each, cleaned and skinned
1 tablespoon olive oil
coarse dried bread crumbs

◉ Prepare a fire in a charcoal grill. To prepare the sauce, in a mortar pound together the coarse salt, pepper to taste and garlic to form a paste. Add the egg yolks and pound again to a paste. Add the mustard and turn with the pestle until a smooth paste forms. Slowly incorporate the olive oil, adding it in a fine thread to the side of the mortar, stirring all the while with the pestle.

◉ Salt the soles to taste and then rub them with the olive oil. Coat them with bread crumbs on all sides. Place on the grill rack over hot coals and grill for 7–8 minutes on each side. Serve hot with sauce on the side.

SERVES 2

Clockwise from top left: Fisherman's Sole with Fisherman's Sauce, Tuna Chartreuse, Provençal Skate

THON À LA CHARTREUSE

Tuna Chartreuse

This preparation is thought to derive from Carthusian monks famed for their production of Chartreuse liqueur. Some cooking authors add the liqueur to the recipe in an abortive attempt to justify its name.

1 thick slice of tuna, about ½ lb (750 g) and 1¼ in (3 cm)
    thick, skinned
8 salt anchovies, rinsed and filleted (see glossary)
3 tablespoons olive oil
1 head leafy lettuce
2 large, garden-ripe tomatoes, peeled, seeded and sliced
2 carrots, about 5 oz (150 g) total weight, peeled and
    thinly sliced
1 large onion, thinly sliced

COQUILLES SAINT-JACQUES À LA PROVENÇALE

Provençal Sea Scallops

If you can find scallops with the golden roe still attached, buy them for this simple dish.

2 tablespoons olive oil
12 sea scallops, each cut in half across the grain and well dried
salt and freshly ground pepper
1 tablespoon unsalted butter
persillade made with 1 clove garlic (see glossary)
½ lemon

▨ Warm the olive oil in a nonstick frying pan over high heat. Season the scallops with salt and pepper to taste. Add to the pan and sauté for not quite 1 minute on each side. Add the butter and, when it foams, add the *persillade.* Toss or stir for a few seconds, squeeze over a bit of lemon juice and serve immediately.

SERVES 4

THON À LA RÉMOULADE

Grilled Tuna with Rémoulade Sauce

The sauce called rémoulade *today is usually mustard, anchovy essence and chopped pickles, capers and fines herbes stirred into a mayonnaise. Traditionally it is made with hard-cooked egg yolks. The anonymous author of* Le cuisinier méridional *(1855) gives two recipes for rémoulade,* provençale *and* languedocienne. *Only the Languedoc* rémoulade *contains mustard.*

1 tuna steak, about 1½ lb (750 g) and 1 in (2.5 cm) thick, skinned

FOR THE MARINADE:

pinch of Provençal mixed dried herbs (see glossary)
1 tablespoon dry white wine
½ lemon
1 teaspoon olive oil

FOR THE RÉMOULADE:

pinch of coarse salt
freshly ground pepper
1 clove garlic
1 tablespoon chopped shallots

Provençal Sea Scallops

A beach along the Bouches-du-Rhône coast, Grilled Tuna with Rémoulade Sauce

1 tablespoon chopped fresh flat-leaf (Italian) parsley
1 tablespoon capers, rinsed and squeezed dry
1 salt anchovy, rinsed and filleted (see glossary)
3 hard-cooked egg yolks
1 uncooked egg yolk
½ cup (4 fl oz/125 ml) olive oil
1 teaspoon fresh lemon juice

salt and freshly ground pepper
2 teaspoons olive oil

✦ Place the tuna steak in a shallow bowl. For the marinade, add the herbs, white wine, a few drops of lemon juice and olive oil to the fish. Marinate for 1 hour or so, turning it over and around in the marinade 2 or 3 times.

✦ To prepare the *rémoulade,* in a mortar pound together the salt, pepper, garlic, shallot and parsley to form a paste. Add the capers and anchovy and pound again to a paste. Add the hard-cooked egg yolks and pound and stir with the pestle to a smooth, homogenous paste. Stir in the raw egg yolk and turn with the pestle for a few moments. Slowly add the olive oil in a fine trickle to the side of the mortar while stirring vigorously with the pestle. Stir in the lemon juice. Set aside.

✦ Prepare a fire in a charcoal grill. Drain the tuna steak and pat it dry with paper towels. Season on both sides with salt and pepper and rub the olive oil over all the surfaces. Place the tuna steak on a well-oiled grill rack over hot coals and grill turning once, until tender, counting 6–7 minutes per side. Use a large, wide spatula to turn the steak and to remove it from the grill. Serve at once with the *rémoulade* on the side.

SERVES 4

CREVETTES GRISES À LA PERSILLADE

Sautéed Shrimp

Medium-sized shrimp in Provence are sold precooked—plunged alive into boiling salted water for 1 minute, drained and cooled. They are called bouquets. *The only shrimp found alive in the market are the tiny (average 1½ inches/4 cm from head to tail)* crevettes grises, *pale grayish, semitransparent shrimp with fragile, parchmentlike shells. Giant shrimp, averaging 8 inches (20 cm) from tip to tail, are called* gambas *and are sold raw but not alive; they are grilled, whole and unshelled, over hot coals for a couple of minutes on each side and served with a* remoulade *sauce (recipe on page 86).*

3 tablespoons olive oil
¾ lb (375 g) live *crevettes grises* or small shrimp (prawn) tails
   in the shell
salt and freshly ground pepper
persillade made with 1 clove garlic (see glossary)
1 lemon

◉ Warm the olive oil in a large, sharply slant-sided frying pan over high heat. Add the shrimp and salt and pepper to taste and sauté, tossing the shrimp repeatedly in the air, until they turn pale pink, 1 minute; count 2 minutes for shrimp tails. Add the *persillade,* toss again, squeeze over a few drops of lemon juice and serve. As with fried whitebait, everything is eaten (if shrimp tails have been substituted, they are shelled at table).

SERVES 4   *Photograph pages 72–73*

RAIE, SAUCE AUX CAPRES

Skate in Caper Sauce

The flesh of skate wings is melting and voluptuous. At table, it separates like magic from the tender, gelatinous bones when the tines of an overturned fork are drawn down the length of the bones.

1½ lb (750 g) skate wings, skinned and cut into 3–4-oz
   (100–125-g) sections if large
4 cups (32 fl oz/1 l) water
½ cup (4 fl oz/125 ml) white wine vinegar
salt

FOR THE SAUCE:
2 egg yolks
1 tablespoon plus 2 cups (16 fl oz/500 ml) water
1 tablespoon fresh lemon juice
1 tablespoon olive oil
freshly ground pepper
3 tablespoons unsalted butter
2 tablespoons all-purpose (plain) flour
salt
3–4 tablespoons (1½ oz/45 g) capers, rinsed and drained

◉ Arrange the skate wings or wing sections, thin parts overlapping, in a large, heavy sauté pan. In a saucepan combine the water, vinegar and salt to taste and bring to a boil. Pour it over the skate, place the sauté pan over the heat and again bring the liquid to a boil. Cover the pan tightly and remove from the heat. Hold, covered, until the sauce is ready.
◉ To prepare the sauce, in a small bowl combine the egg yolks, the 1 tablespoon water, the lemon juice, olive oil and pepper to taste with a fork. Set aside. In a saucepan, melt the butter over low heat. Add the flour and stir with a wooden

spoon until the mixture begins to bubble, a couple of minutes. With a whisk in hand, pour the 2 cups (16 fl oz/500 ml) water into the saucepan, whisking at the same time. Season to taste with salt, raise the heat and continue whisking until the sauce boils. Remove it from the heat and leave to cool for a minute. Whisk in the egg yolk mixture and return the pan to low heat. Turn with the whisk or stir with the wooden spoon until the sauce thickens slightly, about 3 or 4 minutes. It must not boil. Stir in the capers.
◉ Using a flat, perforated skimming spoon, transfer the skate pieces to a heated serving platter, draining as well as possible. Sponge up any liquid that appears in the platter with a paper towel. Ladle a bit of sauce over the fish. Serve the rest of the sauce in a heated bowl.

SERVES 4

ENCORNETS FARCIS

Stuffed Squid

Here are three distinctive stuffings for squid; prepare the one that appeals. Because the squid mantles, or pouches, shrink in cooking, they should be loosely packed with stuffing. Leave a ½-in (12-mm) space at the opening; tack the top sides of the pouches closed with a trussing needle and kitchen string, pulling the ends of the string together, tying and clipping.

FOR THE ANCHOVY–BREAD CRUMB STUFFING:
1 tablespoon olive oil
1 onion, finely chopped
the squids' tentacles and wings, chopped
salt
2 tomatoes, peeled, seeded and chopped
1½ cups (3 oz/90 g) fresh bread crumbs
persillade made with 2 cloves garlic (see glossary)
2 salt anchovies, rinsed, filleted and chopped (see glossary)
freshly ground black pepper and cayenne pepper
2 eggs

◉ To prepare the anchovy–bread crumb stuffing, warm the olive oil in a sauté pan over low heat. Add the onion and cook until softened but not colored, about 10 minutes. Raise the heat, add the tentacles and wings and salt to taste and sauté until the liquid the squid gives off evaporates, 2–3 minutes. Add the contents of the pan to a mixing bowl. Add the tomatoes, bread crumbs, *persillade,* anchovies, black and cayenne peppers to taste and a bit more salt. Mix together loosely, add the eggs and, using your hands, mix thoroughly.

FOR THE RICE STUFFING:
¾ cup (4 oz/125 g) long-grain white rice
1 tablespoon olive oil
1 onion, finely chopped
the squids' tentacles and wings, chopped
salt and freshly ground pepper
1 teaspoon fresh marjoram flower buds and leaves, finely
   chopped
1 tablespoon chopped fresh flat-leaf (Italian) parsley

◉ To prepare the stuffing, bring a saucepan filled with water to a boil. Add the rice and parboil for 15 minutes. Drain into a sieve and rinse under cold running water. Drain again and let stand for 15 minutes.
◉ Warm the olive oil in a sauté pan over low heat. Add the onion and cook until softened but not colored, about 10 minutes. Raise the heat, add the tentacles and wings and sauté until the liquid the squid gives off evaporates, 2–3 minutes. Add the contents of the pan to a mixing bowl with all the remaining ingredients. Using a fork mix thoroughly but gently so as not to break up the rice grains.

Skate in Caper Sauce in the old port of La Ciotat

FOR THE SPINACH-MUSSEL STUFFING:

4 tablespoons olive oil
1 onion, finely chopped
the squids' tentacles and wings, chopped
1 lb (500 g) mussels, opened with white wine over heat
  (see glossary)
2 garlic cloves, finely chopped
1 lb (500 g) spinach, parboiled, squeezed dry and chopped
  (see glossary)
½ cup (1 oz/30 g) fresh bread crumbs
freshly ground pepper
whole nutmeg
2 eggs
salt

◙ To prepare the spinach-mussel stuffing, warm 1 tablespoon of the olive oil in a sauté pan over low heat. Add the onion and cook until softened but not colored, about 10 minutes. Raise the heat, add the tentacles and wings and sauté for 1 minute. Add about ½ cup (4 fl oz/125 ml) of the decanted mussels' cooking liquid and simmer until the liquid is reduced by about two-thirds, about 10 minutes. Set aside.

◙ Heat the remaining 3 tablespoons of olive oil in a sauté pan over medium-high heat. Add the garlic and, when it begins to sizzle, add the spinach and sauté, stirring with a wooden spoon for a minute or so. Add about ¼ cup (2 fl oz/60 ml) of the mussels' cooking liquid and stir until it is absorbed, just a few minutes. Stir in the bread crumbs and remove from the heat to cool partially.

◙ Shell the mussels. In a mixing bowl combine the onion-squid mixture, the shelled mussels and the spinach mixture.

Grind over some pepper and scrape over nutmeg. Add the eggs and, using your hands, mix thoroughly. Taste for salt.

FOR THE SQUID:

4 squid, ½–¾ lb (250–315 g) each, cleaned (see glossary)
3 tablespoons olive oil
1 onion, finely chopped
salt
4 tablespoons marc de Provence (see glossary) or Cognac
persillade made with 2 cloves garlic (see glossary)
3 salt anchovies, rinsed, filleted and chopped (see glossary)
2 tablespoons capers, rinsed, squeezed dry and chopped
½ cup (4 fl oz/125 ml) dry white wine

◙ Stuff the cleaned squid with one of the stuffings, following the directions in the recipe introduction.

◙ In a heavy sauté pan, warm the olive oil over low heat. Add the onion and cook gently until softened but not colored, about 10 minutes. Raise the heat, add the stuffed squid and salt to taste. Shake the pan back and forth, rolling them around, until the flesh has contracted firmly around the stuffing and has turned opaque. Pour over the brandy and ignite with a long-handled match. Shaking the pan, scatter over the *persillade,* anchovies and capers. Roll the squid around by shaking the pan, or turn them around and over with a wooden spoon. When flames die add the wine. Cover the pan tightly and cook over the lowest possible heat for 1 hour, shaking the pan from time to time.

◙ Clip and remove the strings and serve directly from the sauté pan, spooning some of the cooking juices over each squid.

SERVES 4   *Photograph pages 72–73*

DAURADE AU FOUR
Provençal Baked Porgy

1 large onion, cut in half and thinly sliced
4 or 5 cloves garlic, thinly sliced
4–5 tablespoons (2–3 fl oz/60–80 ml) olive oil
1 porgy (bream), red snapper or similar fish, about 4 lb
   (2 kg), cleaned
salt and freshly ground pepper
large pinch of Provençal mixed dried herbs (see glossary)
1 lb (500 g) tomatoes, peeled, seeded and sliced or cut
   into wedges
⅔ cup (3 oz/100 g) black olives
2 green Italian sweet peppers or other sweet peppers (capsicums), seeded, deribbed and cut into long, narrow strips
½ cup (4 fl oz/125 ml) dry white wine

▣ Preheat an oven to 400°F (200°C).
▣ Mix the sliced onions and garlic together. Rub the
bottom of a large gratin dish with 1 tablespoon of the olive
oil and scatter over half of the onion-garlic mixture. Season
the fish inside and out with salt and pepper to taste and the
mixed herbs. Place the fish in the gratin dish and rub it
inside and out with olive oil, turning it around and over.
Scatter the remaining onion-garlic mixture over the fish and
then pile the tomatoes on top, smothering the fish. Scatter
the olives and pepper strips over and around the fish and
sprinkle salt over the surface. Dribble the remaining olive
oil in a thread back and forth over the surface. Pour the wine
into the bottom of the dish. If the fish's tail is not quite
contained in the dish, fold a piece of aluminum foil around
it to prevent its charring.
▣ Place in the oven and bake for about 40 minutes, basting
a couple of times after the first 20 minutes. Test for
doneness with a trussing needle or sharp skewer. Serve
directly from the gratin dish, moving the vegetables to the
side before serving in the same way as for the grilled fish
(recipe follows). Accompany each portion with some
vegetables and juices.

SERVES 4

DAURADE GRILLÉE
Grilled Fish

*Red porgy, scup, sheepshead, black sea bass, red snapper,
and the like are suitable for grilling. Unless the fish is grilled
in its scales (in which case it makes no sense to marinate it),
a hinged, double-faced fish grill is indispensable for turning
the fish over on the grill. The cooking time for a large fish is
judged by the fish's back at its thickest point, counting about
10 minutes per inch (2.5 cm). If a skewer inserted at the thickest
point meets little resistance, or if the first spine of the dorsal fin
can be easily pulled out with its attached bone, the fish is done.
It needs no sauce, but olive oil and lemon wedges, green sauce
(recipe on page 105), pistou (recipe on page 36) or tapénade
(recipe on page 34) are all pleasant accompaniments. If neither
fresh wild fennel nor dried fennel stalk is available, substitute a
pinch of ground fennel seeds.*

1 fish, 3–4 lb (1.5–2 kg), cleaned
fresh wild fennel stalks plus a handful of chopped, feathery
   leaves or, if out of season, sections of dried fennel stalk
freshly ground pepper
¼ cup (2 fl oz/60 ml) olive oil

1 tablespoon *pastis* such as Pernod 51 or Ricard
½ lemon
salt
several fresh thyme branches, stems tied together to
   form a brush

▣ Score the fish on each side two or three times, slicing
shallowly crosswise on the bias, and place the fish in a large
shallow oval dish. Stuff a bundle of fennel stalks, cut or bent
to the right length, into the body and head cavity. If the season is right, sprinkle chopped fennel leaves over the fish, taking care to force a certain amount into the slits in the flesh.
▣ Grind some pepper over the fish, then sprinkle inside and
out, first with the olive oil and then with the *pastis*. Squeeze
over a bit of lemon juice and, using your hands, rub the fish
gently all over.
▣ Leave the fish to marinate while preparing a solid bed of
coals with good depth. They should be slightly on the
decline before putting the fish to grill, with a film of white
ash masking the ardent embers. Meanwhile, turn the fish
over a couple of times, spooning over the marinade.
▣ Open out the fish grill and arrange 2 or 3 lengths of fennel
stalk on one side. Salt the fish and place it on top, head at the
hinge, and lay more fennel stalks on the fish before closing
the grill. Reserve any marinade in the dish.
▣ Place the fish over the coals and turn it over every 4 or 5
minutes. Once it is turned, begin basting with the remaining
marinade by dipping the bundle of thyme into it and dab-
bing it over the surface of the fish. The fish should be done
after 25–30 minutes (see recipe introduction).
▣ Open the grill and slip the fish onto a serving platter,
discarding the outside branches of fennel. At table, cut to the
bone along the lateral line; slit the skin next to the fins and all
the length of the back and from the abdomen to the tail. Then
cut across and lift up serving portions with a spatula.

SERVES 4

BAUDROIE À LA PROVENÇALE
Provençal Monkfish

*Monkfish is sold cleaned and skinned. When filleted, the fillets at
the thickest part of the body are nearly round and can be sliced into
neat, firm medallions.*

1½ lb (750 g) monkfish (anglerfish), filleted and cut into
   slices ¾ in (2 cm) thick
salt and freshly ground pepper
all-purpose (plain) flour
¼ cup (2 fl oz/60 ml) olive oil
¾ cup (¼ lb/125 g) black olives
2 cups (16 fl oz/500 ml) tomato sauce, heated (see glossary)

▣ Preheat an oven to 350°F (180°C). Season the fish slices
with salt and pepper to taste. Coat them with flour and toss
them in your hands or in a sieve to shake off excess flour.
▣ Warm the olive oil in a large sauté pan or frying pan over
medium heat. Add the fish slices and fry, turning once until
golden, about 3 or 4 minutes on each side. Using a slotted
utensil remove to paper towels to drain briefly, then arrange
in a gratin dish. Scatter the black olives over the top, filling
up any empty spaces. Pour the tomato sauce evenly over
the fish.
▣ Place in the oven and bake until the sauce is bubbling,
about 15 minutes. Serve immediately.

SERVES 4   *Photograph pages 92–93*

Top to bottom: Provençal Baked Porgy, Grilled Fish

BAUDROIE BOURGEOIS

Monkfish Durand

This is adapted from a recipe by famed chef Charles Durand, published in the early 19th century. It differs from his Bouil-Abaïsse à la Nimoise in that the latter contains a variety of fish "such as red mullets, half-cooked eels, soles, pageaux, dorades and langouste tails."

Monkfish liver is the sea's answer to foie gras. *It has the same, voluptuous, velvety texture, is delicious simply sautéed and served with lemon sections and is a very useful element in stuffings and sauces.*

FOR THE BROTH:

1 onion, thinly sliced
1 carrot, peeled and thinly sliced
1 bay leaf
1 fresh thyme sprig
stems from a bouquet of fresh flat-leaf (Italian) parsley
monkfish (anglerfish) head and backbone, chopped up
salt
1 cup (8 fl oz/250 ml) dry white wine

½ cup (4 fl oz/125 ml) olive oil
2 leeks, about 5 oz (150 g), including the tender green parts, thinly sliced
2 lb (1 kg) filleted monkfish, cut into about 8 equal pieces
persillade made with 1 clove garlic (see glossary)
the monkfish liver, no larger than ¼ lb (125 g)
3 egg yolks
freshly ground pepper
large handful of ½-in (12-mm) crustless croutons, fried in olive oil until golden and crisp

◉ To prepare the broth, put the vegetables and the herbs in the bottom of a saucepan and place the fish head and back-bone on top. Pour in water to cover and season to taste with salt. Bring to a boil and skim off any froth and scum. Reduce the heat, cover with the lid ajar and simmer for 15 minutes. Add the wine, return to a boil and simmer for 15 minutes longer. Strain the broth through a fine-mesh sieve. Set aside.
◉ Choose a heavy sauté pan or saucepan of a size just to contain the monkfish fillets placed side by side. Warm 3 tablespoons of the olive oil in the pan over low heat. Add the leeks and cook gently, stirring occasionally, until softened but not colored, about 10 minutes. Arrange the pieces of fish atop the leeks, sprinkle the *persillade* over the top and pour in enough of the reserved broth to cover. Bring to a boil and add the liver. Adjust the heat to simmer. Remove the liver when it has firmed up but still remains pink inside, after about 5 minutes. Cook the monkfish for 15 minutes in all.
◉ Meanwhile, in a mortar reduce the liver to a paste. Add the egg yolks and the pepper to taste and stir with the pestle until the mixture forms a smooth, consistent cream. Add the remaining olive oil in a fine trickle to the side of the mortar, stirring constantly with the pestle. The sauce should be quite thick, like a mayonnaise.
◉ When the fish is done, remove the pan from the heat and, using a slotted spoon, transfer the pieces of fish to a warmed deep serving dish. Stir a ladleful of the cooking liquid into the mortar and add the contents of the mortar to the remainder of the cooking liquid, stirring with a wooden spoon. Return the pan to low heat and stir constantly until the sauce thickens slightly and coats the spoon, 8–10 minutes; it must not boil.
◉ Hold a sieve over the fish and pour the sauce into it, moving the sieve back and forth to coat the fish pieces evenly. Stir the sauce in the sieve to help it pass (some of the chopped parsley will cling to the fish and the rest will remain behind in the sieve). Scatter over croûtons and serve.

SERVES 4

SARDINES FARCIES AUX ÉPINARDS

Sardines Stuffed with Spinach

The presentation of the stuffed and rolled sardines, their tails in the air and the dish cloaked in golden crumbs, is startling and beautiful.

18 fresh sardines
6 tablespoons (3 fl oz/90 ml) olive oil
1 onion, finely chopped
persillade made with 1 clove garlic (see glossary)

Clockwise from top: Monkfish Durand, Stuffed Porgy with Crab Sauce (recipe page 95), Sardines Stuffed with Spinach, Provençal Monkfish (recipe page 91)

2 lb (1 kg) spinach, parboiled, squeezed dry and chopped
  (see glossary)
salt and freshly ground pepper
whole nutmeg
2 hard-cooked eggs, chopped
dried bread crumbs

◼ Rub each sardine gently under running water to remove the scales. Cut off the head, slit the abdomen all the way to the tail, gut the fish and carefully pry the rib cage and spine loose with your fingertips and a knife tip. Pinch off the bone near the tail. Leave the fillets attached at the back and tail so that the sardine opens out into a kite shape.

◼ Preheat an oven to 425°F (220°C). Warm 3 tablespoons of the olive oil in a sauté pan over low heat. Add the onion and cook gently until softened but not colored, about 5 minutes. Raise the heat, add the *persillade* and stir around with a wooden spoon. Add the spinach and cook, stirring, over high heat for a minute or so. Add salt to taste, grind over some pepper and scrape over a bit of nutmeg. Stir well and remove from the heat.

◼ Spread half the spinach mixture in an oval 8-cup (48-fl oz/2-l) gratin dish. Stir the eggs into the other half. Lay the sardines out, skin side down. Spoon some stuffing onto the head end of each, roll the sardine up and push it into the bed of spinach in the gratin dish, tail in the air. Place the sardines side by side and touching so they hold their shape. Sprinkle bread crumbs generously over the top and dribble on the remaining 3 tablespoons olive oil in a thread, forming a crisscross pattern.

◼ Place in the oven and bake until the crumbs are golden, 20–25 minutes. Serve immediately.

SERVES 6

93

Herb-Stuffed Fish

VAR

DAURADE FARCIE À LA SANARYENNE

Stuffed Porgy with Crab Sauce

This recipe is adapted from one published in 1928 by Austin de Croze, author of Les plats régionaux de France; *it is signed and dated "Mme. Natte, 1886, Sanary." Sanary is a small fishing port between Bandol and Toulon, perhaps the prettiest and most charming in all the region. The crabs in the original recipe are the local favouilles, or green shore crabs. Blue swimmers, in their soft-shelled phase, may replace hard-shelled crabs.*

FOR THE STUFFING:

1 tablespoon olive oil
1 small onion, finely chopped
¼ lb (125 g) fresh cultivated mushrooms, finely chopped
salt and freshly ground pepper
whole nutmeg
2 tablespoons chopped fresh flat-leaf (Italian) parsley
1 lb (500 g) mussels, opened with white wine over heat (see glossary)
2 hard-cooked eggs, chopped

FOR THE SAUCE:

the mussel's cooking liquid
⅓ cup (3 fl oz/80 ml) dry white wine
1 lb (500 g) small, lively crabs (see recipe introduction)
2–3 tablespoons tomato sauce (see glossary)

1 porgy (bream), about 4 lb (2 kg), cleaned
salt and freshly ground pepper
¼ cup (2 fl oz/60 ml) olive oil
½ cup (4 fl oz/125 ml) dry white wine
tender shoots and feathery leaves of wild fennel

To prepare the stuffing, in a frying pan warm the olive oil over low heat. Add the onion and cook until softened but not colored, about 10 minutes. Add the mushrooms and raise the heat. Add salt and pepper to taste and scrape over a hint of nutmeg. Toss and stir until the liquid the mushrooms release evaporates, about 5 minutes. Add the parsley and sauté for a few seconds, until the odor of cooking parsley fills the air. Transfer the pan's contents to a mixing bowl. Remove the mussels from their shells, reserving their cooking liquid. Stir the mussels and eggs into the mushroom mixture. Set aside.

To prepare the sauce, combine the mussels' cooking liquid and the white wine in a saucepan. Bring to a boil, throw in the crabs, cover and cook, stirring the crabs around from time to time, for 6–7 minutes. Empty into a sieve placed over another saucepan. Remove the crabs, two or three at a time, to a mortar, and pound until broken up, coarse and crumbly. Transfer to a food processor fitted with the metal blade, add 2–3 tablespoons of their cooking liquid and process to a coarse purée. Using the wooden pestle, press the purée through a fine-mesh sieve, small quantities at a time, each time discarding the debris of shells that collects in the sieve. Combine the crab purée, the crabs' cooking liquid and the tomato sauce in a saucepan and set aside.

Preheat an oven to 375°F (190°C). Stuff the fish with the mussel mixture and truss it with skewers and kitchen string as directed in herb-stuffed fish (recipe follows). Season the fish on both sides with salt and pepper. Place it in an oiled gratin dish and dribble the olive oil evenly over the top. Pour the wine into the dish.

Place in the oven and bake for 45–50 minutes, basting often after the first 15 minutes. Begin to test for doneness with a trussing needle or sharp skewer after 40 minutes.

While the fish is cooking, reduce the crab sauce at a light boil to a very light-bodied consistency. Transfer the fish to a heated platter (Mme. Natte suggests that it be placed on a bed of fresh fennel) and remove the skewers and string. Add the fish's cooking juices to the sauce. Return the sauce to a boil and reduce, if necessary. Pour it into a warmed bowl. Serve the fish in the same way as for the grilled fish (recipe on page 91). Pour some of the sauce over both the fish and the stuffing.

SERVES 4   *Photograph pages 92–93*

VAR

CHAPON FARCI AUX HERBES

Herb-Stuffed Fish

FOR THE STUFFING:

1 teaspoon olive oil
the fish's liver or a monkfish (anglerfish) liver
1 cup (2 oz/60 g) fresh bread crumbs
½ lb (250 g) spinach, parboiled, squeezed dry and chopped (see glossary)
½ lb (250 g) Swiss chard (silverbeet) greens, parboiled, squeezed dry and chopped (see glossary)
handful of sorrel leaves, stemmed and finely shredded
persillade made with 1 clove garlic (see glossary)
2 or 3 green (spring) onions, chopped or thinly sliced
salt and freshly ground pepper
2 eggs

1 scorpionfish, about 4 lb (2 kg), cleaned
¼ cup (2 fl oz/60 ml) olive oil
1 yellow onion, thinly sliced
2 cloves garlic, thinly sliced
fresh thyme sprigs and fennel stalk pieces
2 lemons, thinly sliced crosswise
½ cup (4 fl oz/125 ml) dry white wine

To prepare the stuffing, in a small frying pan, warm the olive oil over low heat. Add the liver and cook until it firms up, about 1 minute. Transfer it to a mortar and pound to a purée. Add the bread crumbs and mix together, wiping up all the liver. Transfer the liver mixture to a mixing bowl. Add the spinach, chard, sorrel, *persillade,* and green onions and season to taste with salt and pepper. Mix together, add the eggs and, using your hands mix well, squeezing the mixture repeatedly between your fingers. Taste for seasoning.

Preheat an oven to 375°F (190°C). Stuff the fish, pushing the stuffing well into the head, which, with the abdomen, should form a single cavity. Close the cavity with small, sharp skewers (lengths of bamboo skewer are practical); lace kitchen string back and forth, crossing like a bootlace, and then tie.

Rub the bottom of a large gratin dish with olive oil and scatter the yellow onion, garlic, thyme sprigs and fennel pieces over it. Season the stuffed fish with salt and pepper to taste and pose it in the gratin dish. If the tail is not contained with the dish, wrap it in aluminum foil. Dribble the olive oil evenly over the surface. Arrange a row of lemon slices, slightly overlapping, along the entire length of the fish, from head to tail. Pour the white wine into the bottom of the dish.

Place in the oven and bake for 45–50 minutes, basting often after the first 15 minutes. Begin to test for doneness with a sharp skewer or trussing needle after 40 minutes.

Remove the skewers and string and serve at table in the same way as for the grilled fish (recipe on page 91). Pour a spoonful of pan juices over each serving and place a spoonful of stuffing to the side.

SERVES 6

GRENOUILLES À LA PROVENÇALE

Provençal Frogs' Legs

40 pairs frogs' legs
6 tablespoons (3 fl oz/90 ml) olive oil
juice of ½ lemon
½ cup (2 oz/60 g) all-purpose (plain) flour
salt and freshly ground pepper
persillade made with 2 cloves garlic (see glossary)

◙ Place the frogs' legs in a shallow bowl. Add a few teaspoons of the olive oil and the lemon juice and toss and turn the legs a couple of times. Marinate at room temperature for 1 hour.
◙ Dry the frogs' legs on paper towels. Put the flour in a paper bag, add the frogs' legs, close the bag and shake well. Transfer the legs to a sieve and shake off the excess flour.
◙ Warm the remaining olive oil in a large, nonstick sauté pan over high heat. Add the legs and sauté until golden, 8–10 minutes. Season to taste with salt and pepper and remove to a warmed platter.
◙ Throw the *persillade* into the hot oil remaining in the pan for a couple of seconds. Pour the oil and *persillade* over the frogs' legs and serve immediately.

SERVES 4

PETITE FRITURE

Fried Whitebait

In Provence petite friture *is composed mainly of sardine and anchovy fry* (poutine), *tiny, grayish transparent fish varying from 1 inch (2.5 cm) to 2½ inches (6 cm) in length. Whitebait, from more northerly waters, is thought to contain a large percentage of herring fry.* Poutine *and* whitebait, *in any case, look alike, taste alike and are treated in the same way. In the minds of many, petite friture is vacation food, to be enjoyed with a bottle of chilled Cassis white wine on the terrace of a seaside restaurant to break up a day at the beach. See the glossary for more information on deep-frying.*

⅔ cup (3 oz/90 g) all-purpose (plain) flour
salt, freshly ground black pepper and cayenne pepper
1 lb (500 g) whitebait
about 8 cups (64 fl oz/2 l) corn oil or peanut oil
handful of small bouquets of fresh flat-leaf (Italian) parsley leaves
2 lemons, cut in half

◙ The fish should be fried in three or four batches. Preheat an oven at its lowest setting to keep the first batches warm. Lay out several thicknesses of newspaper covered with paper towels on which to drain the fried fish. Prepare a platter covered with a large folded napkin on which to place them after draining. Put the flour and salt, black pepper and cayenne pepper to taste in a large paper bag. Close it and shake it to mix the flour and seasonings together.
◙ In a large pot or a deep-fat fryer, heat the oil to 375°F (190°C), or until it sizzles at contact when a small, floured fish is thrown in. While the oil is heating, throw a handful of whitebait into the paper bag, close it and shake it well. Remove the fish to a large sieve (leaving behind as much flour as possible). Hold the sieve over a sheet of newspaper and shake it, tossing the fish to rid them of all excess flour. (The flour that is shaken free can be returned to the paper bag.)
◙ When the oil is hot enough, empty the sieve into the oil and stir the fish around in the oil with a fork. A minute later, when the fish are crisp and light gold, remove them, using a slotted spoon, to the paper towels. Prepare another handful of fish in the paper bag, shake off excess flour and add them to the hot oil. Transfer the drained fish to the folded napkin, put the platter in the oven, and so forth until the last batch is fried.
◙ After the last of the fish are removed, add the parsley to the hot oil and remove it as soon as it is crisp. Drain for a second, then scatter it over the fish. Surround with lemon halves and serve, covered with the napkin fold.

SERVES 4

Provençal Frogs' Legs

Top to bottom: Toulon-Style Whiting Fillets, Fried Whitebait

MERLAN À LA TOULONNAISE
Toulon-Style Whiting Fillets

Toulon is famous for its mussels. Any preparation of fish in sauce
à la toulonnaise *is nearly certain to be garnished with mussels,*
to which are often joined black olives.

1 lb (500 g) mussels, opened with white wine over heat
   (see glossary)
2 cups (16 fl oz/500 ml) tomato sauce prepared without salt
   (see glossary)
salt and freshly ground pepper
4 whiting fillets, about 1 lb (500 g) total weight
all-purpose (plain) flour

¼ cup (2 fl oz/60 ml) olive oil

▨ Reduce the mussels' decanted cooking liquid over high heat
to about ⅓ cup (3 fl oz/90 ml). Taste for salt. If it is exces-
sively salty, add only as much of the reduced liquid as necessary to the tomato sauce to salt it correctly. Heat the tomato
sauce and hold it at a simmer while preparing the fish fillets.
▨ Season the fillets with salt and pepper. Cover them
with flour, shaking off any excess flour. Warm the olive
oil in a large frying pan over medium-high heat. Add the
fillets and fry, turning once, until lightly colored, 3–4 minutes on each side. Remove to paper towels to drain, then
arrange on a warmed platter.
▨ Shell the mussels. Add them to the simmering tomato
sauce and pour over the fillets. Serve immediately.

SERVES 4

ENCORNETS À LA PROVENÇALE

Provençal Squid

This preparation is often called à l'americaine, in emulation of lobster (homard) *à l'americaine. It is better suited to squid than to lobster. When octopus is prepared like this, with longer cooking, black olives are added at the end and it becomes* poulpe à la niçoise. *A rice pilaf (recipe on page 195), with or without saffron, is an ideal accompaniment.*

3 tablespoons olive oil
1 onion, finely chopped
2 lb (1 kg) squid, cleaned and pouches cut into rings 1 in
    (2.5 cm) wide (see glossary)
salt, freshly ground black pepper and pinch of
    cayenne pepper
¼ cup (2 fl oz/60 ml) marc de Provence (see glossary)
    or Cognac
½ cup (4 fl oz/125 ml) dry white wine
1 lb (500 g) tomatoes, peeled, seeded and coarsely chopped
2 cloves garlic, finely chopped
bouquet garni (see glossary)

▨ Warm the olive oil in a heavy sauté pan over low heat. Add the onion and cook until softened but not colored, about 10 minutes. Raise the heat, add the squid and stir with a wooden spoon until the liquid the squid gives off evaporates, 2–3 minutes. Season to taste with salt and black and cayenne peppers. Add the brandy and ignite with a long-handled match. When the flames die add the wine and reduce by about half, about 10 minutes.
▨ Add the tomatoes, garlic and bouquet garni and bring to a boil. Adjust the heat to a simmer and cover with the lid ajar. After 30 minutes if the sauce is too abundant, remove the lid and raise the heat slightly to maintain a simmer. If when the squid is tender (45–50 minutes in all), the sauce is still too abundant, remove the squid to a plate and reduce the sauce over high heat, stirring with a wooden spoon. Put the squid back into the sauce to serve.

SERVES 4

CATIGOT À LA CAMARGUAISE

Eel in Red Wine

Eels are sold alive. To kill an eel, run the point of a sharp knife through the brain. To skin it, cut the skin around the base of the head, grasp the head with a towel and pull off the body skin with pliers; it peels off like a glove. Cut off the head and gut the eel.

3 tablespoons olive oil
1 onion, chopped
1 large, garden-ripe tomato, peeled, seeded and
    coarsely chopped
1 eel, about 2 lb (1 kg), skinned, cleaned and cut into
    3-in (7.5-cm) lengths (see recipe introduction)
salt
bouquet garni including a strip of dried orange peel and
    1 dried cayenne chili pepper or other dried chili pepper
    (see glossary)
8–10 cloves garlic
1 cup (8 fl oz/250 ml) dry red wine

boiling water as needed
freshly ground pepper
1 tablespoon chopped fresh flat-leaf (Italian) parsley

▨ Choose a heavy sauté pan of a size just to contain the eel pieces side by side. Warm the olive oil in the pan over medium heat. Add the onion and when it begins to color lightly, in a few minutes, add the tomato. Stir well and raise the heat. Add the eel, salt to taste, bouquet garni and garlic cloves. In a separate pan, bring the wine to a boil. Pour it over the eel and add enough boiling water just to cover the eel. Boil, uncovered, turning the eel around and over from time to time, until tender, about 20 minutes.
▨ Grind over some pepper and remove from the heat. Discard the bouquet garni and sprinkle with the parsley. Serve on warmed plates.

SERVES 4

Top to bottom: Eel in Red Wine, Provençal Squid

ÉCREVISSES À LA PROVENÇALE

Provençal Crayfish

¼ cup (2 fl oz/60 ml) olive oil
1 carrot, peeled, thinly sliced lengthwise and then cut
   across into tiny dice
1 onion, finely chopped
1 small celery heart, finely diced
large pinch of Provençal mixed dried herbs (see glossary)
1 dried bay leaf, crumbled, or fresh bay leaf, finely chopped
salt and freshly ground black pepper
4 dozen crayfish
¼ cup (2 fl oz/60 ml) marc de Provence (see glossary) or Cognac

½ cup (4 fl oz/125 ml) dry white wine
3 tablespoons tomato sauce (see glossary)
large pinch of cayenne pepper
persillade made with 2 cloves garlic (see glossary)

▨ Warm the olive oil in a large, heavy sauté pan over low heat. Add the carrot, onion, celery, herbs, bay leaf and salt and black pepper to taste. Stir with a wooden spoon, cover the pan and sweat over the lowest possible heat for about 15 minutes, stirring occasionally.
▨ Raise the heat to high, add the crayfish and stir briskly until they begin to turn red. Add the brandy and ignite it with a long-handled match. Stir, shaking the pan, until the flames die. Add the wine, tomato sauce and cayenne, cover tightly and cook over medium heat, shaking the pan regularly, until the shellfish are tender, 8–10 minutes. Scatter over the *persillade* and serve.

SERVES 4   *Photograph pages 72–73*

Top to bottom: Grilled Mussel Skewers, Clam and Spinach Gratin, Blanquette of Snails

Tian de Palourdes aux Épinards

Clam and Spinach Gratin

In Provence carpet shells, or palourdes, are used for this gratin. It is also often prepared with mussels.

2 lb (1 kg) little neck or cherrystone clams, opened with
   white wine over heat, as for mussels (see glossary)
4 tablespoons (2 fl oz/60 ml) olive oil

1 clove garlic, finely chopped
2 lb (1 kg) spinach, parboiled, squeezed dry and chopped
   (see glossary)
2 tablespoons all-purpose (plain) flour
about 1 cup (8 fl oz/250 ml) milk
freshly ground pepper
whole nutmeg
salt
dried or semidried bread crumbs

◙ Cook the clams as directed. Remove the clams from the cooking liquid and strain the liquid. Set the liquid and clams aside. Preheat an oven to 375°F (190°C).

100

Warm 3 tablespoons of the olive oil in a sauté pan over medium heat. Add the garlic, disperse it with a wooden spoon and, when it begins to sizzle, add the spinach. Stir regularly until the spinach begins to stick to the pan. Sprinkle over the flour and stir for a minute. Slowly add the clams' decanted cooking liquid, stirring constantly, then add all or part of the milk, depending upon the quantity and the saltiness of the clams' juices. Bring to a boil, adjust the heat to a simmer and cook, uncovered, until slightly thickened, about 15 minutes, stirring from time to time. Grind over some pepper and scrape over some nutmeg. Taste for salt (it will probably need none). Stir in the clams. Spread the mixture in a 6-cup (48-fl oz/1.5-l) gratin dish. Sprinkle with bread crumbs and dribble over the remaining 1 tablespoon olive oil.

Place in the oven and bake until the sauce is bubbling and the surface is nicely colored, about 20 minutes. Serve hot.

SERVES 4

BOUCHES·DU·RHÔNE

PETITS-GRIS EN MATELOTE

Blanquette of Snails

The common striped garden snail, or petit gris *(Helix aspersa), is the type most often eaten in Provence. Before being cooked, petits-gris are starved for a week or so in a cool, dark place, kept in a bucket tightly covered with a screen or an overturned mason's sifter. They are then "disgorged": put into a basin with a large handful of salt and about half a bottle of vinegar, stirred around regularly for 30 minutes, thoroughly rinsed, plunged into boiling water for 5 minutes, drained, refreshed under cold water and twirled out of their shells with a small, two-pronged fork or a nutpick. A court bouillon (see crayfish in court bouillon on page 77) is strained over them and they are simmered, with the lid ajar, for 2 hours. At this point, they are ready for use in other recipes. Many people content themselves with cooking the disgorged snails in their shells and serving them with aïoli (see glossary).*

If you are obliged to use canned snails, it is best to first freshen their flavor by draining them, rinsing them and then simmering them gently for 30 minutes in a half recipe for court bouillon. If using canned snails, cut the number in half; they are twice the size of garden snails.

½ lb (250 g) pickling onions, peeled
3 tablespoons unsalted butter
salt
pinch of sugar
½ lb (250 g) fresh button mushrooms or quartered
    larger caps
juice of 1 lemon
¼ cup (2 fl oz/60 ml) water
80–100 garden snails, cooled in the court bouillon
    (see recipe introduction)
2 tablespoons all-purpose (plain) flour
2 cups (16 fl oz/500 ml) of the snails' court bouillon
3 egg yolks
freshly ground pepper
whole nutmeg
1 tablespoon chopped fresh flat-leaf (Italian) parsley
handful of ½-in (12-mm) croûtons cut from firm-crumbed,
    semidry bread, crusts removed, sautéed in olive oil until
    crisp and golden

Put the pickling onions in a saucepan of a size just to contain them in a single layer. Add ½ tablespoon of the butter, a pinch of salt, the sugar and just enough water to cover barely. Bring to a boil and cover with a lid ajar. Simmer for about 10 minutes, shaking the pan occasionally. If the water has not completely evaporated, remove the lid, turn up the heat and shake the pan gently until no water remains and the onions begin to cook in the butter. Set aside.

In another saucepan combine the mushrooms, ½ tablespoon of the butter, salt to taste, half the lemon juice and the water. Cover and bring to a boil over high heat. Boil for a few seconds, then set aside.

Strain the snails, saving the court bouillon. Put the snails and court bouillon aside separately.

Melt the remaining 2 tablespoons butter in a heavy saucepan over low heat. Add the flour and cook while stirring for 1 minute or so. Add 2 cups (16 fl oz/500 ml) of the snails' court bouillon all at once, whisking briskly at the same time. Raise the heat and continue whisking until the sauce boils. Adjust the heat to a simmer and cook for 15 minutes, stirring occasionally.

Strain the mushrooms, reserving the cooking liquid in a small bowl. Stir the strained mushrooms, the onions and snails into the simmering sauce and remove from the heat. Add the remaining lemon juice and the egg yolks to the bowl containing the mushrooms' liquid. Grind over some pepper, scrape over a bit of nutmeg and beat with a fork. Using a wooden spoon, stir the sauce into the saucepan with the snails. Reduce the heat to low and stir until the mixture thickens slightly, a few minutes; it must not boil.

Pour the snails and their sauce into a warmed deep platter, sprinkle with the parsley, scatter over croutons and serve.

SERVES 6

VAR

BROCHETTES DE MOULES À LA TOULONNAISE

Grilled Mussel Skewers

Slender, sharp-pointed bamboo skewers about 12 in (30 cm) long are ideal for these brochettes, which can also be cooked in a broiler (griller). Save the mussels' cooking liquid for use in a sauce or a soup.

1 slice lean salt pork (green bacon), about ¼ lb (125 g) and
    ½ in (12 mm) thick, cut into lardoons (see glossary)
2 lb (1 kg) large mussels, opened in white wine over heat,
    strained and shells discarded (see glossary)
freshly ground pepper
dried oregano
1 tablespoon olive oil
dried bread crumbs

Prepare a fire in a charcoal grill.

Place the lardoons in a saucepan half filled with cold water and bring to a rolling boil. Drain, rinse in cold running water, and pat dry with paper towels.

Place the lardoons in a mixing bowl and add the mussels. Grind over some pepper, crumble over a little oregano and dribble over the olive oil. Using your hands toss the mussels and lardoons until evenly coated with oil and seasoning.

Thread the mussels and lardoons onto skewers, alternating them; they should be touching but not crowded. Spread a layer of bread crumbs on a tray. Roll each skewer in the crumbs until evenly coated.

Place the skewers on a grill rack over hot coals and grill for 2 minutes on each side. Serve hot.

SERVES 4

POULPE EN DAUBE

Octopus Daube

*A large octopus (*pieuvre*) may take as long as four hours'
cooking to become tender and is usually first beaten to help
it along. On the coast near Toulon, one often sees divers in
their outer-space costumes, heaving large octopus repeatedly
against the rocks. The octopus will be cooked in salted water
and whatever wild aromatic things grow within reach—thyme,
bay, fennel—and eaten hot with vinegar and oil. Sublime. In
Toulon octopus daube is accompanied with a mortar of* aïoli
and diners mix the two sauces together at table.

3 tablespoons olive oil
1 large onion, chopped
2 lb (1 kg) small octopus, weighing less than 1 lb (500 g)
    each, cleaned and hood and tentacles cut into 1-in
    (2.5-cm) squares or lengths
salt
¼ cup (4 fl oz/60 ml) marc de Provence (see glossary)
    or Cognac
2 tomatoes, peeled, seeded and coarsely chopped
8–10 cloves garlic
bouquet garni including fresh fennel stalks and 1 dried
    cayenne chili pepper or other dried chili pepper
    (see glossary)
1 cup (8 fl oz/250 ml) dry red wine
boiling water as needed

◼ Warm the olive oil in a flameproof, earthenware casserole
or heavy sauté pan over low heat. Add the onion and cook
until softened but not colored, about 10 minutes. Add the
octopus and salt to taste and raise the heat to medium. The
octopus will throw off some liquid; cook until nearly all the
liquid disappears. Add the brandy and ignite with a long-
handled match. Stir with a wooden spoon until the flames
subside. Add the tomatoes, garlic and bouquet garni and
cook, stirring, until the tomatoes begin to break up and boil,
about 10 minutes.
◼ Bring the red wine to a boil in a saucepan, pour it over the
octopus and add enough boiling water to cover. Cover with
the lid ajar and simmer for 1 hour. If the cooking juices are
abundant, remove the lid, raise the heat slightly to adjust to
a simmer and continue cooking, stirring occasionally, until
the octopus is tender, about 2 hours in all for small octopus.
The cooking liquid should be mostly reduced, coating the
pieces of octopus. Serve hot.

SERVES 4

LE GRAND AÏOLI

*Aïoli or "garlic-oil," is garlic mayonnaise. The word also desig-
nates the ritual celebration of poached salt cod, boiled vegetables,
hard-cooked eggs and a selection of garden snails, sea snails,
periwinkles, mussels, octopus and other seafoods. When it is
complete, it is called* Le Grand Aïoli. *Everything is served warm,
simply because it is impossible to get it all onto the table hot.*

aïoli (see glossary)
2 lb (1 kg) salt cod, soaked and poached (see glossary)
6 beets (beetroots), wrapped individually in aluminum foil
    and baked at 350°F (180°C) until tender, 45–60 minutes
6 sweet potatoes, baked at 350°F (180°C) until tender,
    about 45 minutes
6 new potatoes, boiled in salted water until just tender,
    about 30 minutes

1 lb (500 g) small carrots, boiled in salted water until just
    tender, 10–15 minutes
1 lb (500 g) green beans, parboiled in salted water for
    5–10 minutes
6 young, tender artichokes, trimmed (see glossary) and
    boiled in salted water until tender, about 20 minutes

Left to right: Octopus Daube, Le Grand Aïoli

2 small heads cauliflower, separated into florets and
    parboiled in salted water for 2–3 minutes
12 garden-ripe plum (Roma) tomatoes, peeled
octopus daube (preceding recipe)
6 hard-cooked eggs, shelled

◉ Prepare the *aïoli* in a mortar and place the mortar in the
middle of the table. Surround it with platters on which all of
the remaining elements, except the octopus, are arranged
decoratively. Serve the octopus hot from its cooking vessel.
Its sauce mingles wonderfully with the *aïoli*.

SERVES 6

Top to bottom: Bourride, Poached Striped Bass or Mullet with Green Sauce

B O U C H E S · D U · R H Ô N E

BOURRIDE

A bourride *usually contains monkfish (anglerfish) plus one or two other varieties—skate wings or any of the fish recommended for* bouillabaisse. *Ask your fish merchant to save the heads (gills discarded) and filleted carcasses, broken up or chopped with a cleaver. The cartilaginous monkfish backbone, rich in gelatin,*

should be cut into small pieces. In the south of France the demand for monkfish heads, which contain abundant flesh and flavor, is so great they are now offered for sale.

FOR THE BROTH:

1 leek, thinly sliced
1 onion, thinly sliced
1 small celery stalk, thinly sliced
3 cloves garlic, crushed

1 bay leaf
1 fresh thyme sprig
stems from a bouquet of fresh flat-leaf (Italian) parsley
strip of dried orange peel
3 or 4 short lengths fennel stalk or large pinch of
    fennel seeds
fish heads and carcasses, gills discarded, chopped up
salt
2 cups (16 fl oz/500 ml) dry white wine

3 lb (1.5 kg) white-fleshed fish (see recipe introduction),
    cut into slices about 1 in (2.5 cm) thick or into 1-in
    (2.5-cm) fillet sections
aïoli (see glossary)
4 egg yolks
slices of baguette partially dried in the sun or in a
    warm oven

◉ To prepare the broth, place leek, onion, celery, garlic, bay leaf, thyme sprig, parsley stems and orange peel in the bottom of a saucepan and arrange the fish heads and carcasses on top. Pour in water to cover and add salt to taste. Bring to a boil and skim off any froth or scum. Reduce the heat, cover with the lid ajar and simmer for 15 minutes. Add the wine, return to a boil, then reduce the heat and simmer for 15 minutes longer. Strain the broth through a fine-mesh sieve.

◉ Arrange the fish pieces, side by side, in a large sauté pan. Pour in enough broth to cover and bring to a boil. Adjust the heat so the broth barely simmers, cover with a lid slightly ajar and simmer for 5 minutes. Cover tightly, turn off the heat and leave to steep for 5 minutes. Using a slotted utensil remove the fish to a warmed platter. Reserve the liquid in the pan.

◉ Put half of the *aïoli* into a mixing bowl. Add the egg yolks and whisk until blended. Slowly add the fish cooking liquid, whisking all the while. Pour the mixture into a saucepan, place it over low to medium heat and stir constantly with a wooden spoon until it acquires a light, creamy consistency and coats the back of the spoon, 8–10 minutes; it must not boil or it will break up.

◉ Place 1 or 2 bread slices in each soup plate. Pour some of the *aïoli* cream into a warmed soup tureen or serve it directly from the saucepan, pouring it over the bread in the soup plates. Serve the fish in the same plates with more cream poured over, accompanied by the remaining *aïoli*.

SERVES 4

P R O V E N C E

Loup de Mer ou Mulet Poché, Sauce aux Herbes

Poached Striped Bass or Mullet with Green Sauce

It makes no sense to attempt poaching relatively large fish without the proper equipment. Poaching a fish that is wrapped in cheesecloth (muslin) or a towel in a makeshift vessel is messy and, with all possible care, it still risks being damaged before ending up on its serving platter. You need a fish kettle, or poaching pan, with a perforated rack on which the fish is placed. Although not essential, a thermometer that clips to the inside of the pan is convenient, for a poached fish should never boil: the ideal poaching temperature is about 185°F (85°C).

Some cooks prefer to prepare a white wine court bouillon for pouring over the fish. In the case of a very fresh sea bass, the court bouillon only masks the exhilarating, clean taste of the flesh. For the same reason, with a sea bass you may prefer to serve only olive oil in place of the sauce.

FOR THE SAUCE:

1 clove garlic
large pinch of coarse salt
freshly ground pepper
1 tablespoon capers, rinsed and drained
3 salt anchovies, rinsed, filleted and chopped (see glossary)
handful of chopped fresh flat-leaf (Italian) parsley
½ lb (250 g) spinach, parboiled, squeezed dry and chopped
    (see glossary)
handful of fresh bread crumbs
2 hard-cooked egg yolks
1 egg yolk, uncooked
1 tablespoon Provençal herb vinegar (see glossary)
about 6 tablespoons (3 fl oz/90 ml) olive oil

1 striped bass or mullet, about 4 lb (2 kg), gutted but
    not scaled
handful of coarse sea salt

◉ To prepare the sauce, in a mortar pound together the garlic, coarse salt and pepper to taste to form a paste. Add the capers and anchovies and pound again to a paste. Progressively add all the remaining ingredients, except the olive oil, and pound, stir and beat until the mixture is smooth and homogenous. Add the olive oil in a fine trickle to the side of the mortar, turning the mixture at the same time with the pestle. Set aside.

◉ Place the fish on a rack, lower it into a poaching pan, pour over water to cover by a generous inch (3 cm) and add the salt. Place the pan over medium heat atop two burners until the water approaches the simmering point or the temperature registers 185°F (85°C). Adjust the heat to very low and control it by keeping the pan's lid ajar; the water must not boil. Hold the kettle at this controlled heat for 20 minutes, then remove it from the heat and leave it, covered, for another 20 minutes. Lift the rack from the water and place it, at an angle, on top of the pan to permit the fish to drain for 1–2 minutes. Gently slip the fish onto its platter.

◉ Remove the skin from the top surface before presenting the fish at table: Using a small, sharp-pointed knife, slit the skin from the top of the head to the gill and the length of the back and underside, slitting closely to either side of the dorsal and anal fins and prying them free along with the tiny bones attached to them. Slit the skin at the base of the tail and carefully peel it free from the flesh, removing at the same time the pelvic and pectoral fins and their attached bones. Do not try to turn the fish over to remove the skin from the other side; it will remain in the platter after the service. Without displacing the fish, sponge the platter clean with paper towels or a tea towel.

◉ To serve, use a sole fillet knife or other medium-sized, supple-bladed, sharp-pointed knife and a spatula or wide palette knife. Have ready an empty platter on which to place the carcass after the top fillets have been served. With the knife tip, cut to the bone the entire length of the lateral line, a more or less curved line, running from the top of the gill to the center of the tail, which corresponds to the path of the spinal column. Slice, crosswise, to the bones, dividing each fillet in two to create individual servings. Slip the blade of the knife into the lateral cut and ease it, at an angle, beneath the section of fillet to be dislodged. Remove the serving to a plate with the spatula (the abdominal quarter will not provide as neat a serving as the rest). When the top fillets are served out, slip the knife tip beneath the spinal column near the base of the tail, slit the skin and lift the tail carefully to free the skeleton from the underlying fillets, holding them in place with the blade of the knife as the skeleton and head are detached from the rest. Move the carcass to the empty platter (don't forget to serve the cheeks to an honored guest) and serve the remaining fillets in the same way as the others. Serve the green sauce on the side.

SERVES 6

FILETS DE MULET AUX FINES HERBES

Mullet Fillets with Fines Herbes

Other fish of approximately the same size can be treated in the same way.

FOR THE BROTH:

1 onion, chopped
2 cloves garlic, crushed
pinch of fennel seeds
flat-leaf (Italian) parsley sprigs
1 bay leaf
1 fresh thyme sprig
heads and carcasses of the mullets, gills discarded, chopped up
salt
1 cup (8 fl oz/250 ml) dry white wine

2 tablespoons olive oil
3 or 4 shallots, finely chopped
1 tablespoon finely chopped flat-leaf (Italian) parsley mixed
    with chopped fresh wild fennel leaves, if available
2 mullets, about 1½ lb (750 g) each, cleaned and filleted
salt
½ cup (4 fl oz/125 ml) dry white wine
3 egg yolks
juice of ½ lemon

freshly ground pepper
whole nutmeg

◉ To prepare the broth, put the onion, garlic and herbs in the bottom of a saucepan and place the fish heads and carcasses on top. Pour in water to cover barely and add salt to taste. Bring to a boil and skim off any froth and scum. Reduce the heat, cover with a lid ajar and keep at a gentle boil for 15 minutes. Add the wine, return to a boil, then reduce the heat and simmer for another 15 minutes longer. Strain, return the broth to the saucepan over high heat and boil until reduced by half. Set aside.

◉ Choose a sauté pan of a size just to contain the fillets side by side. Smear the bottom with 1 tablespoon of the olive oil. Scatter the shallots and parsley over the bottom and place the fillets on top. Sprinkle with salt and pour in the wine. If it does not completely immerse the fillets, add some of the strained broth. Bring to a boil, cover the pan tightly, reduce the heat as low as possible and cook for 5 minutes. Remove from the heat and let stand, tightly covered, to steep for 3–4 minutes longer.

◉ Transfer the fillets to a heated serving platter and add their poaching liquid to the strained broth. In a bowl combine the egg yolks, lemon juice and the remaining tablespoon olive oil. Grind over some pepper and scrape over a bit of nutmeg. Whisk briefly and then whisk in a ladleful of the broth. Stir the egg mixture into the broth with a wooden spoon and place over medium-low heat. Stir until the sauce coats the spoon, about 5 minutes. It must not boil.

◉ Pour the sauce over the fillets and serve immediately.

SERVES 4

Marseilles-Style Mussels

MOULES À LA MARSEILLAISE

Marseilles-Style Mussels

Clams can also be prepared in this way.

2 lb (1 kg) mussels, opened over heat with white wine
    (see glossary)
4 tablespoons (2 fl oz/60 ml) olive oil
1 onion, finely chopped
2 large tomatoes, peeled, seeded and coarsely chopped
persillade made with 2 cloves garlic (see glossary)
salt and freshly ground pepper
dried bread crumbs

◉ Cook the mussels as directed. Remove the mussels from the cooking liquid and snap off and discard one shell from each. Place the mussels in their half shells in a gratin dish. Arrange in two layers, with the bottoms of the top layer reposing on the edges of those below so all the mussels will receive some sauce. Strain the mussel cooking liquid and set aside.

◉ Preheat an oven to 450°F (230°C). Warm 3 tablespoons of the olive oil in a large pan over low heat. Add the onion and sauté until soft but not colored, about 10 minutes. Raise the heat, add the tomatoes and *persillade* and sauté until the tomatoes break up and are boiling, about 6–7 minutes. Add the mussels' decanted cooking liquid and reduce, at a gentle boil, to the consistency of a sauce, about 10 minutes. Taste for salt and grind over some pepper.

◉ Spoon the sauce over the mussels, then sprinkle with bread crumbs. Dribble over the remaining 1 tablespoon olive oil. Place in the oven and bake until the sauce is bubbling and the crumbs are golden, 8–10 minutes. Serve immediately.

SERVES 4

Left to right: Baked Grouper, Sardine Paupiettes, Mullet Fillets with Fines Herbes

MÉROU À LA PROVENÇALE

Baked Grouper

Monkfish (anglerfish) or any large fish with firm, relatively boneless flesh that is sold cut up can be prepared in this way.

salt
4 large, garden-ripe tomatoes, peeled, seeded and cut into slices ½ in (12 mm) thick
¼ cup (2 fl oz/60 ml) olive oil
1½ lb (750 g) grouper fillets without skin, cut into 4 slices 1 in (2.5 cm) thick
freshly ground pepper
¼ cup *tapénade* (recipe on page 34)
persillade made with 2 cloves garlic (see glossary)
dried bread crumbs

◙ Salt the tomato slices on both sides and lay them out on an overturned drum sieve or wire rack to drain for 30 minutes. Place them on a cotton towel or on paper towels to sponge off excess liquid.
◙ Preheat an oven to 375°F (190°C). Choose a gratin dish of a size just to contain the fish slices side by side and rub it with 1 teaspoon of the olive oil. Line the dish with half of the tomato slices. Season the fish slices on both sides with salt and pepper to taste and arrange them atop the tomatoes. Spread some *tapénade* on each fish slice, scatter over the *persillade* and press the remaining tomato slices on top. Sprinkle with salt and bread crumbs and dribble on the remaining olive oil in a thread, forming a crisscross pattern.
◙ Place in the oven and bake until the crumbs are golden, about 25 minutes. Serve hot.

SERVES 4

PAUPIETTES DE SARDINES À LA NIÇOISE

Sardine Paupiettes

Zucchini bear male and female flowers. The fruitless male flowers are picked and sold immediately, before they wilt, in the Provençal morning markets. Usually they are dipped in batter and deep-fried.

4 tablespoons (2 fl oz/60 ml) olive oil
1 large sweet white onion, halved and thinly sliced
4 cloves garlic, thinly sliced
8 fresh sardines, cleaned and filleted
salt and freshly ground pepper
16 sorrel leaves, stemmed
16 freshly picked zucchini (courgette) blossoms, stems cut off at base
6 tablespoons (3 fl oz/90 ml) dry white wine

◙ Preheat an oven to 400°F (200°C). Rub the bottom of a gratin dish with 1 teaspoon of the olive oil. Mix together the onion and garlic and scatter half of the mixture in the dish. Season the sardine fillets with salt and pepper. Roll up a fillet in each sorrel leaf. Slip each sorrel package into a zucchini blossom, folding the pointed petal tips over each other to enclose the package.
◙ Arrange the stuffed blossoms side by side in the gratin dish. Scatter the remaining onion-garlic mixture over the top and dribble with the remaining olive oil. Sprinkle the wine over the top and cover the dish loosely with a sheet of aluminum foil.
◙ Place in the oven and bake for about 10 minutes. Turn off the oven and leave the covered dish in the cooling oven for 15 minutes, or in another warm place before serving.

SERVES 4

BOUCHES·DU·RHÔNE / VAR

BOUILLABAISSE

The original bouillabaisse *was a collection of unsold fish from the day's catch, boiled by fishermen over seaside bonfires in diluted sea water perfumed with the wild herbs that grew within reach. Today, the musts and must-nots of preparing* bouillabaisse *are so numerous and so contradictory that one should be prepared to break rules at will. The water in the following recipe can be replaced by a fish broth made of heads and filleted carcasses; on the Mediterranean coast, many people prepare a saffronless fish soup (recipe on page 42) with which to moisten a* bouillabaisse. *Natives of* bouillabaisse *country are unanimous in their conviction that without* rascasses *(scorpionfish),* bouillabaisse *cannot exist, and they are scornful of Parisians, who add* langoustes, *or lobsters, to their* bouillabaisses; *the Marseillais disapprove of the Toulonnais habit of adding mussels and potatoes and purists are horrified at the notion of adding pastis (the purpose of which is, simply, to reinforce the fennel flavor if fennel stalks are missing). The Martigaux add tiny cuttlefish, whose ink sacks open up, turning the broth black; it is called* la bouillabaisse noire.

Count four or five varieties of firm, white-fleshed fish—monkfish (anglerfish) plus any of those listed in the chapter introduction; if these are in short supply, supplement with halibut, hake or cod. Large fish should be filleted and cut into serving sections; small fish should be cleaned but left whole. The rapid boil, characteristic of bouillabaisse, *may leave the fish looking a bit ragged; the rough treatment is necessary to create the liaison between olive oil and broth, which is one of the dish's most-admired qualities.*

6 lb (3 kg) mixed fish (see recipe introduction)
1½ lb (750 g) potatoes, peeled and quartered

FOR THE MARINADE:

¼ teaspoon powdered saffron
¼ teaspoon ground fennel seeds
¼ cup (2 fl oz/60 ml) olive oil
2 tablespoons *pastis* such as Pernod 51 or Ricard

FOR THE *ROUILLE:*

2 dried cayenne chili peppers or other dried chili peppers
3 cloves garlic
large pinch of coarse salt
large pinch of fresh bread crumbs
¼ teaspoon powdered saffron dissolved in 1 tablespoon
    boiling water

1 egg yolk, at room temperature
1 cup (8 fl oz/250 ml) olive oil, at room temperature

¼ cup (2 fl oz/60 ml) olive oil
1 large onion, finely chopped
2 leeks, including the tender green parts, thinly sliced
3 cloves garlic
1½ lb (750 g) tomatoes, peeled, seeded and coarsely
    chopped
large bouquet garni including a strip of dried orange peel
    (see glossary)
large pinch of saffron threads
salt
boiling water as needed
1 lb (500 g) small, lively crabs such as blue swimmers or
    sand crabs
baguette slices, partially dried in the sun or in a warm oven

◾ Spread the fish and potatoes out on a large platter. To marinate them sprinkle with the saffron and fennel seeds, then with olive oil, turn them all around until evenly coated with oil and colored with saffron. Sprinkle over the *pastis,* turn around again and leave for 1 hour or so. Cover with another platter or with plastic wrap.

◾ To make the *rouille,* in a mortar, pound the chili pepper to a powder. Add the garlic and coarse salt and pound to form a paste. Add the bread crumbs and dissolved saffron and again pound to a paste. Stir in the egg yolk with the pestle until completely integrated. Mount the *rouille* in the same way as an *aioli* (see glossary), adding the olive oil in a trickle to the side of the mortar. Set the *rouille* aside.

◾ Warm the olive oil in a large, heavy pot over low heat. Add the onion and leeks and cook gently until softened but not colored, about 15 minutes. Add the garlic, tomatoes, bouquet garni, saffron and salt and raise the heat to high. Cook, stirring with a wooden spoon, until the tomatoes are broken up and boiling, about 10 minutes.

◾ Add the potatoes, place the fish on top and empty in all of the marinade. Pour in boiling water to cover and bring to a boil over high heat. Boil, uncovered, for 5 minutes, then throw in the crabs, gently displacing the pieces of fish to immerse the crabs completely. Continue to boil for 10 minutes.

◾ Stir 2–3 tablespoons of the boiling broth into the *rouille* to loosen it. Remove and discard the bouquet garni. Remove the fish, potatoes and crab to a warmed serving platter. Place 1 or 2 bread slices in each soup plate and dab some *rouille* on top. Ladle the broth over the bread slices. Serve the fish, crabs and potatoes in the same plates, with a little more broth poured over the top. Pass the remaining *rouille.*

SERVES 8

BOUCHES·DU·RHÔNE

PETITS-GRIS À L'AIXOISE
Aix-Style Stuffed Snails

For stuffed snails, it is convenient to have a snail service: metal or other ovenproof plates with round depressions in which to place the snails before heating them, special snail clamps with which to pick them up at table and small, two-pronged forks with which to remove each snail from its shell. This is done over a piece of bread that will collect the spilled, melted stuffing as well as any remaining in the shell, emptied over the bread when the snail is removed. One tucks the snail into one's mouth along with a bite of the anointed bread.

6 dozen garden snails

FOR THE STUFFING:

pinch of fennel seeds
large pinch of coarse salt

freshly ground pepper
whole nutmeg
3 cloves garlic
2 or 3 shallots, chopped
3 salt anchovies, rinsed and filleted (see glossary)
7 oz (220 g) raw beef marrow (see glossary), chopped
5 tablespoons (3 fl oz/80 ml) olive oil
juice of ½ lemon

◾ Prepare the snails as directed in the introduction for *blanquette* of snails (recipe on page 101). Remove the snails from their shells and cook them as directed in court bouillon; drain and set aside. Rinse and dry the shells and set aside as well.

◾ Preheat an oven to 500°F (260°C).

◾ To make the stuffing, in a mortar pound the fennel seeds to a powder. Add the salt, grind in some pepper and scrape in a bit of nutmeg. Add the garlic and shallots and pound to a paste. Add the anchovies and again pound to a paste. Add the marrow and pound well. Work in the olive oil and lemon juice until smooth and consistent. (Alternatively, transfer the marrow and mortar mixture to a food processor fitted with a metal blade and process until smooth, then mix in the olive oil and lemon juice.)

◾ Put a snail into each shell, twirling it in a spiral. Pack each shell's opening with stuffing, smoothing the surface. Arrange the snails on snail plates—or side by side on a shallow baking dish or dishes—with the stuffed surfaces facing straight up and heat in the oven for a few minutes until the stuffing is bubbling furiously.

◾ Serve immediately. If the snail service is lacking, place all of the snails in the middle of the table. Each person will take one at a time with a teaspoon and remove it from the shell with a cocktail fork or a nutpick.

SERVES 6

Aix-Style Stuffed Snails

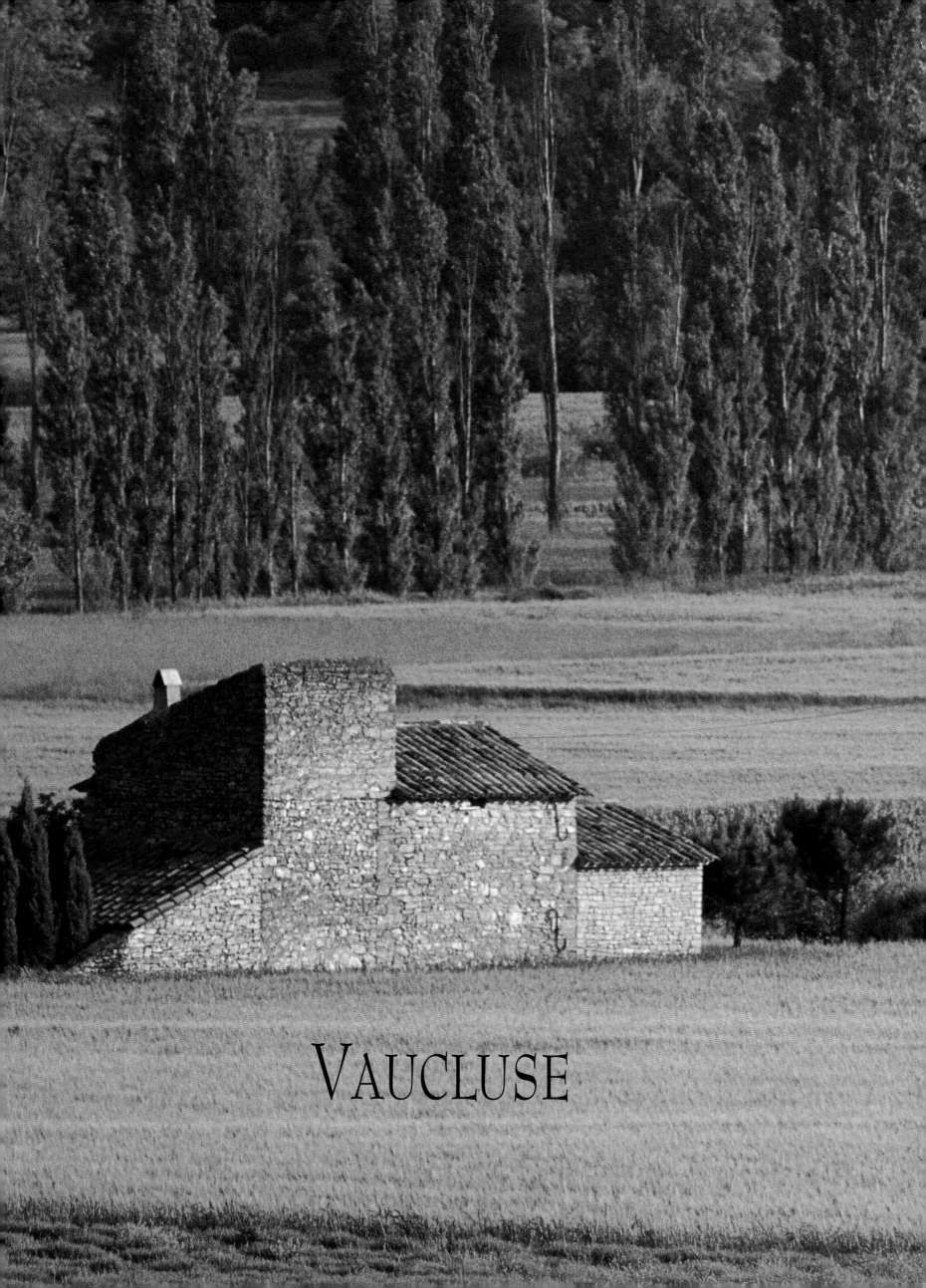

VAUCLUSE

VAUCLUSE

I f the Bouches-du-Rhône is the region of the singsong accent, if the Alpes-de-Haute-Provence are the most solitary in appearance, if the Var knows how to hold its counsel and the Alpes-Maritimes how to cultivate their diverseness, the Vaucluse is indisputably the most elegant and most courted of all Provençal territories.

Here we have villages that capture the fullness of the light (Gordes, Roussillon, Ménerbes, Bonnieux), while others seek the discretion of the shadows (Lourmarin, Mirabeau). We have such opera and theater towns as Avignon and Orange whose lives seem to be one continuous festival, and others like Apt or Cavaillon, intellectual or industrious. But throughout this region, where tomatoes are charmingly called love apples and every village has its citizenry nicknames (slug-eaters, gourd-eaters, herring-suckers, tart-gluttons), where aromatic plants grow and venerable vines and olive trees flourish, where truffles reveal their secrets and vegetables blaze with color, there is a talent for cooking.

The people of the Vaucluse know how to cook and live on very little, as they do everywhere in Provence. They know how to use the things that enabled peasants of the past to toil under a relentless sun out on the *restanques* "terraced fields," or gave them hope at the end of the day on their return from the fields: an anchovy, a tomato, some olives, an onion, a clove of garlic, and, of course, a little bread. Bread once upon a time was cooked on a wood fire, long before the days of large restaurants

Previous pages: Provençal architecture is as diverse as the landscape; here, in the countryside near Gordes, is a characteristic farmhouse known as a mas. *Left: The excellent acoustics inside Senanque, a 12th century Cistercian abbey, are perfectly suited to the Gregorian chants, performed here every summer.*

with gastronomic bakeries all choosing to make their own bread, as they do today. Onion bread, thyme bread, olive bread, walnut bread, Roquefort bread, garlic bread, pepper bread all existed in Apt and Cavaillon, and it is no surprise that a Baker's Museum has been opened in Bonnieux, in the heart of the Lubéron mountain area.

Just as there are Provences, there are Vaucluses. The Vaucluse of the plains is like a royal route: the Vaucluse *comtats* of Orange, Avignon, Cavaillon, Carpentras. It is a region whose towns are rich in history: Orange, the Roman gateway to Provence, where the honey, truffles and olives flourish. Avignon, city of the popes, with its palace-fortress and an unfinished bridge over the Rhône, which, legend has it, was built by a young shepherd. Cavaillon, melon capital and commercial center from time immemorial. Carpentras, with its truffles and its caramels. Vaison-la-Romaine, L'Isle-sur-la Sorgue, birthplace of René Char, one of the great French poets. And Châteauneuf-du-Pape, for which everyone will have something of a soft spot, because its name almost epitomizes the appellation of the Côtes du Rhône wines. Thirteen types of vine are nourished in this soil, all planted from vigorous stocks to resist the onslaught of the mistral. This is the place where the wine blends with the sun, even though it is at Suze-la-Rousse in the Drôme, a little farther north, that the University of Wine has been established.

The Vaucluse of the mountains is instantly summed up by the luminous Lubéron, a place Parisians, foreigners, artists, writers, actors and politicians start squabbling over as soon as summer comes. It is a region coveted by the *tout-Paris,* the chic Provence of the weekend house, although thirty years ago in Gordes, one of the most famous of the Lubéron villages, you would not have found ten telephones.

Oppède-le-Vieux, Ménerbes, Lacoste with the Marquis de Sade's château, Bonnieux, Gordes and the

Carpentras, famous for its truffles, is one of the most important agricultural centers in France.

Cistercian abbey at Senanque, Roussillon with its ocher cliffs each has its special attraction. In Lourmarin Albert Camus, winner of the Nobel Prize for Literature, died in 1960. In a neighboring cottage lived Henri Bosco, the Lubéron's leading writer (although he was born in Avignon), who wrote: "In this deserted countryside you wonder who cultivates the land. You can saunter about all the livelong day in vain, you never see a soul ... these bare open fields between the cultivated valley areas and the meager pastures of the Lubéron guard closely the secrets of these men who ask of them nothing more than a bit of stunted corn and some tart wine."

Those secrets appear to sleep still, in the land of the *bories,* traditional dry-stone houses of the south. Solidly constructed vaulted buildings without a trace of mortar and neither windows nor chimneys, they are refuges against a demented wind, once used to shelter animals or to catch rainwater, or simply heaps of stones removed from fields destined for cultivation. *Bories* are part of the history and legend of this place, used by residents and artists alike: The painter Vasarély had one in Gordes set up as a studio and meditation room.

But the Lubéron is not merely a source of inspiration and special light. It has lost nothing of its colors and flavors, and even if it lacks a cuisine in the proper sense of the word, here too they know how to use and combine the magic of herbs and olive oil, prepare the vegetables that are so valuable for gratins, and make soups fit for a feast. The most robust and popular of these, prepared in all the best kitchens, is the one made with spelt, a noble variety of wheat that was used in the old days for soaking the scraps from a leg of lamb.

As recently as the eighteenth century the wealth of the lower Lubéron was not calculated in country houses or weekenders, but in *banastes* (large wicker baskets) full of beans gathered between Cavaillon and Pays d'Aigues (the Durance River country, from Merindol to Mirabeau). Pertuis was the undisputed bean capital, and its influence was described by Paul Arène, a Provençal writer of the nineteenth century: "Pertuis was sowing its beans. In the town the good citizens sat out in the fresh air and remarked as they watched the moving red and white dots: 'If the rains come in time, France will not be short of beans this year.'" Neighboring Cavaillon contributed its *faiou* beans to this bounty, while in more recent years Cadenet added their red *cocos* (haricot beans).

Finally, Vaucluse means the sweet things of life. There are the jams and preserved fruits from Apt, which were known to the Romans but were truly launched by the Avignon popes (in 1343, Clement VI had a personal "esquire of preserves"). Around 1860 a local confectioner popularized the caramels of Carpentras to the point of flooding the English market, adding to the traditional mixture of white and brown sugars the syrup from fruit preserves and a touch of mint for flavor. This golden age of caramels lasted until the 1950s. Then there are the *papelines* of Avignon, confections of sugar and fine chocolate. According to legend it was their liqueur, made with herbs from the Ventoux, that enabled the people of Avignon to beat cholera in 1884.

At the beginning of the twentieth century, the melons of Cavaillon experienced a period of considerable popularity. They are red- or white-fleshed, sweet and heavy fruits, with some weighing as much as thirty-five pounds (fifteen kilos). The smaller melons are known as Americans, and all of them are used in the making of the Apt fruit preserves. In 1869, Frédéric Mistral expressed his surprise that

Throughout Vaucluse there are clusters of small villages clinging to the hills, each retaining its own unique characteristics, festivals and traditions.

"gourmets eat the Cavaillon melons only with salt."

Here, too, as in the Alpes-de-Haute-Provence, we find honey, gathered by people known locally not as apiarists or beekeepers, but as bee shepherds, because they maintain the practice of moving their charges around the hills as shepherds do their flocks, searching for the perfumes of lavender, thyme or rosemary.

Finally, there are truffles, for which Carpentras still has the largest market in Provence, active between autumn and spring. Every Friday on the Cours des Platanes, the *rabasses*, as the local truffles are called, are weighed on Roman scales. Everything is done with an air of mystery, particularly transactions between the solitary lord of truffles, the *rabassaire* ("truffle picker"), and the purchaser. These precious fungi are tucked into omelets or scrambled eggs (the Provence *brouillade*), cut into strips as a simple yet impressive embellishment to a soup or a salad, or, more simply still, cooked whole buried in ashes. The wonderful brown or black truffle (not the white summer Saint Jean truffle), dug out of the side of the Lubéron, Ventoux, or Lure mountain, is such a precious possession that it is a magnet for secrets and legends.

Meats, Poultry and Game

Sausage, both fresh and cured, can be found in the neighborhood charcuteries of Provence.

MEATS, POULTRY AND GAME

The most important meat production in Provence is that of yearling lamb, called either *mouton* or *agneau,* from the Alpes-de-Haute-Provence. The commercial center is Sisteron. Anyone in Provence will tell you that *agneau de Sisteron* is known to be the best in France. Although beef and veal are not farmed in Provence, the consumption of beef is greater than that of lamb. Veal is less admired than either, unless it be in the useful shape of a breast to contain a stuffing from which emanate all of the flavors of the region. Everyone loves roast kid (*chevreau; cabrí*), which is eaten, if not on Easter day, just before or just after when the kids are severed. From the end of March into May, the butchers display them, hung whole, wrapped with their caul, in which they will be roasted. In its infinite charcuterie disguises, the pig—*le cochon*—is present at all Provençal tables at practically every meal.

Guinea fowl and Muscovy duck (*canard de Barbarie*) are popular and both are often farmed on a small scale locally and offered for sale in the morning open-air markets. Rabbit, usually raised in home hutches, is often consumed in the form of a *gibelotte.* When sautéed tomato or some tomato sauce is added to a *gibelotte,* it is called *chasseur;* if winter savory replaces the thyme, it is called *lapin au pebre d'aï.*

In autumn wild boar and hare excite Provençal passions. Boar (*sanglier*) is increasingly rare on the market. Not so long ago, in November and December, one often saw this majestic beast, hanging whole and bristling,

The Provençal butcher takes as much care with the cutting, trimming and presentation of his meats as the chef does with his preparation.

Previous pages: The grounds of Château d'Ansouis. From left to right: Rabbit in Spicy Sauce (recipe page 133), White Wine Rabbit Stew (recipe page 144)

118

water. They are poached for a quarter of an hour before being hung, steaming, in the front of the shop. In the homes, they are gently grilled and usually served with mashed potatoes.

Of all the local charcuterie, the most glamorous is *andouillettes* prepared *tirées à la ficelle,* chitterling sausages "drawn with string." In this preparation, twisted loops of intermingled, marinated and seasoned strips of pig's gut and long, slender strips of back fat are rolled in *persillade,* pulled with a string into lengths of large sausage casing, and then tucked in at the ends and simmered for hours in a stock or court bouillon. *Andouillettes* are served grilled, with puréed or fried potatoes, accompanied with Dijon mustard.

Entrevaux boasts its local specialty, secca de boeuf, *a type of dried salt beef delicious when eaten with olive oil and lemon juice.*

Most French game can be found in Provence where hunting is a popular sport.

in front of a butcher shop with a sign indicating the date it would be cut up. For a week to follow, the butcher took orders, and the boar was then cut up and dispatched in a few hours' time. Young boar (*marcassin*) is subtle and delicate and treated like venison or lamb: leg or saddle roasted pink, the rib chops grilled semirare, the shoulder cut up and braised with red wine, like a *boeuf bourguignon* or an Avignon daube. The hare is prepared *en civet* ("with its blood"), exactly like a *gibelotte* but with red wine replacing the white and, just before serving, the sauce thickened with the blood. Like an egg-yolk binder, the sauce must not be allowed to boil after the blood is added, lest it break. By unanimous consent, an old Châteauneuf-du-Pape is the ideal companion to a *civet.* Both wild rabbit and hutch rabbit are also often prepared *en civet.*

In the villages, butchers double as *charcutiers* and each also has a daily specialty of some hot preparation to take out. A favorite take-out in the Bouches-du-Rhône and the Var is *pieds et paquets,* whose origins are in Marseilles, where it competes, with *bouillabaisse,* for supremacy of pride. *Pieds et paquets* are lamb trotters and small packages of lamb stomach stuffed with chopped lean salt pork (green bacon), lamb tripe and *persillade.* They are prepared in exactly the same way as *tripe à la marseillaise.* Butchers also offer them raw, with the packages stuffed and ready to be cooked.

Tuesday, for many butchers, is *boudin* or "blood sausage" (black pudding) day, when the long, narrow sausage casings are filled with a *soupe* of blood and stewed onions and then looped and twisted into garlands of sausages that are immersed in a cauldron of hot

PROVENCE

BLANQUETTE D'AGNEAU
Lamb Blanquette

Milk-fed lamb or kid is most often prepared in a blanquette, which is a traditional Easter dish. The following recipe is adjusted for yearling lamb. Accompany with boiled new potatoes or pilaf.

1 lamb shoulder with bone, cut into 8 equal pieces, about 3 lb (1.5 kg)
2 carrots, peeled
1 yellow onion stuck with 2 whole cloves
large bouquet garni (see glossary)
salt
½ lb (250 g) pickling onions
1 tablespoon unsalted butter
pinch of sugar
5 oz (150 g) fresh button mushrooms, quartered if large
juice of 1 lemon
4 egg yolks
freshly ground pepper
whole nutmeg

In a large saucepan arrange the pieces of meat, carrots, yellow onion and bouquet garni so that they may be immersed in a minimum of liquid; do not crowd. Pour in water to cover, add salt to taste and bring slowly to a boil. Skim off any froth and scum. Adjust the heat to maintain a light simmer, cover with the lid ajar slightly and cook for 1½ hours.

Meanwhile, put the pickling onions in a small saucepan of a size to contain them in a single layer. Add half of the butter, the sugar, a pinch of salt and enough water almost to cover them. Bring to a boil, reduce the heat to low, cover and simmer

Top to bottom: Leg of Lamb Braised with Garlic, Lamb Blanquette

for about 8 minutes. Remove the lid, raise the heat and cook, shaking the pan gently, until all the liquid evaporates and the onions are glazed and yellowed, about 5 minutes. Set aside.

In another small saucepan, combine the mushrooms, the remaining ½ tablespoon butter, half of the lemon juice, a pinch of salt and about 3 tablespoons water. Bring to a boil, cover and boil for less than 1 minute. Remove from the heat and set aside.

Remove the saucepan containing the meat from the heat. Discard the carrots, the onion stuck with cloves and the bouquet garni. Add the glazed onions to the meat. Drain the mushrooms' cooking liquid into a bowl and add the mushrooms to the meat. Add the remaining lemon juice and the egg yolks to the mushrooms' liquid. Grind over some pepper and scrape over some nutmeg. Beat with a fork until blended and, using a wooden spoon, stir the mixture into the saucepan. Return to low heat, stirring gently and continuously until the sauce coats the spoon, about 10 minutes. It must not boil. To serve, transfer the lamb and sauce to a warmed serving dish.

SERVES 4

VAUCLUSE

GIGOT À LA CAVAILLONNAISE
Leg of Lamb Braised with Garlic

Braised leg of lamb, for which there are many formulas, is an old-fashioned Provençal favorite rarely encountered today. Have your butcher prepare the leg for braising.

FOR THE LARDOONS (see glossary):

pinch of coarse salt
freshly ground pepper
pinch of Provençal mixed dried herbs (see glossary)
1 clove garlic
1 tablespoon chopped fresh flat-leaf (Italian) parsley
3 oz (100 g) pork back fat, cut into lardoons

1 leg of lamb, about 6 lb (3 kg), pelvic bone removed, leg bone shortened and fat trimmed
8 salt anchovies, rinsed and filleted (see glossary)
1 tablespoon olive oil
1 bay leaf
24 cloves garlic, unpeeled
½ cup (4 fl oz/125 ml) dry white wine
3 tomatoes, peeled, seeded and coarsely chopped
1 cup (5 oz/150 g) black olives

Preheat an oven to 400°F (200°C).

To prepare the lardoons, in a mortar pound together the coarse salt, pepper, herbs and garlic to form a paste. Mix in the parsley. Add the lardoons and mix well until they are evenly coated with the mixture.

With the tip of a small, sharp-pointed knife, pierce the leg repeatedly, on the bias and with the grain. Open the slits with your finger and force in, as deeply as possible, the lardoons and anchovy fillets, alternating between the two.

Rub the leg with the olive oil and place it in an oval ovenproof casserole with a tight-fitting lid. Put the casserole, uncovered, into the oven for 30 minutes. Reduce the oven temperature to 300°F (150°C). Add the bay leaf, garlic, wine and tomatoes, cover and cook for 2 hours, turning the leg several times in its juices. Add the olives and cook until the lamb is tender, another 15 minutes.

Taste the sauce for salt. Transfer the leg to a warmed platter and surround it with the garlic and the olives and a bit of the pan sauce. Serve the remaining sauce in a warmed bowl alongside.

SERVES 8

Lamb and Artichoke Stew

RAGOÛT D'AGNEAU AUX ARTICHAUTS

Lamb and Artichoke Stew

Pilaf, fresh noodles or potatoes are all perfect accompaniments. Little new potatoes, boiled in their skins, can be peeled and added to the stew 10 minutes before serving to simplify things.

3 tablespoons olive oil
1 slice lean salt pork (green bacon), about 3 oz (100 g), cut into lardoons (see glossary)
1 lamb shoulder including shank, about 3 lb (1.5 kg), boned, trimmed of fat and cut into 1½–2 in (4–5 cm) pieces
salt
1 large tomato, peeled, seeded and coarsely chopped
4 cloves garlic, crushed
1 cup (8 fl oz/250 ml) white wine
bouquet garni (see glossary)
4 young, tender artichokes, trimmed, quartered and chokes removed if necessary (see glossary)
½ lb (250 g) pickling onions

◈ Warm 2 tablespoons of the olive oil in a heavy sauté pan over medium heat. Add the lardoons and sauté until colored on all sides, about 10 minutes. Remove them to a plate. Add the lamb pieces to the pan, sprinkle with salt and sauté until nicely colored on all sides, about 20 minutes.

◈ Drain the fat from the pan. Add the tomato, garlic and white wine and raise the heat to high. Stir and scrape the pan bottom with a wooden spoon to dissolve any browned bits. Add the bouquet garni, reduce the heat to low, cover and simmer gently for 1 hour.

◈ Meanwhile, warm 1 tablespoon olive oil in a large, flame-proof earthenware or enameled ironware casserole over low heat. Add the artichokes and the onions and salt lightly. Cover and sweat over very gentle heat, shaking the pan from time to time, for 20 minutes. Add the reserved lardoons and pour in the contents of the sauté pan. Cover and continue to simmer over very low heat until the artichokes and the meat are tender, another 20–30 minutes.

SERVES 4

Daube à la Provençale
Provençal Daube

Everyone agrees that a daube, one of Provence's most revered dishes, should be prepared strictly according to tradition. But traditions vary from one village to another and from one family to another. Some prepare it with white wine, some with red and others insist that a daube must not contain vegetables.

FOR THE LARDOONS (see glossary):

pinch of coarse salt
2 cloves garlic
pinch of Provençal mixed dried herbs (see glossary)
2 tablespoons chopped fresh flat-leaf (Italian) parsley
1 piece pork back fat, ¼ lb (125 g), cut into lardoons

4 lb (2 kg) boneless beef shank (shin), cut into 3 oz (100 g)
    pieces
2 tablespoons olive oil
3 cups (24 fl oz/750 ml) dry red wine
1 pig's foot (trotter), about 1 lb (500 g), split in half lengthwise
¼ lb (125 g) pork rind
1 slice lean salt pork (green bacon), about 5 oz (150 g), cut
    crosswise into sections ½ in (12 mm) wide
2 carrots, peeled and chopped
2 onions, chopped
3 cloves garlic, chopped
1 oz (30 g) dried cèpes, soaked in cold water to cover for 30
    minutes, drained, stem ends trimmed and finely chopped
1 lb (500 g) tomatoes, peeled, seeded and coarsely chopped
⅔ cup (3 oz/100 g) black olives, pitted
salt
large bouquet garni, including strip of dried orange peel
    (see glossary)
½ cup (4 fl oz/125 ml) marc de Provence (see glossary) or Cognac
broth or water, plus any leftover roasting juices
1 lb (500 g) macaroni

◙ To prepare the lardoons, in a mortar pound together the salt, garlic and herbs to form a paste. Mix in the parsley, add the lardoons and mix until each lardoon is well coated with the mixture. Using a small, sharp-pointed knife, pierce each piece of meat 2–3 times, with the grain, and force a lardoon into each slit. Save any leftover lardoons and seasoning.
◙ Put the meat pieces into a bowl, add the olive oil and red wine and marinate at room temperature for 4 hours, turning the meat around in the marinade several times.
◙ In a saucepan place the pig's trotter, pork rind and salt pork and add water to cover. Bring to a boil, drain and rinse well. Cut the pork rind into 1-in (2.5-cm) squares.
◙ In a large bowl mix together the pork rind, salt pork pieces, carrots, onions, garlic, cèpes, tomatoes and olives. Put a layer of the pork rind mixture in the bottom of an earthenware vessel, preferably a *daubière,* or a heavy pot. Place the pig's trotter halves on top and finish the layer with pieces of the larded meat. Sprinkle to taste with salt. Continue layering the pork rind mixture and the meat pieces, embedding the bouquet garni in the middle and finishing with the rind mixture. Pour over any red wine marinade remaining in the bowl, the brandy and almost enough broth to immerse the contents.
◙ Cover and place over medium-low heat, protected by a flame-tamer. Bring to a boil (this will take about 1 hour) and adjust the heat to very low to maintain only a murmur at the liquid's surface for about 6 hours. Skim off, as well as possible, all the fat. (If, toward the end of skimming, you spoon up juices with the fat, empty the skimming spoon into a bowl and refrigerate the bowl; when the fat solidifies, it can be lifted off and discarded and the jellied juices returned to the leftover daube.)
◙ Preheat an oven to 400°F (200°C).
◙ Bring a large pot filled with salted water to a boil. Add the macaroni and cook according to the package instructions,
10–15 minutes for most types of macaroni. Drain well and empty the macaroni into a gratin dish. Spoon over some of the daube's cooking juices and put into the oven for a few minutes until the juices are bubbling.
◙ Serve the daube directly from its cooking vessel, accompanied with the macaroni.

SERVES 8

Poulet Sauté à la Barthelasse
Barthelasse Sautéed Chicken

La Barthelasse is an island in the Rhône River, between Avignon and Villeneuve-lès-Avignon. In the last century, it was a favorite rendezvous for Sunday lunch, when residents of both towns flocked to the restaurants there to eat poulet à la Barthelasse.

1 frying chicken, about 2½ lb (1.2 kg), cut into serving pieces
salt and freshly ground pepper
¼ cup (2 fl oz/60 ml) olive oil
¼ cup (2 fl oz/60 ml) dry white wine
persillade made with 2 cloves garlic (see glossary)

◙ Season the chicken pieces with salt and pepper to taste. Warm the olive oil in a sauté pan over medium-high heat. Put all the pieces in the pan except the breasts. Sauté, turning the pieces, for 15 minutes. Add the breasts and sauté until all the pieces are nicely colored on both sides, about 10 minutes longer. Add the wine, moving the chicken pieces around and scraping the pan bottom with a wooden spoon until the browned bits dissolve.
◙ Add the *persillade,* turn the pieces around and, when the characteristic odor of cooking parsley and garlic fills the air, serve directly from the pan.

SERVES 4   *Photograph page 4*

Aillade de Veau
Veal and Garlic Stew

Stews with abundant garlic garnish are favorite Provençal fare. The garlic cloves remain intact but collapse into a sweet purée in the mouth.

1½ lb (750 g) stewing veal, cut into 1½-in (4-cm) pieces
salt and freshly ground pepper
3 tablespoons olive oil
2 tablespoons dried bread crumbs
½ cup (4 fl oz/125 ml) white wine
1 lb (500 g) tomatoes, peeled, seeded and chopped
16 cloves garlic
double recipe pasta dough made without saffron, cut into
    noodles (see Provençal fish soup on page 42)

◙ Season the pieces of veal with salt and pepper to taste. Warm the olive oil in a sauté pan over medium heat. Add the veal and brown until colored on all sides, about 30 minutes. Remove the meat to a plate.
◙ Add the crumbs to the pan and stir well. Pour in the wine and deglaze the pan, stirring and scraping the pan bottom with a wooden spoon until all the browned bits dissolve. Add the tomatoes, garlic and a pinch of salt and cook for 10 minutes. Put the meat and its juices into the sauce, reduce the heat to very low, cover and simmer until the meat is tender, about 45 minutes.
◙ Fill a large saucepan with salted water, bring to a boil and add the noodles. Parboil for about 2 minutes and drain. Stir the noodles into the sauce, simmer for a few minutes longer and serve.

SERVES 4

Overlooking the village of Gordes, from left to right:
Provençal Daube, Veal and Garlic Stew

Clockwise from top: Camargue Veal Rib Tips, Shoulder of Lamb on a Bed of Potatoes, Camargue Lamb Stew

ÉPAULE D'AGNEAU À LA BOULANGÈRE

Shoulder of Lamb on a Bed of Potatoes

Epaule (or gigot) à la boulangère is so named because, traditionally, it was prepared in a baker's oven after the last batch of morning's bread was removed.

1 tablespoon unsalted butter
2 lb (1 kg) potatoes, peeled and thinly sliced but unrinsed
2 large onions, thinly sliced
about 1 cup (8 fl oz/250 ml) broth or salted water
1 lamb shoulder, including shank, about 3 lb (1.5 kg)
pinch of Provençal mixed dried herbs (see glossary)
salt and freshly ground pepper
1 tablespoon olive oil

◼ Preheat an oven to 375°F (190°C).
◼ Butter a large baking dish. In a saucepan combine the potatoes and onions. Pour in the broth to immerse them barely. Bring to a boil, stirring with a wooden spoon to prevent them from sticking. Pour them into the baking dish. Smooth the surface and bake for 20 minutes.
◼ Trim any superficial fat from the shoulder. Sprinkle it with the herbs, salt and pepper and rub the surfaces with the olive oil.

Place the shoulder on the bed of onions and potatoes. Bake for 30 minutes, basting 2 or 3 times with the baking juices. Turn the oven off and leave the baking dish in the oven for 20 minutes before removing.

◎ Carve the lamb in the kitchen and arrange the slices atop the potatoes and onions. Pour over any carving juices.

SERVES 4

CÔTELETTES D'AGNEAU AU GRIL
Grilled Lamb Loin Chops

Grilled lamb is best pink all the way through, neither rare nor well done. Thick pieces of meat give the best results. The bed of coals should have good depth and a veil of white ash masking its intensity.

4 lamb loin chops, each about 3 in (7.5 cm) thick, at
    room temperature
2 cloves garlic
pinch of Provençal mixed dried herbs (see glossary)
freshly ground pepper
1 tablespoon olive oil
salt

◙ Prepare a fire in a charcoal grill.
◙ With a sharp knife, remove all the visible fat, including the sheath of back fat, from the chops. Take care not to separate the apron from the loin. Rub the sawn bone surfaces repeatedly with the garlic cloves, smearing the resulting purée over the meat's surface. Sprinkle lightly with the herbs and grind some pepper over all the surfaces. Wrap the apron around the chop and fix it in place with a sharpened rosemary branch or a 4-in (10-cm) length of bamboo skewer. Rub the chops all over with the olive oil. The chops have five sides: the two cut sides, the fillet, the filet mignon and the bone surface, around which the apron is wrapped.
◙ Salt the chops and place them on the grill rack. Grill them for 3–4 minutes on each side, the two cut surfaces first. When all the sides are colored, leave the chops, bone surface down, facing the dying coals, for 8–10 minutes.

SERVES 4

TENDRONS DE VEAU À LA GARDIANE
Camargue Veal Rib Tips

Like boeuf à la gardiane, *this is a Camargue cowboys' stew. A saffron-flavored pilaf is a good accompaniment.*

3 tablespoons olive oil
2 lb (1 kg) veal rib tips
salt
½ lb (250 g) pickling onions
3 cloves garlic, crushed
¼ lb (125 g) fresh cultivated mushrooms, finely sliced
pinch of Provençal mixed dried herbs (see glossary)
1 tablespoon all-purpose (plain) flour
1 cup (8 fl oz/250 ml) dry white wine
1 lb (500 g) tomatoes, peeled, seeded and coarsely chopped
⅔ cup (3 oz/100 g) black olives
⅔ cup (3 oz/100 g) green olives, blanched for a few seconds
    in boiling water and drained

◎ Warm the olive oil in a large sauté pan over medium heat. Salt the rib tips, add to the pan and brown until well colored on all sides, about 15 minutes. Remove to a plate. Add the onions, garlic and mushrooms, sprinkle with the herbs and salt to taste and turn up the heat. Shake the pan and stir the contents with a wooden spoon until the mushrooms' liquid evaporates. Sprinkle the flour over the top, reduce the heat and cook, stirring, for 1–2 minutes.
◎ Pour in the white wine and deglaze the pan, stirring and scraping the pan bottom with a wooden spoon. Add the tomatoes, bring to a boil and slip the meat and its juices into the sauce. Reduce the heat to low, cover and simmer for 1¼ hours. Add the olives and simmer until the meat is tender, 15 minutes longer.

SERVES 6

GARDIANE D'AGNEAU
Camargue Lamb Stew

This is Provence's answer to Irish stew, simple and satisfying.

2 tablespoons olive oil
1 lb (500 g) neck chops, superficial fat removed
4 cloves garlic, crushed
1 lb (500 g) russet potatoes, peeled and thinly sliced
1 bay leaf
salt
boiling water as needed

◎ Warm the olive oil in a sauté pan over medium heat. Add the chops and cook, turning once, until colored on both sides, about 10 minutes.
◎ Add the garlic, potatoes, bay leaf and salt to taste and pour in boiling water to cover barely. Reduce the heat to very low, cover and simmer until the potatoes begin to fall apart to thicken the sauce, about 1 hour.

SERVES 4

Grilled Lamb Loin Chops served with potatoes au gratin

PROVENCE

GIGOT RÔTI À LA PROVENÇALE
Roast Leg of Lamb

A leg of lamb should always be carved at table. The ritual ceremony adds an important dimension to the pleasure taken in the meal. To carve, hold the leg end with the other end resting on the platter. Carve away from yourself, at a sharp bias, nearly parallel to the bone, lifting off thin slices, first from the rounded, fleshy part of the leg, then from the leaner muscle to the other side and, finally, slice off small pieces of meat from the leg end. Each has a different flavor and degree of doneness. Serve a slice of each to each guest.

pinch of coarse salt
freshly ground pepper
pinch of Provençal mixed dried herbs (see glossary)
41 firm cloves garlic
pinch of fine salt
1 tablespoon dry white wine
1 leg of lamb, about 6 lb (3 kg), leg bone unsawn and pelvic
    bone boned out, at room temperature
1 tablespoon olive oil
mirepoix (see glossary)
3 cups (24 fl oz/750 ml) dry red wine

◙ In a mortar pound together the coarse salt, pepper to taste, herbs and 1 garlic clove to form a paste. Stir in the white wine.
◙ Trim off any superficial fat from the lamb leg. With a small, sharp-pointed knife, cut several deep slits in the leg, on the bias and with the grain. Open up each slit with your finger and, with a teaspoon, insert some of the herb mixture. Smear any remaining mixture over the meat's surface. Rub the leg all over with the olive oil, cover with plastic wrap and leave to marinate at room temperature for 1 hour or so.
◙ Meanwhile, prepare the *mirepoix* and combine in a small saucepan with the wine. Bring to a boil and simmer, uncovered, until reduced by two thirds, or to about 1 cup (8 fl oz/250 ml). Pass the reduced wine through a sieve, pressing the vegetables with a wooden pestle to extract all the liquid.

Roast Leg of Lamb

◙ Preheat an oven to 400°F (200°C). Put the leg in a shallow, oval ovenproof dish. Place in the oven and roast for 10 minutes. Reduce the oven heat to 350°F (180°C); 20 minutes later reduce the heat to 325°F (160°C). When the leg has been in the oven for 45 minutes, turn the oven off and leave the leg to rest, in the oven, for 20 minutes (if your oven is very hermetic, open the oven door for a couple of minutes to cool it down).
◙ While the leg is resting, in a small saucepan combine the garlic cloves with water to cover and the fine salt. Bring to a boil and simmer for 15 minutes. Drain, reserving the cooking water. Combine the cooked garlic cloves and the red wine reduction in a small saucepan and gently reheat.
◙ Transfer the leg of lamb to a heated serving platter. Place the roasting pan on the stove top over high heat and deglaze it with some (or all, depending on what remains) of the garlic cooking liquid, scraping the pan bottom with a wooden spoon until all the browned bits dissolve. Add it to the wine reduction and bring to boil.
◙ Pour the boiling wine reduction into a warmed bowl. At table after carving, add the juices from the carved leg to the bowl. Ladle the juices and garlic cloves over the slices of lamb on each serving plate.

SERVES 8

PROVENCE

GRILLADE DE BOEUF À LA PROVENÇALE
Provençal Grilled Beef

Panfried steak is shunned in Provence. Steaks are grilled over hot coals and many feel that grilled beef can achieve its perfect expression only if it is finished with anchovy. Fruit woods, grapevine stock and broom are the woods preferred for preparing the embers; olive wood makes a wonderful, long-lasting bed of coals. The butcher's cut (l'onglet; le morceau du boucher), also known as hanging tender or bloody skirt, is especially favored. It is composed of a single muscle joining the flanks inside the body. When pared of all external fat and nervous tissue, it falls into two elongated oval strips, 2½–3 inches (6–7.5 cm) thick, the juiciest and most flavorful of all grilling cuts.

freshly ground pepper
1 butcher's cut, 1½ lb (750 g), trimmed (see recipe introduction)
2 teaspoons olive oil

FOR THE SAUCE:

small pinch of coarse salt
2 cloves garlic
2 salt anchovies, rinsed and filleted (see glossary)
3 tablespoons olive oil
1 tablespoon chopped fresh flat-leaf (Italian) parsley

◙ Grind the pepper over the steak, rub it with olive oil and marinate at room temperature for 2 hours. To prepare the sauce, in a mortar pound together the salt and garlic to form a paste. Add the anchovies and pound again to a paste. Stir in the olive oil with the pestle, and then stir in the parsley with a spoon. Set aside.
◙ Prepare a fire in a charcoal grill. When the flames have died and the coals are glowing, place the steak on the grill rack and grill the steak, turning 3 or 4 times, 8–10 minutes.
◙ Transfer the steak to a carving board and slice it thinly, on the bias, without displacing the slices of meat. Slip the sliced steak, in its original form, onto a warmed platter. Pour over any juices that have escaped in carving. Spoon on the sauce the length of the steak.

SERVES 4

Along the backroads of the Vaucluse, Provençal Grilled Beef

Top to bottom: Sausages in Rice, Roast Pork with Olives and Anchovy, Grilled Pork Chops with Piquant Sauce

BOUCHES·DU·RHÔNE

SAUCISSES À LA MÉNAGÈRE

Sausages in Rice

8 fresh pork link sausages
1 leek, including the tender green parts, finely chopped
1½ cups (8 oz/250 g) long-grain white rice

salt and cayenne pepper
large pinch of saffron threads
3 cups (24 fl oz/750 ml) water, boiling

◙ Separate the sausages and prick each several times with a trussing needle or sharp skewer. Pour only enough water into the bottom of a sauté pan to form a film. Add the sausages and cook over low heat, shaking the pan and turning the sausages,

128

until the water evaporates and the sausages are lightly browned on all sides in their own fat, about 10 minutes. Remove the sausages to a plate.

▒ Add the leeks to the pan with the sausage drippings and cook, stirring, over low heat until softened, about 10 minutes. Add the rice, salt and cayenne pepper to taste and the saffron. Stir with a wooden spoon over low heat until the rice turns milky and opaque in appearance, about 5 minutes. Add the boiling water, stir once, cover tightly and simmer over very low heat for 10 minutes. Remove the lid, lay the sausages on top of the rice, re-cover and cook until the rice is tender, about 12 minutes longer.

SERVES 4

V A R

RÔTI DE PORC À LA TOULONNAISE
Roast Pork with Olives and Anchovy

In Provence sage is nearly always associated with pork. The sage must be fresh, as dried sage has a musty flavor.

1 section of pork loin, about 3 lb (1.5 kg), boned without separating the loin and the tenderloin
salt and freshly ground pepper
persillade made with 1 clove garlic (see glossary)
8 salt anchovies, rinsed and filleted (see glossary)
⅔ cup (3 oz/100 g) black olives, pitted and chopped
several fresh sage sprigs
½ cup (4 fl oz/125 ml) dry white wine

▒ Preheat an oven to 450°F (230°C). Lay out the boned loin, back side down. Sprinkle with salt and pepper to taste and then with the *persillade*. Distribute the anchovy fillets and chopped olives along the sides of the tenderloin. Roll up the loin, tie it and, on the fat surface, pierce the flesh at regular intervals with the tip of a sharp knife. Insert tiny sprigs or single, larger leaves of fresh sage into the slits. Sprinkle the roast with salt and place in a roasting pan.

▒ Place in the oven and roast for 10 minutes. Reduce the oven temperature to 325°F (160°C). Begin basting regularly with the drippings after 30 minutes. After 45 minutes, spoon most of the fat out of the roasting pan, add a few spoonfuls of the wine and continue basting, every 3–4 minutes, adding more wine to the pan if it begins to dry up. After about 1¼ hours, the roast will be nicely glazed.

▒ Remove the pork to a carving board, snip the strings and carve into slices ⅓ in (8 mm) thick. Lay the slices, overlapping, on a heated serving platter. Pour over the carving juices and the basting juices from the roasting pan.

SERVES 6

V A R

BÉQUETS AU FOUR
Baked Lamb Shanks

The unpeeled garlic cloves are squeezed and spread on bread at table. After long cooking, they are transformed into a sweet purée.

4 lamb shanks, about 1 lb (500 g) each
salt
pinch of Provençal mixed dried herbs (see glossary)
1 tablespoon olive oil
16 garlic cloves, unpeeled

2 carrots, peeled and cut into 1-in (2.5-cm) pieces
2 onions, coarsely chopped
½ cup (4 fl oz/125 ml) dry white wine

▒ Preheat an oven to 400°F (200°C).
▒ Sprinkle the shanks with salt and herbs and rub them with olive oil. Place in a roasting pan and roast for 30 minutes.
▒ Remove the shanks from the oven and reduce the oven temperature to 300°F (150°C). Transfer the shanks to a lidded oven casserole and add the garlic, carrots and onions. Sprinkle with a little salt. Pour off the fat in the roasting pan and place the pan over high heat. Pour in the wine and deglaze the pan, scraping the pan bottom with a wooden spoon until all the browned bits dissolve. Pour the deglazing juices over the contents of the casserole and cover.
▒ Place in the oven and bake until the shanks are tender, about 1½ hours.

SERVES 4   *Photograph pages 130–131*

P R O V E N C E

CÔTES DE PORC, SAUCE HACHÉE
Grilled Pork Chops with Piquant Sauce

Sauce hachée—"chopped sauce"—is such a wonderfully descriptive name that it is a pity to lose it. Today, it is called sauce piquante, but only the name has changed.

FOR THE SAUCE:

1 tablespoon olive oil
1 onion, finely chopped
salt and cayenne pepper
1 tablespoon all-purpose (plain) flour
1 cup (8 fl oz/250 ml) broth or water
persillade made with 1 clove garlic (see glossary)
2 or 3 shallots, finely chopped
2 or 3 fresh cultivated mushrooms, finely chopped
6 tablespoons (3 fl oz/90 ml) red wine vinegar
1 tablespoon capers, rinsed and chopped
2 salt anchovies, rinsed, filleted and mashed (see glossary)
4 sour gherkins, finely chopped

4 pork chops, each about 1 in (2.5 cm) thick
2 teaspoons olive oil
24 fresh sage leaves
salt and freshly ground pepper

▒ Prepare a fire in a charcoal grill. To prepare the sauce, warm the olive oil in a saucepan over low heat. Add the onion and sauté over low heat until softened and lightly colored, about 10 minutes. Add salt and cayenne pepper to taste and the flour and stir well. Raise the heat to medium-high. Slowly pour in the broth or water, whisking constantly. Continue to whisk until the mixture comes to a boil. Reduce the heat to a gentle simmer.

▒ In a small saucepan over high heat, combine the *persillade*, shallots, mushrooms and vinegar. Bring to a boil and simmer gently until nearly dry, just a few minutes. Then pour the mushroom mixture into the broth mixture. Add the capers, anchovies and gherkins, stir well and hold over very low heat.

▒ Rub the pork chops with the olive oil. Press 3 sage leaves onto each side of each chop. Season to taste with salt and grind over some pepper. Place on the grill rack over dying embers. Grill until cooked, about 5 minutes on each side.

▒ Reheat the sauce, if necessary, and serve with the pork chops.

SERVES 4

GRILLADE DES MARINIERS
Braised Beef Slices with Anchovy

This was once a specialty of the riverside bistros frequented by the Rhône river sailors, who called it la grillade, *not because the meat was grilled but because it was cut into slices like a* grillade.

3 lb (1.5 kg) boneless beef shank (leg), cut into slices ⅓ inch
   (8 mm) thick
2 bay leaves
large pinch Provençal mixed dried herbs (see glossary)
6 tablespoons (3 fl oz/90 ml) olive oil
4 cloves garlic, finely chopped
1 lb (500 g) sweet white onions, coarsely chopped
½ cup (4 fl oz/125 ml) dry white wine
¼ cup (2 fl oz/60 ml) Provençal herb vinegar (see glossary)
¼ cup (2 fl oz/60 ml) marc de Provence (see glossary) or Cognac
salt and freshly ground pepper
3 tablespoons capers, rinsed, squeezed dry and chopped
6 sour gherkins, chopped
3 salt anchovies, rinsed, filleted and mashed (see glossary)

◉ In a large bowl sprinkle the beef slices with the herb mixture and then turn them around with the 3 tablespoons of the olive oil and the bay leaves. Leave to marinate at room temperature for 3–4 hours.
◉ In a bowl mix together the garlic and onions. In another bowl stir together the wine, vinegar and brandy. Put a layer of the onion-garlic mixture in the bottom of a flameproof earthenware *daubière* or a heavy pot. Top with a layer of meat slices and then more of the onion-garlic mixture. Sprinkle 2–3 tablespoons of the wine mixture over the top and season to taste with salt and pepper. Continue layering, tucking the bay leaves in a middle layer and finishing with a layer of the onion-garlic mixture. Add any remaining wine mixture and marinade. Cover tightly and cook over very low heat for 2 hours.
◉ Add the capers and gherkins, swirl the pot and cook for 2 hours longer. Add the mashed anchovies, swirl the pot and leave to simmer for a few minutes. Sprinkle over the remaining 3 tablespoons olive oil and serve directly from the pot.

SERVES 8

ÉPAULE D'AGNEAU À LA VENAISSINE
Braised Stuffed Lamb Shoulder

A boned lamb shoulder, when laid out flat on a work surface, has four irregular corners, recalling the map of France. After pressing the stuffing in place, bring opposite corners to meet, tacking them with a trussing needle and kitchen string. Tie a length of string around the circumference and then, with a good yard (meter) of string, at least four times vertically around to form a melon shape.

1 whole lamb shoulder including shank about, 3 lb (1.5 kg),
   boned and trimmed of fat
pinch of Provençal mixed dried herbs (see glossary)
2 tablespoons olive oil
1 cup (8 fl oz/250 ml) dry white wine
1 cup (2 oz/60 g) fresh bread crumbs
persillade made with 1 clove garlic (see glossary)
2 oz (60 g) lean salt pork (green bacon), chopped
1 egg
salt and freshly ground pepper
mirepoix (see glossary)

◉ Sprinkle the boned shoulder lightly on both sides with the herbs. Place it flat in a dish. Pour over ½ cup (4 fl oz/125 ml) of the wine and about 2 teaspoons of the olive oil. Marinate for 2–3 hours at room temperature, turning the shoulder over a couple of times.
◉ Preheat an oven to 400°F (200°C). In a bowl, combine the bread crumbs, *persillade*, salt pork, egg and 1 tablespoon of the olive oil. Season lightly with salt, grind over some pepper and mix thoroughly.
◉ Drain the shoulder, reserving the marinade, and pat it dry with paper towels. Spread the crumb mixture on the shoulder and press it on firmly; tie it up as directed in the recipe introduction. Rub with the remaining 1 teaspoon olive oil.

Left to right: Braised Stuffed Lamb Shoulder, Braised Beef Slices with Anchovy, Baked Lamb Shanks (recipe page 129)

Sprinkle the tied lamb with salt and place in a small, ovenproof frying pan or a round baking dish.

❈ Place in the oven and roast for 40 minutes. Meanwhile, prepare the *mirepoix* in the bottom of a heavy saucepan of a size just to contain the shoulder. Place the shoulder on top. Pour off the fat from the roasting pan and place the pan on the stove top over high heat. Pour in the marinade and the remaining ½ cup (4 fl oz/125 ml) wine and deglaze the pan, scraping the pan bottom with a wooden spoon until all the browned bits dissolve. Pour the deglazed pan juices over the lamb shoulder. Cut a sheet of parchment (kitchen) paper to the dimensions of the saucepan, smear one side lightly with olive oil, and place, oiled side down, over the meat. Cover with a lid and simmer,

over very low heat until tender when pierced with a trussing needle, about 1 hour.

❈ Preheat an oven again to 400°F (200°C). Carefully clip and remove the strings from the shoulder and return it to its roasting pan. Strain the braising juices through a sieve, pressing the vegetables with a wooden pestle to extract all the liquid. Remove any fat from the surface, if necessary, and pour the juices over the shoulder. Place in the oven and baste every couple of minutes until the surface is glazed, 10–15 minutes.

❈ With a wide spatula, transfer the shoulder to a heated platter. Pour the juices into a warmed bowl and pass at the table. Cut the shoulder into wedges to serve.

SERVES 4–6

From left to right: Boiled Beef Gratin, Stuffed Pork Chops

HACHIS AU GRATIN

Boiled Beef Gratin

Leftover beef from pot-au-feu *(recipe on page 45) should be cooled out of its broth, enclosed in plastic wrap and refrigerated. When cold, a gelatinous cut, like leg of beef, is very firm and can be thinly*

sliced easily or cleanly chopped. Try also boeuf à l'arlésienne, *thin slices of broiled beef overlapping in a gratin dish, sprinkled with a* persillade, *covered with a layer of hot ratatouille (recipe on page 56) and put into a 400°F (200°C) oven for 10 minutes.*

3 tablespoons olive oil
1 onion, finely chopped
1 lb (500 g) *pot-au-feu* beef (recipe on page 45), chilled, thinly
   sliced, cut into narrow strips and chopped

persillade made with 2 cloves garlic (see glossary)
salt
1 cup (8 fl oz/250 ml) tomato sauce (see glossary)
freshly ground pepper
whole nutmeg
2 lb (1 kg) russet potatoes, peeled and quartered
¼ cup (2 oz/60 g) unsalted butter, chilled and diced
handful of dried bread crumbs
2 tablespoons freshly grated Parmesan cheese

◙ Warm 2 tablespoons of the olive oil in a heavy saucepan over low heat. Add the onion and cook gently until soft but not colored, about 5 minutes. Add the chopped meat, raise the heat and stir with a wooden spoon for a couple of minutes. Add the *persillade* and the tomato sauce, stir, bring to a boil, reduce the heat to low and simmer gently for 10 minutes. Grind over pepper and scrape over a bit of nutmeg.

◙ Meanwhile, place the potatoes in a saucepan with lightly salted water just to cover. Bring to a boil, cover and boil until just tender, about 30 minutes. Drain them into a sieve placed over a bowl, saving their water. With a wooden pestle, push them, without turning the pestle, through the sieve back into their saucepan. Add the butter and some of their cooking water, grind over some pepper and stir but do not beat with a wooden spoon. Continue to add cooking water and to stir until the mixture is quite fluid—almost pourable. This may use up all of the cooking liquid.

◙ Preheat an oven to 350°F (180°C). Spread the meat–tomato sauce mixture in the bottom of a 6-cup (48-fl oz/1.5-l) gratin dish or other baking dish. Spread the potato purée evenly on top. Drag the tines of a fork back and forth across the surface to create a textured design. In a small bowl stir together the bread crumbs and cheese and sprinkle evenly over the potato layer. Dribble the remaining 1 tablespoon olive oil in a fine thread over the top, forming a crisscross pattern.

◙ Place in the oven and bake until golden, about 20 minutes.

SERVES 4

PROVENCE

CÔTES DE PORC FARCIES À LA PROVENÇALE
Stuffed Pork Chops

Wild mushrooms can be substituted for cultivated; prepared with cèpes, these chops are sumptuous.

FOR THE STUFFING:

1 tablespoon olive oil
1 onion, finely chopped
2 oz (60 g) fresh cultivated mushrooms, finely chopped
small pinch of Provençal mixed dried herbs (see glossary)
persillade made with 1 clove garlic (see glossary)
a few drops of lemon juice
salt, freshly ground pepper, and freshly scraped nutmeg
handful of fresh bread crumbs
1 egg

4 double-rib pork chops, trimmed of fat except for thin layer of back fat
salt and freshly ground pepper
2 tablespoons olive oil
2–3 tablespoons dry white wine

◙ To prepare the stuffing, warm the olive oil in a frying pan over low heat. Add the onion and cook gently until softened but not colored, about 10 minutes. Add the mushrooms, raise the heat and sauté until nearly all the liquid released from the mushrooms evaporates, about 5 minutes. Add the herbs, *persillade,* lemon juice and salt, pepper and nutmeg to taste.

Empty into a bowl and let cool for a few minutes. Add the bread crumbs and egg and, using your hands, mix thoroughly.

◙ Using a small, sharp-pointed knife, pierce the back of each chop deeply, ¾ in (2 cm) from the spine end to ¾ in (2 cm) from the tip, to form a pouch. Divide the stuffing equally among the pouches and stuff them. Close each opening with a pair of crossed toothpicks. Season the chops to taste with salt and pepper.

◙ Warm the olive oil in a heavy sauté pan over medium heat. Add the chops and brown, turning once, over moderate heat, 7–8 minutes on each side. Cover and cook over very low heat until the chops are tender, about 45 minutes. Turn the chops in their juices several times; if the juices appear to be drying up, add some of the wine once, or as often as necessary.

◙ Serve the chops with cooking juices spooned over the top.

SERVES 4

PROVENCE

SAUPIQUET DE LAPIN
Rabbit in Spicy Sauce

In the villages and countryside of Provence, literally half the population has rabbit hutches. Gibelotte and saupiquet *are favorite and often-prepared dishes. Cookbooks not destined to be read by native Provençaux often substitute chicken—rabbit is better.*

1 rabbit, about 3½ lb (1.7 kg), with liver
pinch of Provençal mixed dried herbs (see glossary)
2 bay leaves
3 cloves garlic, unpeeled, plus 1 clove, peeled
freshly ground pepper
½ cup (4 fl oz/125 ml) olive oil
salt
½ cup (4 fl oz/125 ml) dry white wine
pinch of coarse salt
1 clove garlic
4 salt anchovies, rinsed and filleted (see glossary)
2 tablespoons capers, rinsed and squeezed dry
1 tablespoon finely chopped fresh flat-leaf (Italian) parsley
⅔ cup (3 oz/100 g) black olives, pitted and coarsely chopped

◙ Cut the rabbit into 8 pieces: 2 forelegs; 2 hind legs; the saddle cut in two, kidneys left attached; and rib cage split in two.

◙ Place the rabbit pieces in a bowl and sprinkle with the Provençal herbs. Add the bay, unpeeled garlic, pepper to taste and 3 tablespoons of the olive oil. Toss together, cover and marinate in the refrigerator for several hours or overnight.

◙ Preheat an oven to 350°F (180°C). Spread the rabbit pieces and their marinade in a shallow oven dish. Place in the oven and roast until the rabbit is tender, 45 minutes, turning the pieces at regular intervals. After 20 minutes, baste from time to time with 2 or 3 tablespoons of the wine, never letting the dish become dry.

◙ Meanwhile, in a small frying pan over high heat, sauté the liver in a few drops of olive oil until slightly firmed up but still rare. Remove from the heat and set aside.

◙ In a mortar pound together the coarse salt, pepper to taste and the peeled garlic to form a paste. Add the anchovies and the capers and continue to pound to a paste. Add the liver, pound to a paste, and stir in the remaining olive oil (about 5 tablespoons/3 fl oz/80 ml) slowly with the pestle. Finally, stir in the parsley and olives. Transfer the mixture to a small, flameproof earthenware casserole and warm over very low heat; it should not cook.

◙ Transfer the rabbit pieces to a warmed platter. Discard the bay leaves and garlic and stir the roasting juices into the warmed anchovy-caper sauce. Spoon the sauce over the rabbit to serve.

SERVES 4   *Photograph on pages 116–117*

GRAS-DOUBLE À LA MARSEILLAISE

Tripe à la Marseillaise

Whether pieds et paquets or beef tripe is prepared this way, it is one of the great dishes of Provence. Beef tripe is sold partially precooked. In some countries, it is sold "bleached," which makes it tasteless and useless. Buy it unbleached in ethnic neighborhoods and, if possible, include a mixture of all four stomachs: blanket, honeycomb, bible and reed. Bible tripe, so-named because of its bible page–thin, ripply extensions, is the loveliest of all. Boiled potatoes are excellent with this dish.

1 pig's foot (trotter), split in half lengthwise
2 leeks, white and tender green parts, thinly sliced
2 onions, coarsely chopped
10 oz (300 g) carrots, peeled and thinly sliced
1½ lb (750 g) tomatoes, peeled, seeded and coarsely
   chopped
3 cloves garlic
large pinch of Provençal mixed dried herbs (see glossary)

2½ lb (1.25 kg) tripe, cut into strips ¾ in (2 cm) by 4 in (10 cm)
salt
bouquet garni, including a strip of dried orange peel
   (see glossary)
⅓ cup (3 fl oz/80 ml) marc de Provence (see glossary)
   or Cognac
about 2 cups (16 fl oz/500 ml) dry white wine

◙ Place the split pig's foot in a saucepan and add water to cover. Bring to a boil, drain and rinse in cold running water. Drain again and set aside.
◙ Mix together all the vegetables, garlic and the dried herbs and put a handful of the mixture in the bottom of a large earthenware pot or other large pot. Place the trotter halves and a handful of the tripe on top. Sprinkle with salt. Repeat the layers, sprinkling each one with salt and burying the bouquet garni in the middle. Finish with a layer of vegetables. Add the brandy and enough white wine just short of immersing the contents.
◙ Place a flame-tamer between the pot and the heat source, cover and bring slowly to a boil, counting about 1 hour. Simmer over very low heat for at least 7 or 8 hours.
◙ Slowly rewarmed and simmered for an hour the following day, the tripe is even better.

SERVES 4

Tripe à la Marseillaise

The entry to Château d'Ansouis, Jellied Daube

DAUBE EN GELÉE

Jellied Daube

A daube's intoxicating, dense harmony of flavors is even more clearly defined when served in its jelly than when hot. At lunch on a hot summer's day, a green salad is the perfect accompaniment. A daube is often prepared specially to be served cold. This recipe assumes about half of the daube is left over.

leftover daube in its cooking pot (recipe on page 122)
fresh flat-leaf (Italian) parsley bouquets, black olives and
    tomato sections

⊞ While the daube is still warm, drain off all the cooking liquid. Put a spoonful onto a small metal dish and chill it in the coldest part of the refrigerator (but not the freezer). If the spoonful does not set to a firm jelly, pour the cooking juices into a saucepan and reduce over high heat to the correct consistency when a spoonful is tested.

⊞ Discard the bouquet garni, pressing it between 2 spoons to recuperate the juices. Bone the trotter and cut the flesh into small pieces. In a mixing bowl (preferably metal, which facilitates unmolding) of a size to contain the solids and the cooking liquid without excessive leftover space, distribute the pieces of beef, trotter, rind and salt pork evenly. Pour over the cooking liquid, leave to cool, cover and refrigerate until the following day.

⊞ To unmold, first loosen the rim of jelly from the bowl by running the tip of a small knife around the edge. Then immerse the bowl very rapidly, almost to the level of its contents, in hot water. Place it on a towel, place an overturned round platter on top and turn the platter and the mold over together. Surround the unmolded daube with parsley bouquets, tomato sections and black olives. Present it at table before slicing, then slice and serve the slices with the aid of a spatula.

SERVES 4

FARCI BRAISÉ
Braised Stuffed Breast of Veal

Here, the stuffed veal breast is slowly braised in the oven and then served with the pan juices.

3 lb (1.5 kg) veal breast, stuffed with stuffing of choice
  (recipes on page 152)
1 tablespoon olive oil
salt
mirepoix (see glossary)
1 bay leaf
½ cup (4 fl oz/125 ml) dry white wine
2 cups (16 fl oz/500 ml) broth, boiling

◉ Preheat an oven to 400°F (200°C).
◉ Smear the surface of the stuffed breast with the olive oil and sprinkle with salt to taste. Place it in a shallow roasting pan and roast for 30 minutes, basting with the pan juice after 15 minutes. Remove from the oven and turn the oven down to 325°F (160°C).
◉ Meanwhile, prepare the *mirepoix* and spread it in the bottom of an oval ovenproof casserole of a size to contain the breast. Add the bay leaf and place the meat atop the *mirepoix*. Drain off any fat in the roasting pan and place the pan over medium-high heat. Pour in the wine and deglaze the pan, scraping the pan bottom with a wooden spoon until all the browned bits dissolve. Pour the deglazing juices and the boiling broth over the meat. Cut a sheet of parchment (kitchen) paper to the dimensions of the casserole, smear one side lightly with olive oil and place the paper, oiled side down, on top of the meat. Cover the casserole and place in the oven 1½ hours. Remove the casserole from the oven and increase the heat to 400°F (200°C).
◉ Put the breast back into the roasting pan. Pass the braising juices through a sieve; press the solids firmly but do not purée them into the juices. Put the juices into a small saucepan and bring to a boil. Move the saucepan half off the heat, adjusting the heat to maintain a very light boil on one half of the surface, until a skin forms on the still side, collecting the fat. Ladle some of the fatless juice from the boiling side of the pan over the stuffed breast and place it in the oven. Keep a small bowl and a tablespoon beside the saucepan to skim off the fatty skin from time to time, pulling it to the edge of the pan with the side of the spoon. Baste the meat often, either with the juices in the roasting pan or with fat-free juices from the saucepan. When no more fat collects on the still side of the saucepan, remove the pan from the heat.
◉ When the surface of the veal breast presents a glistening, bronzed surface, after about 20 minutes, remove it to a heated platter and snip the strings. Pour the remainder of the sauce into a warmed bowl. Present the glazed breast at table, then slice.

SERVES 6

BOEUF À LA PROVENÇALE
Sautéed Boiled Beef

Similar rapid sautés can be made from other well-cooked meats (but not from rare roasts, which turn tough with this treatment). Potatoes, pasta and rice are good accompaniments.

3 tablespoons olive oil
1½ lb (750 g) tomatoes, peeled, seeded and coarsely chopped
salt
persillade made with 1 clove garlic (see glossary)
1 lb (500 g) *pot-au-feu* beef, chilled and cut into ¾-in (2-cm)
  cubes (recipe on page 45)
⅔ cup (3 oz/100 g) black olives
several fresh basil sprigs with flower buds
freshly ground pepper

◉ Warm the olive oil in a sauté pan over high heat. Add the tomatoes, sprinkle with salt to taste, and add the *persillade*. Sauté to evaporate the tomatoes' juices as rapidly as possible.
◉ Add the beef cubes, reduce the heat to low, cover and simmer for 10 minutes. Add the olives, cover and simmer until heated through and flavors are blended, 3–4 minutes.
◉ Just before serving tear the basil leaves into fragments and crumble the flower buds. Add the leaves and buds to the pan. Grind over some pepper, stir the sauce and serve.

SERVES 4

ALOUETTES SANS TÊTE; PAUPIETTES DE BOEUF À LA PROVENÇALE
Provençal Beef Birds

Charles Durand's all-purpose stuffing (see poached stuffed breast of veal, page 152) can replace the stuffing used here. Red wine often replaces white wine in the sauce for this dish. Serve with boiled potatoes, mashed potatoes, pilaf or macaroni.

2 lb (1 kg) beef rump
FOR THE STUFFING:
½ lb (250 g) lean salt pork (green bacon), chopped
the chopped beef trimmings
persillade made with 3 garlic cloves (see glossary)
salt and freshly ground pepper

¼ cup (2 fl oz/60 ml) olive oil
1 onion, finely chopped
½ cup (4 fl oz/125 ml) dry white wine
2 tomatoes, peeled, seeded and chopped
salt
bouquet garni (see glossary)
1 cup (8 fl oz/250 ml) broth or water
⅔ cup (3 oz/100 g) black olives

◉ Cut the beef into 12 slices ⅓ in (8 mm) thick and about 3 in (7.5 cm) by 4 in (10 cm). Reserve the trimmings and chop them. Flatten the slices of meat slightly with the side of a heavy knife blade or a meat mallet.
◉ In a bowl mix together thoroughly all of the stuffing ingredients, including salt and pepper to taste. Separate the mixture into 12 equal portions. Cut twelve 1-foot (30-cm) lengths of kitchen string. Place a portion of the stuffing near a narrow end of a meat slice and roll up the slice. Loop the string around the middle of the rolled slice, then cross it and loop it lengthwise around the roll. Finish up with a double knot. Clip off the excess string and tuck the ends of the meat roll in to make a neat package. Repeat with the remaining stuffing and meat slices.
◉ In a heavy sauté pan of a size to contain the rolls without crowding, warm the olive oil over medium heat. Add the rolls and brown lightly on all sides, about 15 minutes. Add the onion and keep turning the meat regularly until the onion is lightly colored, about 5 minutes. Pour in the white wine and deglaze the pan, moving the meat around and scraping the pan bottom with a wooden spoon. Add the tomatoes, salt, bouquet garni and almost enough broth to cover the meat. Bring to a boil, reduce the heat to low, cover, and simmer, turning the meat regularly in its sauce about 1¼ hours. Add the olives and continue simmering until the rolls are tender, about 1¼ hours longer. When ready, the beef birds should be richly glazed and very little sauce should remain.
◉ Clip and remove the strings. Place on a warm platter and serve.

SERVES 6

Clockwise from top: Braised Stuffed Breast of Veal, Provençal Beef Birds, Beef and Potato Stew, Sautéed Boiled Beef

BOEUF À LA GARDIANE

Beef and Potato Stew

This is the traditional beef stew of the gardians, horsemen, or cowboys, who guard the bulls and horses of the Camargue.

2 tablespoons olive oil
2 lb (1 kg) stewing beef (leg or chuck), cut into 1¼ in (4 cm) cubes
salt
1 slice lean salt pork (green bacon), about ¼ lb (125 g), cut crosswise into finger-thick sections
1 large onion, chopped
3 cloves garlic, crushed
boiling water as needed
bouquet garni including a strip of dried orange peel (see glossary)
1 lb (500 g) russet potatoes, peeled and sliced ¼ in (6 mm) thick
⅔ cup (3 oz/100 g) black olives
freshly ground pepper

In a heavy sauté pan over medium heat, warm the olive oil. Add the beef pieces and brown on all sides, shuffling them around with a wooden spoon. This should take about 15 minutes. Season to taste with salt, add the salt pork and stir occasionally until lightly colored, about 6 minutes. Add the onion, lower the heat and stir regularly.

When the onion is lightly browned, after about 5 minutes, add the garlic, pour in 1 cup (8 fl oz/250 ml) boiling water and deglaze the pan, scraping the pan bottom with the wooden spoon until all the browned bits dissolve. Tuck the bouquet garni into the center, pack in the potatoes, sprinkle with salt and add more boiling water until the potatoes are nearly covered. Cover tightly and cook over the lowest possible heat until the meat is tender and the potatoes are falling apart, 2½–3 hours.

A few minutes before serving, stir in the olives and grind over the pepper.

SERVES 4

ALPES·MARITIMES

ESTOUFFADE À LA NIÇOISE

Niçois Braised Beef

The presence of tomato and black olives place this stew in the south of France. It is a recipe type that exists under different names all over France. If, for instance, the white wine is replaced by red, the tomato sauce is eliminated and the olives replaced by little onions, it becomes a boeuf bourguignon.

1 slice lean salt pork (green bacon) 5 oz (150 g) cut into
    lardoons (see glossary)
4 tablespoons (2 fl oz/60 ml) olive oil
1 lb (500 g) onions, coarsely chopped
2 lb (1 kg) stewing beef, cut into 3-oz (100-g) pieces
salt
2 tablespoons all-purpose (plain) flour
2 cups (16 fl oz/500 ml) dry white wine
½ cup (4 fl oz/125 ml) tomato sauce (see glossary)
bouquet garni (see glossary)
broth or water as needed
5 oz (150 g) fresh cultivated mushrooms, quartered
⅔ cup (3 oz/100 g) black olives
freshly ground pepper

▨ Place the lardoons in a saucepan, add water to cover and bring to a boil. Drain immediately, rinse in cold water and dry. Set aside.
▨ In a large sauté pan over medium-low heat, warm 2 tablespoons of the olive oil. Add the lardoons and color very lightly on all sides, about 7 minutes. Remove them to a dish and add the onions to the pan. Cook over medium-low heat until softened and beginning to color, about 10 minutes. Turn them into a sieve placed over a bowl to collect the oil. Add 1 tablespoon of the remaining oil and the oil from the onions to the sauté pan. Add the beef pieces and brown over medium heat on all sides, salting them as they are turned, about 15 minutes. Sprinkle the flour over the meat and continue to turn the meat pieces until the flour is lightly browned. Return the onions to the pan and stir well. Pour in the wine and deglaze the pan, scraping the pan bottom with a wooden spoon until all browned bits dissolve. Add the tomato sauce, the bouquet garni and enough broth just to immerse the meat. Bring to a boil, reduce the heat to low, cover and simmer, until the meat is tender, 2½–3 hours.
▨ While the meat is cooking, warm the remaining 1 tablespoon oil in another sauté pan over high heat. Add the mushrooms and salt to taste. Sauté until lightly colored and their liquid is reabsorbed. Set aside.
▨ Remove the meat pieces to a plate and pour the contents of the sauté pan into a sieve placed over a bowl. Return the meat to the sauté pan, add the reserved lardoons, mushrooms and olives. Grind over some pepper and cover the pan to keep its contents warm.
▨ Squeeze and discard the bouquet garni and press the sauce through the sieve, puréeing the onions. Put it into a saucepan of a size just to contain it, bring to a boil and hold, half off the heat, at a light boil to one side. Skim the still side with a spoon occasionally until no more fat rises. Pour the sauce into the pan holding the meat. Bring to a boil and simmer for 10 minutes before serving.

SERVES 4

An 18th century home on a hillside vineyard in the Var,
Niçois Braised Beef

PAIN DE VEAU À LA PROVENÇALE
Provençal Veal Loaf

Other chopped leftover meats or ground uncooked meats may be added if the necessary quantity of cooked veal is lacking. The sorrel leaves melt in cooking, leaving a delicate, veined pattern on the surface of the unmolded loaf.

1 lb (500 g) roasted or braised veal, finely chopped
2½ cups (5 oz/150 g) fresh bread crumbs, moistened with a
　few tablespoons of hot milk
persillade made with 1 clove garlic (see glossary)
pinch of Provençal mixed dried herbs (see glossary)
3 eggs
salt, freshly ground pepper and freshly scraped nutmeg
1 tablespoon unsalted butter, softened
8–10 large sorrel leaves, stemmed
boiling water as needed
2 cups (16 fl oz/500 ml) tomato sauce, heated (see glossary)

▦ Preheat an oven to 350°F (180°C).
▦ In a mixing bowl combine the meat, moistened bread crumbs, *persillade,* herbs, eggs and salt, pepper and nutmeg to taste. Using your hands mix well.
▦ Grease a 6-cup (48-fl oz/1.5-l) charlotte mold with the butter. Line it with sorrel leaves, pressing their top surfaces firmly against the buttered bottom and sides of the mold. Fill the mold carefully, to avoid displacing the leaves (or refrigerate the mold first to set the butter and hold the leaves in place). Smooth the surface and tap the bottom of the mold against a work surface to settle the contents. Place the mold in a larger, deep oven dish and add boiling water to reach halfway up the sides of the mold. Place in the oven for 45 minutes. Remove from the oven and from the oven dish and leave to settle for 10 minutes.
▦ To unmold, place a round platter upside-down over the mold; using a folded towel, grasp the edges of the platter and the ears of the mold and invert the platter and mold together. Lift off the mold. Pour a ribbon of hot tomato sauce around the loaf and serve, accompanied with the remaining sauce in a bowl.

SERVES 4

ROUELLE DE VEAU À L'ANCHOIS
Veal Shank with Anchovy

Fresh egg noodles, parboiled, drained and tossed with butter are a good accompaniment to the veal shank.

1½ lb (750 g) veal shank, boned
4 salt anchovies, rinsed, filleted and cut in half crosswise
　(see glossary)
3 tablespoons wine vinegar
3 tablespoons olive oil
salt
about ½ cup (4 fl oz/125 ml) dry white wine
persillade made with 1 clove garlic (see glossary)
1 teaspoon grated orange zest

▦ With a small, sharp-pointed knife, pierce the meat repeatedly, with the grain, on both sides and slip a half anchovy fillet into each slit. Put the meat into a large bowl and sprinkle over

the vinegar and 1 teaspoon of the olive oil. Marinate for 4 hours at room temperature, turning it around two or three times.
▦ Drain the meat and pat it dry with paper towels. Warm the remaining olive oil in a heavy saucepan of a size just to contain the meat with ease. Put the meat in the pan, salt lightly, cover and cook over very low heat, turning it regularly. Watch the meat carefully. At first, it will release some of its own liquid and

Top to bottom: Veal Shank with Anchovy, Provençal Veal Loaf

begin to simmer before the liquid evaporates and the meat begins to color in the oil. Tease the cooking along, adding a couple of spoonfuls of the wine each time the pan becomes dry. It will be ready in about 1½ hours. Remove the meat to a heated serving platter. Slice and keep warm.

▣ Simmer the juices over medium-low heat until the pan is dry and the juices have turned solid and are adhering to the pan bottom. Pour off the fat and deglaze the pan with a few spoonfuls of the wine, scraping the bottom with a wooden spoon to dissolve all browned bits. Pour these juices over the meat. Mix together the *persillade* and orange zest and sprinkle on top.

SERVES 4

141

Braised Stuffed Duck with Olives

CANARD FARCI AUX OLIVES
Braised Stuffed Duck with Olives

FOR THE STUFFING:

3 oz (100 g) *brousse* (see glossary) or ricotta cheese
1 egg
1 tablespoon olive oil
1 onion, finely chopped
the duck heart, liver and fleshy lobes of the gizzard, cut into
    small pieces
pinch of coarse salt
1 clove garlic
½ cup (1 oz/30 g) fresh bread crumbs
1 lb (500 g) Swiss chard (silverbeet) greens, parboiled,
    squeezed dry and chopped (see glossary)
dried oregano flowers, salt and freshly ground pepper and
    freshly scraped nutmeg

1 duck, about 4 lb (2 kg)
1 teaspoon olive oil
salt
mirepoix (see glossary)
¼ cup (2 fl oz/60 ml) dry white wine
2 cups (16 fl oz/500 ml) broth, boiling
⅔ cup (3 oz/100 g) green olives in brine, parboiled for
    1 minute and drained
½ lemon

◉ To prepare the stuffing, combine the cheese and egg in a
mixing bowl and mash together well with a fork. Warm the
olive oil in a small frying pan over low heat. Add the onion and
cook until softened but not colored, about 10 minutes. Add the
heart, liver and gizzard and cook, stirring, until they turn gray,

just a few minutes. Remove from the heat.
◉ In a mortar pound together the coarse salt and garlic to form
a paste. Stir in the bread crumbs.
◉ Add the onion mixture, the crumb-garlic mixture and the
chard to the mixing bowl. Crumble over dried oregano flowers
to taste, then season with salt, pepper and a few scrapings of
nutmeg. Using your hands mix thoroughly.
◉ Preheat an oven to 450°F (230°C). Remove the wishbone
from the duck as directed for roast chicken with anchovies
(recipe on page 150). Cut off the wing tips at the second joint;
cut the tips in two at the first joint. Cut the neck into short
sections. Set these pieces aside. Stuff the abdomen of the duck
with the chard mix and sew up or skewer closed. Truss the duck
with kitchen string. Rub it with the olive oil and sprinkle all over
with salt. Put into a roasting pan, breast side up, with the neck
and wing tip pieces. Wrap the bone tip of each drumstick with
a fragment of aluminum foil to prevent its charring.
◉ Place in the oven and roast for 35–40 minutes, basting often
with the pan juices after the first 15 minutes. Remove from the
oven and reduce the oven temperature to 300°F (150°C).
◉ Meanwhile, prepare the *mirepoix* and spread it on the bottom
of an oval Dutch oven or other heavy pot with a lid of a size just
to contain the duck.
◉ Remove the foil drumstick wrappings and place the duck on
the *mirepoix,* scattering the wing and neck pieces around the
bird. Pour off all the fat from the roasting pan and place the pan
on the stove top over high heat. Pour in the wine and deglaze
the pan by scraping the pan bottom with a wooden spoon until
all browned bits dissolve. Pour the deglazing juices and the
boiling broth over the duck. Lightly oil a piece of parchment
(kitchen) paper cut to the dimensions of the casserole and
place, oiled side down, on top of the duck. Cover and braise in
the oven for 1 hour. Remove from the oven. Raise the oven
temperature to 375°F (190°C).

◉ Transfer the duck to a shallow, oval oven dish. Pour the braising juices through a sieve placed over a small saucepan, pressing the *mirepoix* with a wooden pestle to extract all the liquid. Bring the juices to a boil, then move the saucepan half off the heat, adjusting the heat to keep a gentle boil on the heated surface. Ladle some of the fat-free juices from the boiling side over the duck and put it into the oven. When a skin forms on the still surface in the saucepan, pull it to the side with the edge of a spoon and remove it. Continue cleansing the sauce and basting the duck in this manner until no more fat rises to the surface in the saucepan. Add the olives to the saucepan.

◉ When the duck is richly glazed, after about 20 minutes, remove it to a warmed platter. Snip and remove the trussing strings. Pour the juices from the oven dish into the saucepan. Sharpen the mixture with a squeeze of lemon juice. Pour the sauce and the olives into a heated bowl. Carve the duck and ladle some of the juices and olives over each serving.

SERVES 4

VAR

POULET FARCI EN CRAPAUDINE
Baked Stuffed Chicken

FOR THE STUFFING:

¼ lb (125 g) *brousse* (see glossary) or ricotta cheese
2 tablespoons olive oil

1 egg
½ lb (250 g) spinach, parboiled, squeezed dry and chopped (see glossary)
handful of fresh bread crumbs
¼ cup (1 oz/30 g) freshly grated Parmesan cheese
persillade made with 1 clove garlic (see glossary)
salt, pepper and freshly scraped nutmeg

1 chicken, about 3 lb (1.5 kg)
1 tablespoon olive oil
salt and freshly ground pepper

◉ To prepare the stuffing, combine all the ingredients in a mixing bowl. Using your hands, mix thoroughly.

◉ Preheat an oven to 450°F (230°C). Split, flatten and remove the breastbone from the chicken as directed for chicken grilled with Provençal herbs (recipe on page 151). Using your fingertips and starting at the neck, gradually loosen the skin from the breasts and legs, being careful not to tear it. With one hand, introduce the stuffing, small quantities at a time, between the skin and the flesh, distributing and molding it from outside with the other hand. Truss the chicken with chicken string. Rub it with the olive oil and sprinkle with salt and pepper. Place the bird, breast side up, in a round, shallow baking dish of a size to just hold the chicken, and roast for about 10 minutes. Reduce the oven temperature to 350°F (180°C) and continue to roast, without turning, until juices run clear when pierced at the thigh joint, about 40 minutes. Baste the bird with the pan juices two or three times during the last 30 minutes of roasting.

◉ To serve, move the chicken to a carving board and carve in the same way as for the grilled chicken.

SERVES 4

Baked Stuffed Chicken

POULET À LA VAUCLUSIENNE
Vaucluse-style Chicken

1 chicken, about 3 lb (1.5 kg), trussed
salt and freshly ground pepper
1 tablespoon olive oil
2 oz (60 g) lean salt pork (green bacon), diced
1 onion, finely chopped
½ cup (4 fl oz/125 ml) dry white wine
1 lb (500 g) tomatoes, peeled, seeded and coarsely chopped
⅔ cup (3 oz/100 g) black olives
1 elongated eggplant (aubergine), about ¼ lb (250 g)
all-purpose (plain) flour
vegetable oil as needed

◉ Remove the breast bone from the chicken as directed for roast chicken with anchovies on page 142. Season the chicken with salt and pepper to taste. Put it into a deep, oval flameproof casserole or Dutch oven with the olive oil and salt pork and place over medium-low heat. Move the ingredients around in the pan, cover and uncover it, turn the chicken and stir the pork for 10–15 minutes. Add the onion and keep stirring. When the onion is lightly colored, raise the heat, add the wine, and stir and move the contents. Add the tomatoes and salt. When the tomatoes begin to fall apart and boil, after about 10 minutes, cover and reduce the heat to low. Cook, gradually turning the chicken completely around in the juices, over the next 45 minutes. Stir in the olives at the end of the cooking period.
◉ Meanwhile, slice the eggplant into rounds ¼ in (6 mm) thick. Salt them on both sides.
◉ Remove the chicken from the casserole; clip and remove the trussing strings. Carve the bird and arrange the pieces and slices in a warmed deep platter or large earthenware gratin dish. Pour the contents of the casserole over the chicken and keep warm.
◉ In a large frying pan over medium-high heat (375°F/190°C), pour in vegetable oil to a depth of ½ in (12 mm). Sponge the eggplant slices dry with paper towels. Coat them with flour, shaking off any excess. When the oil is hot, slip the slices into the pan. Fry, turning once, until golden brown, about 2–4 minutes on each side. Remove to paper towels to drain.
◉ Arrange the eggplant slices around the chicken and serve.

SERVES 4

POULET AU RIZ À LA PROVENÇALE
Chicken Pilaf

A pilaf is the perfect way to dispose of the giblets, necks and wing tips that remain after trussing birds for roasting. Livers should be sautéed rapidly, kept pink and added only a moment before serving. This is a perfect family meal.

¼ cup (2 fl oz/60 ml) olive oil
1 frying chicken, about 3 lb (1.5 kg), cut into serving pieces
salt and freshly ground pepper
1 onion, finely chopped
1 sweet red pepper (capsicum), seeded, deribbed, cut into
   ½-in (12-cm) strips wide and then cut crosswise into squares
1½ cups (8 oz/250 g) white long-grain rice
⅛ teaspoon powdered saffron
small pinch of cayenne pepper
persillade made with 1 clove garlic (see glossary)
2½ cups (20 fl oz/625 ml) water, boiling
2 large tomatoes, peeled, seeded and coarsely chopped

◉ Warm the olive oil in a large, heavy sauté pan over medium-high heat. Season the chicken pieces with salt and pepper to taste. Put all the chicken pieces except the breasts in the pan. Sauté, turning the pieces, for 10 minutes. Add the breasts and sauté until all the pieces are nicely colored on both sides, about 10 minutes longer. Transfer the chicken pieces to a plate.
◉ Pour most of the oil from the sauté pan into a large frying pan and reserve it. Add the onion and the pepper to the sauté pan and stir them around over low heat until softened. Add the rice, salt to taste, saffron and cayenne and stir with a wooden spoon until the rice turns opaque, about 5 minutes. Stir in the *persillade,* pour in the boiling water, stir once, and place the chicken pieces on top. Pour over any juices that have drained from the pieces, cover the pan tightly and cook over very low heat until the rice is tender and the chicken is cooked, about 25 minutes.
◉ Meanwhile, heat the leftover oil in the frying pan. Add the tomatoes and a pinch of salt and sauté over high heat until most of their liquid evaporates. After the rice and chicken mixture has cooked for 15 minutes, spread the tomatoes over the surface without disturbing the contents. Recover and continue cooking until done.

SERVES 4

GIBELOTTE DE LAPIN
White Wine Rabbit Stew

In the last century, a gibelotte often included an eel, skinned, cut up and sautéed with the rabbit. The pieces of eel were then held aside until the rabbit was nearly done and then simmered for a few minutes in the sauce.

1 rabbit, about 3½ (1.7 kg), with liver
salt and freshly ground pepper
3 tablespoons olive oil, plus a few drops
1 slice lean salt pork (green bacon), about ¼ lb (125 g), cut into
   lardoons (see glossary)
1 large onion, coarsely chopped
3 cloves garlic, crushed
3 tablespoons all-purpose (plain) flour
¼ cup (2 fl oz/60 ml) marc de Provence (see glossary) or Cognac
2 cups (16 fl oz/500 ml) dry white wine
boiling broth or water (as needed)
bouquet garni (see glossary)
1 lb (500 g) small new potatoes, peeled

◉ Cut the rabbit into 8 pieces: 2 forelegs; 2 hind legs; the saddle cut in two, kidneys left attached; and rib cage split in two.
◉ Season the rabbit pieces with salt and pepper. Warm the 3 tablespoons olive oil in a large sauté pan over medium heat. Add the rabbit pieces and tuck the lardoons into the empty spaces. Turn the lardoons regularly, either by shaking the pan or by flipping them over with a knife tip or a fork. When the rabbit pieces are all colored on one side and turned, after about 20–30 minutes, add the onion. Displace the contents of the pan by pushing, nudging and stirring with a wooden spoon until the onion is softened and beginning to color, about 10 minutes.
◉ Add the garlic, sprinkle the flour evenly over the top and turn the rabbit pieces over. Continue to move and displace everything for a couple of minutes, then pour over the brandy.
◉ Turn, stir and scrape the pan bottom. If it flames, keep stirring. Pour over the wine and continue to stir and scrape until it comes to a boil. Tuck the bouquet garni into the middle and pour over enough broth or water to immerse the rabbit pieces. Cover and simmer at very low heat for 45 minutes. After 15 minutes, add the potatoes, one by one, here and there, making certain they are completely immersed in the sauce.
◉ A minute before serving, remove any visible fat from the sauce's surface. Cut the liver into small pieces and sauté it for a few seconds in a few drops of olive oil. Scatter the pieces over the surface of the dish. Serve directly from the sauté pan.

SERVES 4   *Photograph pages 116–117*

Sunset vista from Bonnieux, from left to right: Vaucluse-style Chicken, Chicken Pilaf

PROVENCE

BROCHETTES D'ABATS
Brochettes of Mixed Meats

In the south of France, the word brochette, *unless qualified, means a skewer of mixed lamb offal. Some cooks like to include cubes of tender meat from the leg or the loin. Whatever the mixture, everyone adores it. It is practical to skewer the meats an hour or so ahead of time and leave them to marinate at room temperature. Saffron-flavored pilaf and Provençal baked tomatoes (recipe on page 173) are typical and ideal accompaniments.*

2 slices lean salt pork (green bacon), about ¼ lb (125 g) and ½ in (12 mm) thick, cut into lardoons (see glossary)
large pinch of coarse salt
freshly ground pepper
pinch of Provençal mixed dried herbs (see glossary)
2 cloves garlic
2 tablespoons olive oil
2 lamb hearts, trimmed of fat and arterial tubes, quartered lengthwise and then each quarter halved crosswise
2 veal kidneys, halved lengthwise, trimmed of fat and then each half cut into ¾-in (2-cm) pieces
fresh rosemary, optional

◙ Place the lardoons in a saucepan and add water to cover. Bring to a boil, drain and refresh under cold running water. Drain again and pat dry with paper towels; set aside.

◙ In a mortar pound together the coarse salt and freshly ground pepper, herbs and garlic to form a paste. Stir in the olive oil with the pestle and empty the mortar into a large mixing bowl. Wipe out the mortar with a handful of meat pieces. Add

them to the mixing bowl, along with all the other meat pieces. Turn the mixture all around with your hands, until meat and marinade are intimately intermingled.

◙ Count your pieces ahead of time to portion them equally among the skewers. You will have 4 heart pieces, probably 5 lardoons and 6 or 7 kidney pieces per skewer. Thread them onto the skewers, more or less alternately, touching but not packed. Lay them on a platter or a tray, pour over any marinade left in the bowl and hold until the fire is ready.

◙ Prepare a fire in a charcoal grill. Place the skewers on the grill rack over glowing coals and grill, turning every couple of minutes, for 8–10 minutes. If fresh rosemary is available, throw a handful of leaves or a couple of branches onto the coals a few seconds before removing the brochettes (do not use dried rosemary—it will blaze up instead of smoking).

SERVES 4

PROVENCE

PINTADE AUX CHOUX
Guinea Fowl with Cabbage

The classic is partridge with cabbage. Guinea fowl replaces partridge out of the game season. Old pheasants are treated in the same way. For the poaching sausage, select a pork sausage, coarsely ground and well-seasoned but not smoked.

1 large savoy cabbage
salted boiling water as needed
1 guinea fowl, about 3 lb (1.5 kg), trussed
1 tablespoon olive oil
salt and freshly ground pepper
2 slices lean salt pork (green bacon), about ¼ lb (125 g) each
2 large onions, coarsely chopped
¼ cup (2 fl oz/60 ml) dry white wine
1 poaching sausage, ½ lb (250 g), pricked in several places
large bouquet garni (see glossary)
½ lb (250 g) carrots, peeled and cut into slices ¾ in (2 cm) thick
about 2 cups (16 fl oz/500 ml) broth, boiling

◙ Preheat an oven to 450°F (230°C). Remove and discard the dark green, outer leaves from the cabbage. Quarter the cabbage vertically and cut out the core from each quarter. Trim off visible thick ribs and then coarsely shred the quarters. Pack them into a large saucepan and pour in salted boiling water to cover. Cook at a gentle boil for 10 minutes. Drain into a colander, refresh the cabbage beneath cold running water and then squeeze to extract as much liquid as possible.

◙ Rub the guinea fowl with the olive oil and sprinkle all over with salt and pepper. Put into a Dutch oven or other oval roasting dish, breast side up. Place in the oven and roast for 20 minutes. Remove from the oven and reduce the oven temperature to 300°F (150°C).

◙ Meanwhile, place the salt pork in a saucepan and add water to cover. Bring to a boil over high heat and drain. Rinse under cold running water and drain again; set aside.

◙ In the bottom of a heavy oval pot, scatter a handful of the parboiled cabbage and all of the onions. Place the guinea fowl on top, breast side up. Place its roasting pan on the stove top over high heat. Pour in the wine and deglaze the pan by scraping the pan bottom with a wooden spoon until all the browned bits dissolve. Pour the deglazed juices over the bird. Tuck a slice of salt pork alongside each side of the bird. Place the poaching sausage along one side and the bouquet garni along the other. Scatter the carrots around the bird. Cover everything with the remaining cabbage, pressing it into place, and pour over enough boiling broth to cover barely.

◙ Cover and place in the oven until the bird is very tender, about 2 hours. The bird will have given most of its goodness to the cabbage, but that is what is wanted. Remove the sausage

Guinea Fowl with Cabbage

Left to right: Brochettes of Mixed Meats, Provençal Quail Pilaf

and salt pork after the first hour, then put them back in to warm up 10 minutes before removing the pan from the oven.

▣ Put the bird on one plate and the sausage and salt pork on another; keep warm. Place a large sieve over a large saucepan and pour the cabbage and juices into it. Mound the cabbage in the center of a warmed platter. Put the saucepan over high heat and boil to reduce the juices to ½–⅔ cup (4–5 fl oz/125–150 ml).

▣ Using poultry shears cut the bird into quarters; discard the trussing strings. Slice the sausage thickly and cut the salt pork slices in half; distribute around and on top of the cabbage. Pour the reduced juices over the top.

SERVES 4

CAILLES AU RIZ À LA PROVENÇALE

Provençal Quail Pilaf

4 quail
4 tablespoons (2 fl oz/60 ml) olive oil
1 onion, finely chopped
1½ cups (8 oz/250 g) long-grain white rice
small pinch of Provençal mixed dried herbs (see glossary)
1 bay leaf

salt
3 cups (24 fl oz/750 ml) broth, boiling
freshly ground pepper
½ cup (4 fl oz/125 ml) dry white wine
¼ cup (2 fl oz/60 ml) tomato sauce (see glossary)

▣ Using poultry shears, split each quail down the back. Open the birds out flat, skin side up, and flatten them with your hand. Set aside.

▣ Warm 1 tablespoon of olive oil in a flameproof earthenware casserole or heavy sauté pan over low heat. Add the onion and sauté gently until softened, about 10 minutes. Add the rice, mixed herbs and bay, salt lightly and stir with a wooden spoon until the rice turns milky and opaque, about 5 minutes. Pour in the boiling broth, stir once, cover tightly and cook over very low heat for 25 minutes.

▣ As soon as the rice is covered, heat the remaining 3 tablespoons olive oil in a sauté pan over medium heat. Season the quail with salt and pepper and place in the pan. Cook, turning once, until nicely colored, 5–6 minutes on each side.

▣ Place the quail on top of the cooking rice and cover tightly again. Place the sauté pan over high heat. Pour in the wine and deglaze the pan by scraping the pan bottom until all browned bits dissolve. Boil until reduced by half, then stir in the tomato sauce and simmer for a couple of minutes.

▣ When the rice and quail are ready, pour the sauce over the quail. Serve directly from the pan.

SERVES 4

Clockwise from top left: Gratin of Pork and Beans, Pork and Red Wine Stew, Pork Cutlets with Tapénade

CIVET DE PORCELET
Pork and Red Wine Stew

A civet, strictly speaking, is a meat stew, the sauce of which is thickened at the last minute with the animal's blood. Civet de porcelet, which is a popular specialty in Provençal country auberges, is usually a simple pork and red wine stew. If you are able to obtain pork blood, mix ½ cup (4 fl oz/125 ml) of the blood with the anchovy-garlic mixture in the following recipe, stir some of the sauce into it and, off the heat, stir it into the stew. Stir over low heat until the bright red color of the blood turns chocolate brown; it must not boil or the sauce will break.

2 lb (1 kg) boneless pork shoulder butt or blade, cut into 2-in (5-cm) pieces
3 cups (24 fl oz/750 ml) dry red wine
4 tablespoons (2 fl oz/60 ml) olive oil
pinch of Provençal mixed dried herbs (see glossary)

1 slice lean salt pork (green bacon), ¼ lb (125 g), cut into lardoons (see glossary)
fine salt
½ lb (250 g) yellow onions, coarsely chopped
2 tablespoons all-purpose (plain) flour
4 tablespoons marc de Provence (see Glossary) or Cognac
1 bay leaf
1 fresh sage sprig
½ lb (250 g) pickling onions
1 teaspoon unsalted butter
pinch of sugar
⅔ cup (3 oz/100 g) black olives
pinch of coarse salt
freshly ground pepper
1 clove garlic
2 salt anchovies, rinsed and filleted (see glossary)

◙ In a bowl combine the meat, wine, 1 tablespoon of the olive oil and the herbs. Mix well and marinate in the refrigerator several hours or overnight.

◙ Drain and dry the meat pieces. Warm 2 tablespoons of the olive oil in a heavy sauté pan over medium-low heat. Add the lardoons and sauté until lightly colored but not crisp, about 10 minutes. Remove to a plate. Add the meat pieces to the same pan. Season to taste with fine salt and brown over medium heat. When the pieces are turned to brown the second side, add the yellow onions. Sauté until the onions are lightly colored, about 10 minutes. Add the flour, stir around for a couple of minutes, then add the brandy and marinade. Raise the heat and deglaze the pan, scraping the pan bottom with a wooden spoon until all the browned bits dissolve. Add the bay leaf and sage and bring to a boil. Reduce the heat to low, cover and simmer and cook until the meat is tender, about 1½ hours.

◙ Meanwhile, in a small saucepan combine the pickling onions, butter, sugar, a pinch of fine salt and enough water almost to cover the onions. Bring to a boil, cover and simmer over low heat for 8 minutes. Remove the lid, raise the heat and cook until the liquid evaporates and the onions begin to color. Put them aside with the lardoons.

◙ Remove the pieces of meat from the sauce and discard the bay leaf and sage. Empty the sauté pan into a sieve placed over a bowl to catch the liquid. Put the meat back into the sauté pan and add the lardoons, pickling onions and olives. Cover and set aside. Pass the sauce through the sieve, puréeing the onions. Pour the sauce into a small saucepan, bring to a boil and move half off the heat. Adjust to a light boil on half the surface and allow a skin of fat to form on the still surface. Pull the skin to the side of the pan with a spoon and remove it; repeat until no more fat appears.

◙ Pour the sauce over the meat, onions and olives. Return the sauté pan to low heat, cover and simmer gently for 15 minutes.

◙ In a mortar pound together the coarse salt, pepper to taste, garlic and anchovies to form a paste. Stir in the remaining 1 tablespoon olive oil. Stir the garlic mixture into the stew and serve.

SERVES 4

V A U C L U S E

TIAN DE HARICOTS
Gratin of Pork and Beans

If fresh white shell beans (cocos; see glossary) are available, substitute 4 lb (2 kg) shell beans in their pods for the dried beans. Cook them in salted boiling water, with the same aromatic elements, for 30–40 minutes before joining them to the meat.

1¾ cups (¾ lb/350 g) small dried white beans such as Great Northerns
1 carrot, peeled
1 onion stuck with 2 whole cloves, plus 1 large onion, thinly sliced
bouquet garni including 1 fresh sage sprig (see glossary)
boiling water as needed
salt
2 teaspoons olive oil
¼ lb (125 g) lean salt pork (green bacon), diced
1½ lb (750 g) boneless pork shoulder butt or blade
freshly ground pepper
2 tomatoes, peeled, seeded and coarsely chopped

◙ Place the beans in a large bowl. Add water to cover and let stand for several hours or as long as overnight. Drain the beans, empty them into a large saucepan and add cold water to cover abundantly. Bring to a boil and boil gently for 10 minutes. Drain the beans, return them to the saucepan and add the carrot, onion stuck with cloves and the bouquet garni. Pour over boiling water to cover by about 1 in (2.5 cm). Bring to a boil, reduce the heat to low, cover and simmer until nearly but not quite done, about 45 minutes. Season to taste with salt.

◙ Meanwhile, warm the olive oil and salt pork in a heavy saucepan over medium heat. Season the pork shoulder or blade with salt and pepper and add it to the pan. Color the meat on all sides, about 20 minutes. Add the sliced onion and continue to cook, stirring and turning the meat, until the onion is lightly colored, about 10 minutes. Add the tomatoes, raise the heat and cook until they begin to fall apart and boil, 5–10 minutes. Reduce the heat to low, cover and simmer until the beans are ready.

◙ Preheat an oven to 350°F (180°C). Transfer the meat to a large, deep oven dish, preferably earthenware. Drain the beans, reserving their liquid. Remove and discard the carrot, the onion stuck with cloves and the bouquet garni. Add the beans and about 1 cup (8 fl oz/250 ml) of their liquid to the sauce in the saucepan, stirring and pouring around the piece of pork. Add enough additional beans' cooking liquid to immerse all the ingredients. Put the dish in the oven and, as soon as the surface is bubbling, reduce the oven temperature to 300°F (150°C). Stir the beans a bit every 20 minutes or so, immersing the skin that forms on the surface. Add more cooking liquid from time to time; the beans should never dry out. Bake until beans are tender, about 1½ hours.

SERVES 4

P R O V E N C E

ESCALOPES DE PORC À LA TAPÉNADE
Pork Cutlets with Tapénade

Because they take up so much space, breaded cutlets for more than two servings must be prepared either in relays or in two large frying pans at the same time.

4 pork loin cutlets, each about ⅓ in (8 mm) thick
salt and freshly ground pepper
4 tablespoons (3 oz/90 g) *tapénade* (recipe on page 34)
½ cup (2 oz/60 g) freshly grated Parmesan cheese
2 eggs
½ teaspoon olive oil
semidried bread crumbs
peanut oil or corn oil for frying
1 lemon, quartered

◙ Press the cutlets firmly with the side of a large knife blade to flatten them slightly. Sprinkle on both sides with salt and pepper. Spread 1 tablespoon *tapénade* on one side of each cutlet. Cover and chill to firm up the *tapénade*.

◙ Assemble side by side: a plate spread with half the grated cheese; a soup plate in which the eggs, olive oil and a few drops of water have been beaten with a fork; and an opened newspaper spread abundantly with bread crumbs. Place a cutlet, *tapénade* side up, on the bed of Parmesan. Sprinkle some of the remaining Parmesan on top, pressing it in lightly with the palm of your hand. Transfer the cutlet to the beaten eggs, spoon some of the egg over the top and lift the cutlet rapidly to the bread crumbs. Sprinkle crumbs generously over the top and press on gently. Repeat with the remaining cutlets and leave the cutlets on the bed of crumbs to dry for 1 hour or so before frying.

◙ In a large frying pan over high heat, pour in oil to a depth of ½ in (12 mm). Slip in the cutlets and turn down the heat to medium or medium-low if necessary to prevent the cutlets from browning too rapidly. When they are golden around the edges, turn them by piercing, near the edge of the cutlet, with a single tine of a long-handled, two-pronged fork. When both sides are golden and crisp, after about 8 minutes, use a spatula to transfer them to paper towels to drain. Serve accompanied with the lemon quarters.

SERVES 2

POULET AUX ANCHOIS
Roast Chicken with Anchovies

This is adapted from Le cuisinier méridional *(1855). The original recipe is for a spit-roasted bird turned before open flames.*

FOR THE STUFFING:

2 oz (60 g) lean salt pork (green bacon), finely chopped
3 salt anchovies, rinsed, filleted and finely chopped (see glossary)
1 oz (30 g) *brousse* (see glossary) or ricotta cheese
3 tablespoons finely chopped fresh flat-leaf (Italian) parsley
3 tablespoons finely chopped shallots
freshly ground pepper

1 chicken, about 3 lb (1.5 kg)
1 tablespoon olive oil
salt and freshly ground pepper

◼ Combine all the ingredients for the stuffing in a bowl. Using a fork mash together very thoroughly.
◼ To make the eventual carving of the bird easier, remove the wishbone: Carefully pull the neck skin over the breast to expose the flesh. With a small knife tip, slit the flesh against the contours of the wishbone, freeing the vertex at its attachment to the breastbone. Hook your finger at the angle of the bone and pull it loose from its attachment at the wing joints.
◼ Preheat an oven to 450°F (230°C). Using your fingertips and starting at the neck, gradually loosen the skin from the breasts and the legs, being careful not to tear it. With one hand, introduce the stuffing, small quantities at a time, between the skin and the flesh, distributing and molding it from outside with the other hand. Truss the chicken with kitchen string. Rub it with the olive oil and sprinkle with salt and then grind over some pepper.
◼ Place the bird in a roasting pan, breast side up, and roast for about 10 minutes. Reduce the oven temperature to 350°F (180°C) and continue to roast, without turning, until the juices

salt and freshly ground pepper
all-purpose (plain) flour
¼ cup (2 fl oz/60 ml) olive oil
1 small onion, finely chopped
½ cup (4 fl oz/125 ml) dry white wine
1½ lb (750 g) tomatoes, peeled, seeded and coarsely chopped
persillade made with 1 clove garlic (see glossary)
⅔ cup (3 oz/100 g) black olives
fresh basil leaves

▣ Season the chicken pieces with salt and pepper, then coat with flour, shaking off any excess. In a large sauté pan over medium heat, warm the olive oil. Put all the pieces in the pan except the breasts. Sauté, turning the pieces, for 10 minutes. Add the breasts and sauté until all the pieces are nicely colored on both sides, about 10 minutes longer. Reduce the heat to low, cover and cook for 10 minutes.

▣ Transfer the chicken pieces to a warmed platter; keep warm. Add the onion to the pan and stir it around with a wooden spoon. When it begins to color, pour in the wine. Raise the heat to high and deglaze the pan, scraping the pan bottom with a wooden spoon until the browned bits dissolve and the wine is almost completely reduced. Add the tomatoes and salt to taste and continue to cook over high heat, shaking the pan and stirring, until their excess liquid evaporates. A couple of minutes before removing from the heat, add the *persillade* and olives.

▣ Just before serving, tear some basil leaves into small fragments and stir them into the sauce. Pour the sauce over the chicken pieces and serve.

SERVES 4

Clockwise from top: Roast Chicken with Anchovies, Provençal Sautéed Chicken, Chicken Grilled with Provençal Herbs

run clear when pierced at the thigh joint, about 40 minutes. Baste the bird with the pan juices two or three times during the last 30 minutes of roasting. Carve at table.

SERVES 4

PROVENCE

POULET SAUTÉ À LA PROVENÇALE
Provençal Sautéed Chicken

Chicken sautéed with tomatoes is a recurrent theme in Provençale cuisine. Often the chicken is sautéed more briefly and finishes cooking in the tomato sauce.

1 frying chicken, about 3 lb (1.5 kg), cut into serving pieces

PROVENCE

POULET GRILLÉ AUX HERBES DE PROVENCE
Chicken Grilled with Provençal Herbs

Young guinea fowl, pigeons (squabs) and quail are prepared in the same way. Guinea fowl requires the same cooking time as chicken; pigeons are done in 15–18 minutes and quail in 12–15 minutes.

1 frying chicken, about 3 lb (1.5 kg)
pinch of Provençal mixed dried herbs (see glossary)
salt and freshly ground pepper
1 tablespoon olive oil

▣ Cut off the wing tips from the chicken at the second joint. Using poultry shears, split the back, from tail to neck, cutting along one side of the neck. Cut along the other side of the neck to remove the neck and a section of the spine to the mid-back. Open the chicken out, skin side facing up. Press hard on the breastbone to fracture it and the rib-cage structure. Turn the chicken over and pull out the breastbone. Turn it over once again, skin side up. Using a small knife tip, pierce the skin of the abdomen between the thigh and the tip of the breast, to each side, and force the drumstick up to push its tip through the slit to the underside.

▣ Prepare a fire in a charcoal grill and position the grill rack about 4 in (10 cm) from the coals. Season the chicken with the herbs and salt and pepper to taste and rub all the surfaces with the olive oil. Place on the grill rack and grill for about 35 minutes, turning several times. When the skin side is facing the coals, watch it carefully as the skin chars easily and rapidly. Most of the grilling, once the skin is golden brown, should be done skin facing up.

▣ Present the bird on a carving board. To carve the chicken, split it the length of the breast and slit the skin from around the thighs to the back. It will fall into quarters.

SERVES 4

151

FARCI BOUILLI

Poached Stuffed Breast of Veal

This first stuffing is a simplified adaptation of a recipe by Charles Durand. He recommends the addition of chopped truffles and writes that it can be used to stuff all kinds of poultry or breasts of veal or lamb, poached or braised. Remove the marrow from the sawed sections of marrow bone using a knife tip. Each recipe makes enough stuffing for a 3 lb (1.5 kg) veal breast.

STUFFING 1

½ lb (250 g) each spinach, Swiss chard (silverbeet) greens and sorrel leaves, stemmed and finely chopped
5 oz (150 g) veal, chopped
¼ lb (125 g) lean salt pork (green bacon), chopped
3 oz (100 g) raw beef marrow (see glossary)
pinch of coarse salt
2 cloves garlic
handful of chopped fresh flat-leaf (Italian) parsley
1 teaspoon finely chopped fresh tarragon
2½ cups (5 oz/150 g) fresh bread crumbs
3 oz (100 g) shank end of raw ham such as prosciutto, cut into ⅛-in (3-mm) dice
1 slice pork back fat, 2 oz (60 g), cut into narrow strips and then diced
3 eggs
salt, freshly ground pepper, ground allspice and freshly scraped nutmeg

◙ Layer the chopped spinach, chard and sorrel leaves together in a bowl, salting the layers well. Let stand for 30 minutes. Squeeze the leaves dry and set aside.
◙ Combine the veal, salt pork and marrow in a food processor fitted with the metal blade and process to a purée. Set aside.
◙ In a mortar pound together the coarse salt and garlic to form a paste. Mix in the parsley, tarragon and bread crumbs.
◙ In a mixing bowl combine all the ingredients, including salt, pepper, allspice and nutmeg to taste. Using your hands mix thoroughly until the mass is absolutely homogenous.

STUFFING 2

Trimmed and finely sliced young artichokes are often added to this typical stuffing from Nice. In season, tender, peeled broad (fava) beans can replace or be added to the peas. Sometimes, shelled hard-cooked eggs, tips removed, are placed end to end at the heart of the stuffing so that each slice contains a round of yellow and white at its center.

½ lb (250 g) sausage meat (see glossary)
½ lb (250 g) ground veal
1 lb (500 g) Swiss chard (silverbeet) greens, parboiled, squeezed dry and chopped (see glossary)
¼ cup (3 oz/90 g) long-grain white rice, parboiled for 15 minutes, drained and rinsed
1 large handful of shelled small green peas (about 1 lb/500 g unshelled)
persillade made with 1 clove garlic (see glossary)
½ cup (2 oz/60 g) freshly grated Parmesan cheese
pinch of Provençal mixed dried herbs (see glossary)
2 eggs
salt and freshly ground pepper

◙ Assemble all the ingredients, including salt and pepper to taste, in a mixing bowl. Using your hands mix thoroughly until all the elements are evenly incorporated.

FOR THE VEAL:

To ready a breast of veal for stuffing, slice the ribs and backbone section free of the flesh. Using your fingertips and a knife tip, open the two layers of muscle separated by a fatty membrane. (If you like, ask your butcher to prepare the breast for stuffing.) Stuff the pouch loosely with stuffing, fold the flaps over to enclose it and sew together with looped stitches at intervals of 1–1½ in (2.5–4 cm).

A poached stuffed breast of veal can be treated in the same way as a pot-au-feu: the broth served as a first course, poured over crusts of bread, with grated cheese on the side. In this case, ⅛ teaspoon powdered saffron enhances the soup. Often the broth is reserved for another use and a tomato sauce accompanies the poached breast. Or the stuffed breast is removed from its broth, cooled completely, cut into thin slices and served cold with tapénade (recipe on page 34).

1 veal breast, 3 lb (1.5 kg), stuffed with stuffing of choice (preceding recipes)
2 whole cloves
2 onions
3 carrots, peeled and cut into sections
3 cloves garlic, crushed
bouquet garni (see glossary)
handful of coarse sea salt

◙ Place the stuffed breast in a heavy oval pot. Stick the cloves into 1 of the onions. Surround the breast with the onions, carrots, garlic and bouquet garni. Pour in water to cover and add the salt. Bring slowly to a boil and skim off any scum and froth. Adjust the heat to maintain a gentle simmer and cover with the lid slightly ajar. Simmer for 2 hours.
◙ Clip and remove the strings before serving, either hot or cold.

SERVES 6

BOEUF MIRONTON À LA PROVENÇALE

Beef in Onion Sauce

Mironton (or miroton) is a great classic, a symbol of fulfilling, rustic, family food. Sometimes a few filleted salt anchovies are mashed and added to the sauce.

4 tablespoons olive oil
10 oz (300 g) onions, finely sliced
2 tablespoons all-purpose (plain) flour
2 cups (16 fl oz/500 ml) *pot-au-feu* broth (recipe on page 45)
2 tablespoons Provençal herb vinegar (see glossary)
persillade made with 1 clove garlic (see glossary)
1 bay leaf
1 fresh thyme sprig
salt
1 lb (500 g) *pot-au-feu* beef, chilled and thinly sliced (recipe on page 45)
1 tablespoon capers, rinsed
freshly ground pepper
dried bread crumbs

◙ Warm 3 tablespoons of the olive oil in a saucepan over medium-low heat. Add the onions and cook, stirring, until lightly colored, about 10 minutes. Add the flour and cook, stirring, for 1 minute. Add the broth and vinegar, stirring. Add the *persillade,* bay leaf and thyme and bring to a boil, stirring. Adjust the heat to low and simmer for 20 minutes. Season to taste with salt.
◙ Preheat an oven to 350°F (180°C). Layer half of the beef slices, overlapping, in a gratin dish. Grind some pepper, scatter some capers and pour some sauce over the top. Repeat the layers, ending with sauce. Sprinkle with crumbs and dribble the remaining tablespoon of oil in a thin thread back and forth over the top. Put into the oven and bake until the sauce is bubbling and the surface is lightly browned, 15–20 minutes.

SERVES 4

Top to bottom: Beef in Onion Sauce, Poached Stuffed Breast of Veal

Paquets de Lapin au Four

Roast Rabbit Packages

The upper part of a rabbit doesn't lend itself to this preparation; save it for a stew. Any potato gratin is a good accompaniment.

2 hind legs and the saddle, cut in half, of 1 rabbit
1 tablespoon olive oil
4 fresh winter savory sprigs
2 bay leaves
2 cloves garlic, crushed
freshly ground pepper
½ lemon
salt
about ½ oz (15 g) caul, soaked briefly in tepid water with a
    dash of wine vinegar and drained (see glossary)

◙ In a bowl combine the rabbit pieces, olive oil, savory, bay and garlic. Grind over some pepper, squeeze over a few drops of lemon juice and toss with your hands. Marinate at room temperature for 1 hour or so, turning everything around a couple of times.

◙ Preheat an oven to 400°F (200°C). Discard the bay leaves and garlic. Salt the rabbit pieces and press a sprig of savory onto each. Lay the caul out flat on a work surface. Cut it into 4 squares, each measuring 6–8 in (15–20 cm). Wrap a piece of rabbit with its savory sprig in each caul square.

◙ Place a small wire rack in the bottom of a shallow oven dish. Place the rabbit packages on top, pleat side of the caul facing down. Roast until the caul has melted and browned into a lovely lacework, 20–25 minutes.

SERVES 4

Poulet aux Quarante Gousses d'Ail

Chicken with 40 Cloves of Garlic

A classic, Provençal method for preparing roast chicken.

1 roasting chicken, about 4 lb (2 kg), cut into serving pieces
    with thighs and legs separated
salt and freshly ground pepper
½ lb (250 g) cloves firm, crisp garlic, unpeeled
2 bay leaves or 2 or 3 fresh thyme sprigs
1 fresh savory sprig
½ cup (4 fl oz/125 ml) olive oil
large bouquet garni (see glossary)

◙ Season the chicken pieces to taste with salt and pepper. Put them in a mixing bowl with the garlic, loose herbs and olive oil. Using your hands mix well. Cover and leave to marinate at room temperature for 1–2 hours.

◙ Preheat an oven to 300°F (150°C). Discard the herbs from the marinade (or incorporate them into the bouquet garni). Place the bouquet garni in the middle of an ovenproof earthenware casserole. Arrange the chicken pieces and garlic cloves around the bouquet, neither packed nor with wasted space. Empty over any remaining oil from the marinade, cover tightly (if the lid is not tight fitting, first place a sheet of heavy aluminum foil over the casserole before pressing the lid in place) and bake until the chicken is tender, about 1¾ hours.

◙ Serve directly from the casserole.

SERVES 6

Roast Rabbit Packages

In Lourmarin, Vaucluse, Chicken with 40 Cloves of Garlic

Veal Sweetbreads Braised with Artichokes

RIS DE VEAU BRAISÉS AUX ARTICHAUTS

Veal Sweetbreads Braised with Artichokes

Sweetbreads should be plump and full in appearance, white, with a slight pink cast, moist and glistening. Whatever the final preparation of the sweetbreads, the preliminary steps are the same. First soak the sweetbreads in repeated changes of cold water for 12–24 hours. Then place them in a large saucepan, cover generously with cold water, bring to a boil over medium-low heat and hold beneath the boil for 15 minutes. Drain, plunge into a basin of cold water and, when cool enough to handle, pull off and discard all visible fat, gristly tubes and membrane. The fine, interior membranes, which hold together the lobular structure, should be left intact.

mirepoix (see glossary)
4 young, tender artichokes, trimmed, quartered and chokes removed if necessary (see glossary)

2 lb (1 kg) veal sweetbreads, soaked, boiled and cleaned (see recipe introduction)
bouquet garni (see glossary)
salt
¼ cup (2 fl oz/60 ml) dry white wine
freshly ground pepper

◉ Prepare the *mirepoix* in a large, flameproof earthenware casserole or heavy sauté pan. Place the artichokes, sweetbreads and bouquet garni on top and sprinkle with salt. Cover and sweat over very low heat, turning everything over a couple of times, for about 10 minutes.

◉ Sprinkle the wine over the top. Lightly oil one side of a sheet of parchment (kitchen) paper cut to the dimensions of the pan and place over the sweetbreads oiled side down. Cover with a lid and simmer over very low heat for 45 minutes. Turn the sweetbreads and artichokes over halfway through the cooking, and, if moisture is lacking, add a couple spoonfuls of boiling water or white wine.

◉ Serve directly from the pan.

SERVES 4

FOIE DE VEAU À LA MOISSONNEUSE

Harvesters' Calf's Liver

Foie à la moissonneuse, *which also often made with lamb's liver, is essentially the same as the Venetian specialty,* fegato di vitello alla veneziana. *It is said to have been a favorite dish of the wheat harvesters in the Vaucluse in the last century.*

5 tablespoons (3 fl oz/80 ml) olive oil
1 lb (500 g) large sweet white onions, halved and sliced
    paper-thin
1 bay leaf
1 fresh thyme sprig
persillade made with 3 cloves garlic (see glossary)
salt
½ cup (4 fl oz/125 ml) red wine
¾ lb (375 g) calf's liver
freshly ground pepper
all-purpose (plain) flour
2 tablespoons red wine vinegar

◙ Warm 2 tablespoons of the olive oil in a large, flame-proof earthenware casserole or heavy sauté pan over very low heat. Add the onions, bay, thyme, *persillade* and salt to taste. Cover and sweat, stirring a couple of times, for about 45 minutes. At this point, the onions will have cooked in their juices without coloring. Remove the lid, turn up the heat slightly and permit them to color lightly, stirring regularly with a wooden spoon. Add the wine, bring to a boil and simmer, uncovered, over low heat, until reduced to the consistency of a sauce, about 15 minutes. Grind over some pepper.

◙ Cut the liver into slices about ½ in (12 mm) thick, then cut each slice into 1-in (2.5-cm) squares. Season the squares with salt and pepper. Coat them with flour and then toss them in a sieve to rid them of any excess flour.

◙ Warm the remaining 3 tablespoons olive oil in a large sauté pan. Add the liver squares and sauté them, tossing and stirring, until slightly firmed up but still rare, no more than a couple of minutes.

◙ Add the liver pieces to the onion sauce. Pour the vinegar into the sauté pan over high heat. Deglaze the pan by scraping the pan bottom until all the browned bits dissolve. Stir the deglazing juices into the onion sauce and serve.

SERVES 4

Harvesters' Calf's Liver

BOUCHES-DU-RHÔNE

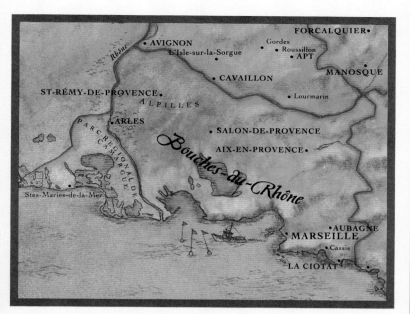

BOUCHES-
DU-RHÔNE

W
hen a river meets the sea everything becomes possible. The ancient love story between the Rhône and the Mediterranean seems to have given birth to the multitude of contrasts we find in this peaceful and whimsical *département*. It lies among the dry stones of the Alpilles, the Valley of the Durance, the *étangs* of the Camargue, the luminous Aix country, the mingled beauty and ugliness of Marseilles and the last remaining coves around Cassis.

Marseilles represents a concentration of the most marked features of Mediterranean civilization. The *ville* is open, colorful, secret, excessive and often impossible for the visitor. This is a city that never loses sight of the Provençal traditions without which it would simply be a community like any other, but at the same time the door is always open to influences and flavors filtering in from elsewhere. And the port of Marseilles? "It is the market France offers to the vendors of the vast world," wrote Albert Londres in *Marseille porte du Sud* (Marseilles, Gateway of the South).

It is a matter of both fragrance and color, a characterization epitomized by the local *bouillabaisse. Lou bouiabaisso* means "when this boils, turn down the heat!" This simple dish has more than once lost its soul in third-rate restaurants in the port area and along the coast, and its composition is a subject of debate, not to say war, between purists and heretics. These days in Marseilles it is also the subject of a charter, and we still find it on the

Previous pages: The poppy fields and picturesque mountains outside Aix-en-Provence inspired Picasso to spend his final years here. Left: A fisherman pulls fish from his net in Marseilles, the largest port in the Mediterranean.

The intricately carved cloisters of the Cathedral of Saint-Trophîme in Arles, erected between the twelfth and fourteenth centuries, provide exquisite examples of both Romanesque and Gothic architecture.

family table in a form dictated by the various rock fish brought into port by the little local fishing boats known as *pointus.* It comes flavored, of course, with saffron, which in days gone by was brought from the Orient; sometimes it is accompanied with pasta or even sprinkled with grated cheese and includes among its ingredients a lobster or *muscardins,* those little cuttlefish whose sacs spread ink to make the soup black. There are as many variations as there are moods.

Now we turn to the undeniable king of Marseilles cuisine, who also reigns well beyond these boundaries: on the hills of Aubagne, in the countryside around Aix and alongside the Alpilles, in a magic triangle between Salon-de-Provence, Arles and Saint-Rèmy. Along the little Mediterranean coves known as *calanques* where the blue sea sparkles and in the open country lashed by the mistral, this sun king is called garlic. It flavors every dish, invites itself to every table. You will find it in plaits on the butchers' stalls along the Cours Belzunce, on trestles in little Provence markets, hanging in kitchens within the cook's reach, or a few cloves carefully preserved in the huts along the seashore. Certainly the cuisine of Provence and the cooks of Marseilles have no exclusive rights when it comes to the use of garlic. But this extraordinary plant, which arrived several thousand years ago from Central Asia, is part of the legend and of the landscape in Provence. It can revive the most tasteless of cuisines, and its beneficial properties are legion.

Reinvigorating, diuretic and antiseptic garlic is believed to cure colds, arthritis, cholesterol and melancholy, as well as prolong life. Provençal writer Jean Giono speaks in *Le hussard sur le toit* (The Hussar on the Roof) of this heaven-sent garlic that must be harvested before the peak of the hot season. So it is perfectly normal that the people of Provence should use and abuse this sun king, which has its local capital in Piolenc. Chefs these days offer it on their menus almost reluctantly: It is "sweet garlic" that flavors their dishes, not the robust and formidable variety that, according to the

great cook Curnonski, obliges anyone who has eaten it "to use only indirect speech"!

Thus garlic is omnipresent, in all sorts of ways, in the cuisine of Provence. It is the indispensable companion of spring lamb in the Alpilles, and is immortalized in *aïoli,* the garlic sauce that, according to the poet Frédéric Mistral, heats up the body and bathes the soul in rapture.

Here, in the Bouches-du-Rhône more than in other places happiness is built on very little. On basil, for example, which responds perfectly to olive oil, appearing in a *soupe au pistou* or teaming up with a couple of red mullet happened on from the catch of the day. Or on the sea urchins, so memorably sketched by Raoul Dufy, which are the true fruits of the Mediterranean, to be eaten raw with a drop of lemon juice. *Panisses,* poor man's pancakes made from chick-pea flour, speak of Greek and Roman civilizations. These same chick-peas are preferred eating for traditionalists on Palm Sunday, as a way of remembering the great famines of the fifteenth century. Then there is *pieds et paquets,* a dish of sheep tripe that is part of the culinary heritage of Marseilles, as are *navettes,* elongated boat-shaped cookies for Candlemas, traditionally made from November through Easter.

It may appear as if Marseilles is dictating the rules for a whole *département.* But the Bouches-du-Rhône does not live under the thumb of the city. Marcel Pagnol's Provence also passes through Aubagne, the land of the *santons* (clay figures for the Christmas crib) and the rock-anchored village of Cassis, with its coves, and its white wine pressed from terrace-grown vines. Mistral wrote that "it sparkles like some limpid diamond and tastes of the rosemary, the mist and the myrtle that envelop our hills." Here, too, they have their *bouillabaisse,* or rather, around La Ciotat, their *choupin,* a chunk of bread that fishermen at sea in days of old dipped into a fish bouillon, a sort of ragout seasoned with a few onions and a bit of vinegar.

The Provence of Aix has a totally different style from

that of Marseilles. Here the tone was set in the sixteenth century by middle-class traders, men of influence and magistrates who invested in land and established country houses and mansions that were all front, the better to maintain the secrecy of their affairs. Aix-en-Provence is a city of water; in evoking its fountains the poet Jean Cocteau said of it: "A blind man would think it is raining, but were he able to see into his cane as in a mirror, he would behold the blue fountains singing the glory of Cézanne." It is a city of art and architecture, with its Archbishop's Palace, its grand town houses, its squares and parks with their air of melancholy.

The great impressionist painter Paul Cézanne spent his youth here, walking the paths of the Sainte-Victoire Mountain so dear to the people of Aix, and painting, as did Renoir, the mineral landscape and harsh light of this enchanting mountain. The renowned writer Émile Zola, an unrepentant gourmand, recited poems there as he nibbled *calissons,* the city's famed pastries made from home-grown almonds, preserved melon and fruit syrup, or fished for crayfish.

According to the celebrated nineteenth-century cook Auguste Escoffier, Zola "loved freshly caught sardines seasoned with pepper and salt, sprinkled lightly with olive oil and grilled over vine embers, then arranged on an earthenware plate rubbed with garlic, and coated with a *persillade* made with the local Aix oil. . . . He was also fond of a *blanquette* of milk-fed lamb *à la Provençale* served with saffron noodles, of scrambled eggs with cheese and thinly sliced white Piedmont truffles, of risotto with small birds and black truffles, and of the famous polenta with white truffles that was also dear to the heart of the Emperor Napoleon."

And there are other moods still. There are those of the Camargue, land of many waters, where the stones to build the characteristic farmhouses known as *mas* have come down from the quarries of the Alpilles; where there are ponds and marshes, white horses and black bulls, and an internal sea (the Vaccarès). It is a threatened area with a secret vegetation, a domain of dead wood that tourists seldom attempt to penetrate. For a big celebration in these parts, a bull might be basted with spicy oil and roasted all night on a spit, or perhaps *la gardiano,* a hearty ragoût prepared with shoulder of lamb and potatoes, will be put on to cook.

Here we have the moods of La Crau and its stony spaces, of Salon-de-Provence, where Nostradamus lived and wrote a *Treatise on Preserves and Cosmetic Making,* after the manner of *mères de famille* at the time. It was in Salon where, at the beginning of the century, everyone was something of an olive oil merchant, selling to Parisians and "people from the north" who liked their oil more fresh than fruity (sacrilege!).

The bright sunlight Mistral wrote about is the sun of the Arles and Alpilles region. Its rays are never so pure as in Maillane, the town where Mistral was born, and where he lived in a home named the House of the Lizard. This is the heart of Provence, a place of poetry and the cradle of the Provençal language. Here, as in Fontvieille where the memory of Alphonse Daudet and his famous mill is preserved, in Maussane-les-Alpilles and in the Baux where Van Gogh transformed the olive trees into burning, tortured creatures, the land is harsh, and it is a crazy wind that whistles through the reeds of Vallabrègues bearing legends.

In Arles the wind calms down, and all the world knows that this, the earliest of the Roman colonies, which later became a capital port, a city of sailors, is where the knowing Provence draws on its memories to rediscover its heritage. Here are the Musée Arlaten, repository of regional folklore and costume, the amphitheatre, the cemetery and the walks of the Alyscamps painted by Gauguin. This is a country of golden hues and flame colors that, of course, has its distinguishing culinary features.

The joy of the market garden is present in eggplants (aubergines) *à la boumiano,* the new season's broad (fava) beans, or purslane. We still find the sailors' traditional *fricot,* a stew of beef, onions, oil, anchovies and, of course, garlic simmered together in a clay *toupin.* Garlic is also present in the local Arles sausage. Nothing has been lost, not even the little white vineyard snails that are still enjoyed *à la suçarelle* (noisily sucked out their shells, without the aid of a fork) with onion, tomato, parsley, garlic and anchovies. The goat cheeses, flavored with thyme or bay leaf, are also known by a very Camargue name: *guardians.* And again, these Provençals of the Rhône delta make use of what is at hand in a simple and instinctive cuisine. For fruity wines (especially whites), which express in their own way the joy of being in Provence, they need look no further than the Côteaux des Baux or the Côteaux d'Aix.

The Provençaux are serious about boules, *their sport of choice and will gather in the village square at any opportunity to practice it.*

VEGETABLES AND GRAINS

Fresh red peppers and eggplant are basic to many Provençal summer recipes.

VEGETABLES AND GRAINS

T he several cuisines of Provence and Italy find a philosophical common ground in their treatment of vegetables and grains. Nowhere are these dietary staples treated with greater respect, variety or wit, always with a direct and uncomplicated clarity of flavor and often in similar styles. Not surprisingly, the similarities are most marked in the cooking of Nice, which has been part of France only since 1860. Except for brief occupations by France under Louis XIV and twenty years under the Convention and Napoléon, Nice belonged to the house of Savoy for five centuries and was part of the kingdom of Piedmont and Sardinia. Its history is reflected in its treatment of vegetables and in its affection for pastas, gnocchi, polenta and rice. Only in Nice does a *rizotto* resemble that of Piedmont; elsewhere in Provence, a *rizotto* is a pilaf. Pilaf is dry; *rizotto* is wet.

Many of the preparations in this chapter are equally at home as starters and as garnishes to roasts. In Provence people like to savor single flavors or well-considered combinations of two flavors. Cluttered plates do not exist; a roast takes one garnish. A typical Provençal menu reserves a place apart for a vegetable service, between the first course and the main course. Mixed vegetable stew; any artichoke, eggplant (aubergine), zucchini (courgette) or mushroom preparation; stuffed vegetables; and most gratins are all admirable vegetable entrées. In April a dish of tender broad (fava) beans in *sauce poulette* (white sauce bound with egg yolks and flavored with mushrooms)

Fresh green shallots resemble green onions yet their flavor is more complex and intense.

Previous pages: A terrace in Solliès-Pont. Clockwise from top left: Braised Artichokes (recipe page 189), Provençal Green Beans (recipe page 196), White Beans with Sausage and Salt Pork (recipe page 183).

The produce stand is often the first stop of the day dictating the direction of an entire menu.

Zucchini blossoms, a summer delicacy, add a splash of sunshine to the vibrant displays of vegetables.

with a pinch of finely chopped spring shoots of savory is exquisite savored alone. In May little peas braised with lettuce and onions are *de rigueur*.

Vegetables never take a back seat. Even as a garnish to a roast, the signature depends on the way the vegetables are treated. Roast beef is no different in Provence than in any other part of the world until it is escorted by an eggplant gratin, Provençal baked tomatoes or garlicky potatoes. Then, it is Provençal roast beef.

At the height of summer, the morning street markets, a riot of vegetable colors undulating in a dapple of light filtered through the shade of plane trees, bring to mind the reflected light of Provence on Renoir's blue and purple eggplant, red and yellow peppers, and tomatoes stroked with green at their stem ends. They spark memories and anticipation of cool wine and relaxed summer lunches shared with friends on vine-covered terraces, of well-being and ritual communion.

ALPES-MARITIMES

ARTICHAUTS FARCIS

Stuffed Artichokes

These stuffed artichokes will be best appreciated as a separate course.

4 large, young artichokes, trimmed (see glossary)
2 oz (60 g) raw ham such as prosciutto, chopped
persillade made with 1 clove garlic (see glossary)
2 oz (60 g) semidry bread, crusts removed, soaked briefly in water to cover, squeezed dry and chopped
1 egg
¼ cup (1 oz/30 g) freshly grated Parmesan cheese
salt and freshly ground pepper
4 tablespoons (2 fl oz/60 ml) olive oil
1 onion, chopped
2 tomatoes, peeled, seeded and chopped coarsely
1 bay leaf
1 fresh thyme sprig
½ cup (4 fl oz/125 ml) dry white wine

▩ Preheat an oven to 350°F (180°C).

▩ Fill a large saucepan with water and bring to a boil. Add the trimmed artichokes and boil for 7–8 minutes; drain well.

▩ Using a teaspoon, carefully pry free and pull out the tender leaves from the hearts of the artichokes; reserve. Pry out and discard the chokes. Chop the leaves and add them to a bowl with the ham, *persillade,* bread, egg, cheese and salt and pepper to taste. Mix well and stuff the artichokes, mounding the stuffing and molding the surface with an overturned tablespoon. Set aside.

▩ In a flameproof earthenware casserole or other shallow flameproof vessel of a size to hold the artichokes snugly, warm 2 tablespoons of the olive oil over low heat. Add the onion and cook gently until softened, about 10 minutes.

▩ Spread the tomatoes over the onions and sprinkle with salt to taste. Place the artichokes on top, tuck in the bay leaf and thyme sprig and dribble the remaining 2 tablespoons of olive oil over the surfaces of the artichokes. Pour the wine around the artichokes, cover and bake until tender, about 45 minutes. Remove the cover after 30 minutes to permit the surfaces to color and the pan juices to reduce.

SERVES 4

PROVENCE

FÈVES À LA MÉNAGÈRE

Broad Beans in Poulette Sauce

In Provence broad beans are at their best in April, when winter savory is also sending forth its tender new shoots. The two are always allied.

2 tablespoons olive oil
1 onion, finely chopped
4 lb (2 kg) young, tender, thumbnail-sized broad beans (favas), shelled and each bean peeled
salt
1 fresh winter savory sprig
3 tablespoons water, boiling
3 egg yolks
2 tablespoons cold water
freshly ground pepper

Stuffed Artichokes

Left to right: Broad Bean Purée, Broad Beans in Poulette Sauce

 Warm the olive oil in a flameproof earthenware casserole or other heavy pot over low heat. Add the onion and cook gently until softened, about 10 minutes. Add the beans, savory and salt to taste; cover and cook, shaking the pan regularly, 4–5 minutes. Add the boiling water, cover and shake regularly for a few minutes longer until the beans are heated through.

 Combine the egg yolks and cold water in a small bowl and grind over some pepper. Whisk with a fork, then, using a wooden spoon, stir the mixture into the broad beans. Rotate the pan to swirl the contents gently and serve.

SERVES 4

PURÉE DE FÈVES

Broad Bean Purée

For a purée, broad beans should be somewhat larger than those prepared in a poulette sauce (see recipe on page 168). They must be quite firm and beginning to turn starchy, but still a bright, clear green color when skinned. Reject any that are beginning to turn yellow. Especially good as an accompaniment to roast lamb or pork.

4 lb (2 kg) large, tender broad (fava) beans, shelled and each bean peeled
1 large onion, coarsely chopped
2 or 3 fresh winter savory sprigs, tied together
salt and freshly ground pepper
½ cup (4 oz/125 g) unsalted butter, diced

 Fill a saucepan with salted water and bring to a boil. Add the beans, onion and savory and cook at a gentle boil until the beans are tender enough to purée, 10–15 minutes.

 Drain, reserving the cooking liquid; discard the savory and, using a wooden pestle, pass the beans and onion through a fine-mesh sieve back into the pan. Add a little cooking liquid when necessary to ease the passage. If the finished purée seems stiff, loosen it by stirring in more cooking liquid. Taste for salt and grind over a little pepper.

 Reheat over medium heat, stirring and beating constantly with a wooden spoon, until heated through. Remove from the heat, beat in the butter, and serve immediately.

SERVES 4

Left to right: Lentils in Red Wine, Lentil Purée with Celery

PROVENCE

LENTILLES À LA PROVENÇALE
Lentils in Red Wine

If available, use the small greenish brown–speckled lentils called lentilles du Puy *or* lentilles vertes.

1½ cups (10 oz/300 g) lentils
1 tablespoon olive oil
5 oz (150 g) lean salt pork (green bacon), cut into ½-in (12-mm) dice
1 onion, thinly sliced
bouquet garni (see glossary)
2 cloves garlic
2 cups (16 fl oz/500 ml) broth or water
½ cup (4 fl oz/125 ml) dry red wine
½ cup (4 fl oz/125 ml) tomato sauce (see glossary)
salt and freshly ground pepper

❂ Place the lentils in a bowl and add water to cover. Let stand for several hours.
❂ Warm the olive oil in a large flameproof earthenware casserole or heavy pot over medium-low heat. Add the salt pork and cook until its fat begins to melt. Add the onion and cook, stirring occasionally, until softened and lightly colored, 8–10 minutes. Add the bouquet garni and garlic and pour in the broth or water, wine and tomato sauce. Bring to a boil, cover and reduce the heat to a simmer.
❂ Drain the lentils and put them into a saucepan. Cover generously with cold water and bring to a boil. Drain and empty them into the pan holding the wine mixture. Cover and simmer until the lentils are tender, 45–60 minutes, depending upon the quality and age of the lentils. Add a little boiling water if the lentils begin to dry out.
❂ Taste for salt and grind over some pepper before serving.

SERVES 4

PROVENCE

PURÉE DE LENTILLES AU CÉLERI
Lentil Purée with Celery

Especially good as an accompaniment to guinea fowl or to small, furred or feathered game. If possible, use lentilles du Puy *or* lentilles vertes.

1½ cups (10 oz/300 g) lentils
bouquet garni (see glossary)
1 onion stuck with 2 whole cloves
1 carrot, peeled and cut in half
boiling water as needed
salt
¼ cup (2 oz/60 g) unsalted butter, diced
1 heart of celery, crisped in ice water and cut into small dice

❂ Place the lentils in a bowl and add water to cover. Let stand for several hours.
❂ Drain the lentils and put them into a saucepan. Cover generously with cold water and bring to a full boil. Drain and return them to the saucepan. Add the bouquet garni, onion and carrot. Pour in boiling water to cover by about 1 in (2.5 cm), cover and simmer until lentils are purée-tender, about 1 hour. Add salt to taste after 30 minutes.
❂ Drain, reserving the cooking water.
❂ Pass the lentils through a fine-mesh sieve, pressing them with a wooden pestle and adding a little of the cooking water from time to time to help them pass.
❂ Reheat over medium heat, stirring constantly with a wooden spoon. Remove from the heat and stir in the butter and celery. Taste for salt and serve at once.

SERVES 4

OIGNONS FARCIS

Stuffed Onions

*As these stuffed onion sheaths cook, the enclosing seam melts
and your guests may wonder how it was possible to stuff a
seemingly whole, elongated onion without opening it up.
A lovely separate course.*

4 very large, sweet white onions, about 2 lb (1 kg) total
 weight, split in half lengthwise

FOR THE STUFFING:

chopped hearts of the parboiled onions
1 lb (500 g) spinach, parboiled, squeezed dry and chopped
 (see glossary)
½ lb (250 g) *brousse* (see glossary) or ricotta cheese
½ cup (2 oz/60 g) freshly grated Parmesan cheese
2 oz (60 g) raw ham such as prosciutto, chopped
pinch of finely chopped fresh marjoram
2 eggs
whole nutmeg
salt and freshly ground pepper

2 cups tomato sauce, heated (see glossary)
handful of freshly grated Parmesan cheese

❖ Bring a large pot filled with water to a boil and drop in the
onions. Cook at a light boil for 20 minutes. Drain the onions
and refresh in a basin of cold water.

❖ Drain the onions again and carefully pull them apart, layer
after layer. Lay the layers out on towels. Chop the centers,
whose sheaths are too small for stuffing, and place them in a
mixing bowl. Add all the remaining stuffing ingredients,
including a scrape of nutmeg and salt and pepper to taste.
Using your hands mix thoroughly.

❖ Preheat an oven to 350°F (180°C). Pour enough of the hot
tomato sauce into the bottom of a large gratin dish to form a
thin layer. Place a heaping tablespoonful of stuffing on each
of the onion layers, roll up and place them, seam sides down,
in the gratin dish. They should be arranged side by side and
touching but not packed too tightly. Pour over the remaining
hot tomato sauce; the stuffed onions should be not quite
immersed. Cover the dish loosely with aluminum foil, place
in the oven and bake for 30 minutes.

❖ Remove the foil, sprinkle with cheese and bake until the
onion rolls are tender and the sauce is bubbling, 15–20 minutes longer. Serve at once.

SERVES 4

Preheat an oven to 375°F (190°F). Salt the drained tomato halves again and grind over some pepper. Heat 3 tablespoons of the olive oil in a large frying pan over high heat. Add the tomato halves, cut side down, and fry until the liquid they give off evaporates and the pan contains a slightly caramelized residue. Reduce the heat, turn the tomatoes over and cook gently on the skin sides for a few minutes, shaking the pan to keep them from sticking.

Arrange the tomato halves, cut sides up, in a gratin dish just large enough to accommodate them. Return the frying pan to high heat; throw in the *persillade* and stir it around for a few seconds. Remove from the heat and add a large pinch of bread crumbs—enough to absorb the oil and juices from the pan. With a teaspoon, evenly distribute the *persillade*-crumb mixture among the tomato halves, gently forcing it into the seed pockets. Sprinkle crumbs over the surfaces and dribble evenly with the remaining 1 tablespoon olive oil.

Place in the oven and bake until the tomatoes have shrunken a little and the tops are browned, 10–15 minutes. The tomatoes will be fragile, so serve with a spatula.

SERVES 4

CHAMPIGNONS À LA BÉRIGOULE
Mushrooms Durand

In his seminal work on Provençal cookery, Charles Durand proposed this recipe for oronges *(Caesar's mushrooms,* Amanita caesarea*), which, in fact, are never better than when anointed with olive oil, seasoned with salt and pepper and grilled. The following preparation is best adapted to cultivated mushrooms.*

1 lb (500 g) large, firm, unopened fresh cultivated
    mushrooms, stem ends trimmed
2 cloves garlic
pinch of coarse salt
3 tablespoons olive oil
½ cup (4 fl oz/125 ml) dry white wine
salt
freshly ground pepper
2 tablespoons chopped fresh flat-leaf (Italian) parsley
2 salt anchovies, rinsed, filleted and chopped (see glossary)
dried bread crumbs

Gently force the stem of each mushroom, from one side, then from another, until it breaks off at the point where it joins the cap. Chop the stems.

In a mortar pound together the garlic and coarse salt to form a paste. Rub a little garlic paste inside each mushroom cap where the stem was broken off. Put the caps and chopped stems in a saucepan. Add 2 tablespoons of the olive oil, the wine and a pinch of salt. Bring to a boil over high heat, cover and simmer for 15 minutes, turning the mushroom caps over a couple of times.

Meanwhile, preheat an oven to 450°F (230°C). Transfer the mushroom caps to a gratin dish just large enough to accommodate them, hollow sides up and lightly touching. Grind over some pepper. Add the parsley and anchovies to the chopped stems and the juices in the saucepan and cook, uncovered, at a gentle boil until very little liquid remains. Spoon the mixture into the mushroom caps, sprinkle with the dried bread crumbs and dribble a few drops of the remaining olive oil over each cap.

Place in the oven until the crumbs have browned and the mushrooms are piping hot, about 10 minutes. Serve at once.

SERVES 4

In Bonnieux, Vaucluse, from left to right: Stuffed Onions, Provençal Tomatoes, Mushrooms Durand

TOMATES À LA PROVENÇALE
Provençal Tomatoes

Throughout Provence this is a beloved dish. In summer it appears at many tables daily, served separately or as a garnish to roast and grilled meats or poultry. There are slight variations: sometimes the bread is fresh, soaked, squeezed and chopped; sometimes the persillade *is not fried. This is the* Toulonnaise *version.*

8 firm, garden-ripe tomatoes
salt and freshly ground pepper
4 tablespoons olive oil
persillade made with 4 cloves garlic (see glossary)
semidried bread crumbs

Cut the tomatoes in half horizontally, to expose cross sections of the seed pockets. With your little finger, loosen the seeds in each pocket and give the tomato half an abrupt upside-down shake to empty it without damaging the flesh. Sprinkle the cut surfaces with salt and place the halves, cut surface down, on a wire rack for 30 minutes to drain.

173

ALPES·MARITIMES

GNOCCHI AUX POMMES DE TERRE

Potato Gnocchi

Potato gnocchi are often served with the braising juices from a daube or estouffade (recipe on page 139) or with tomato sauce (see glossary). They are also delicious served with pistou (recipe on page 36).

2 lb (1 kg) baking potatoes, peeled and cut into pieces
salt
whole nutmeg
1 egg
2 cups (8 oz/250 g) all-purpose (plain) flour
¼ cup (2 oz/60 g) unsalted butter, melted and kept warm
¾ cup (3 oz/100 g) freshly grated Parmesan cheese

◙ Fill a saucepan with salted water and add the potatoes. Bring to a boil and boil just until tender, about 20 minutes. Drain well and pass through a sieve, food mill or ricer into a mixing bowl.
◙ Season the potatoes with salt to taste and scrape over some nutmeg. Add the egg and work in the flour, progressively, to make a firm but still supple, workable dough. Using your knuckles, knead the dough in the mixing bowl until smooth, then transfer it to a floured work surface. Flour your hands well and, using your palms, roll out orange-sized sections of the dough into logs about ½ in (12 mm) thick. Cut the logs into 1-in (2.5-cm) lengths. Press the center of each piece with a floured thumb or forefinger, to form a hollow. Alternatively, place each piece on a fork, press and give the dough a quarter roll, leaving one side indented and the other decoratively striated by the tines of the fork.
◙ Bring a large saucepan filled with water to a boil. Working in batches to prevent the gnocchi from sticking together, drop a batch into the boiling water. As soon as the gnocchi rise to the surface, after about 3 minutes, remove them with a large, flat, perforated skimming spoon. Let drain for a few seconds

Potato Gnocchi

and then put them into a warmed deep serving dish. Repeat with the remaining gnocchi.
◙ When all the gnocchi are cooked, pour over the melted butter, sprinkle over the cheese and serve.

SERVES 6

VAUCLUSE

TIAN À LA COMTADINE

Potato Gratin with Garlic

When this gratin accompanies a leg of lamb, the leg is placed directly on top of the potatoes to roast.

2 lb (1 kg) potatoes, peeled, thinly sliced and wiped dry
¼ cup (2 fl oz/60 ml) olive oil
12 cloves garlic
salt
1 bay leaf
boiling water as needed

◙ Preheat an oven to 350°F (180°C). In a mixing bowl toss together the potato slices and olive oil until all the slices are evenly coated. Spread half the slices in the bottom of a large, shallow 6-cup (48-fl oz/1.5-l) gratin dish, preferably earthenware. Distribute the garlic cloves evenly amongst the potatoes and sprinkle with salt. Add the bay leaf then top with the remaining potato slices. Pour over boiling water almost to cover, sprinkle with salt to taste and dribble over any oil remaining in the bowl.
◙ Place in the oven and bake until all the water is absorbed, 50–60 minutes. If the surface is well colored before then, cover loosely with aluminum foil to protect it from darkening further. Serve at once.

SERVES 4

VAR

BOULANGÈRE À L'OSEILLE

Potato Gratin with Sorrel

The acidity of the sorrel and the sweetness of the onions do wonderful things to potatoes. A perfect accompaniment to any roast.

2 tablespoons unsalted butter
5 oz (150 g) young sorrel leaves, stemmed, tightly rolled up and thinly sliced
salt
¾ cup (6 fl oz/175 ml) heavy whipping (double) cream
2 lb (1 kg) large potatoes, peeled and sliced lengthwise as thinly as possible, preferably with a mandoline
½ lb (250 g) sweet white onions, thinly sliced

◙ Preheat an oven to 350°F (180°C). Butter a 8-cup (64-fl oz/2-l) gratin dish.
◙ Melt 1 tablespoon of the butter in a sauté pan over low heat. Add the sorrel, sprinkle with salt to taste and cook for a few minutes, stirring with a wooden spoon, until the sorrel turns gray and begins to dissolve. Add the cream and simmer for a few minutes. Remove from the heat.
◙ Combine the potatoes (unrinsed and undried) and onions in a saucepan. Season to taste with salt and pour over enough water almost to cover. Bring to a boil, shaking the pan and displacing the potatoes with a wooden spoon to prevent them from sticking to the bottom. Pour into the gratin dish and smooth the surface. Spread the creamed sorrel evenly on top.
◙ Place in the oven and bake until the potatoes are tender, about 1 hour. Serve immediately.

SERVES 4

Left to right: Potato Gratin with Garlic, Potato Gratin with Sorrel

POMMES DE TERRE SAUTÉES À LA PROVENÇALE

Provençal Sautéed Potatoes

These potatoes are delicious cooked in their skins, but the French never consider the possibility of eating potato skins, and peel them carefully at table before eating them.

3 tablespoons olive oil
1½ lb (750 g) small new potatoes
12 cloves garlic, unpeeled
salt
freshly ground pepper
1 tablespoon chopped fresh flat-leaf (Italian) parsley

◉ Warm the olive oil in a flameproof earthenware casserole or heavy sauté pan over low heat. Add the potatoes and garlic cloves and season to taste with salt. Cover and cook until the potatoes are tender, about 40 minutes. Shake the pan from time to time to turn the potatoes over. When removing the lid to check their progress, do not tilt it, and be sure to wipe it dry before putting it back in place.
◉ Just before serving, grind over some pepper, sprinkle with the parsley and toss the contents of the pan well.

SERVES 4

MOUSSELINE AU GRATIN

Gratin of Mashed Potatoes and Garlic with Cheese

A perfect accompaniment to grilled sausages of any kind—andouillettes, blood sausages (black pudding), link sausages.

2 lb (1 kg) potatoes, peeled and quartered
8 cloves garlic
salt
boiling water as needed
4 tablespoons (2 fl oz/60 ml) olive oil
½ cup (2 oz/60 g) freshly grated Parmesan cheese
3 eggs
freshly ground pepper
whole nutmeg

◉ Preheat an oven to 400°F (200°C). Combine the potatoes and garlic in a saucepan. Add a pinch of salt and enough boiling water just to cover. Cover and cook at a gentle boil until the potatoes are just done, about 30 minutes.
◉ Drain, saving the cooking water, and pass the potatoes and garlic through a fine-mesh sieve with the help of a wooden pestle. Using a wooden spoon, stir in enough of the cooking water to form a loose, not quite pourable purée.
◉ Smear a 6-cup (48-fl oz/1.5-l) gratin dish with olive oil. In a small bowl combine 2 tablespoons of the olive oil, half of the cheese, the eggs and a little of the cooking water. Grind over some pepper, scrape in some nutmeg and whisk together. Stir the oil mixture into the sieved potatoes. Pour into the gratin dish, sprinkle with the remaining cheese and dribble with the remaining 2 tablespoons olive oil.
◉ Place in the oven and bake until swelled and golden, 15–20 minutes. Serve hot.

SERVES 4–6   *Photograph pages 8–9*

PIMENTS DOUX AU GRATIN
Gratin of Sweet Peppers

Serve either as a course apart or as an accompaniment to a roast; especially good with lamb. The anchovies and olives provide good salty counterpoints to the sweetness of the peppers in this colorful dish.

2 large red sweet peppers (capsicums) and 2 large yellow
    sweet peppers

Left to right: Gratin of Sweet Peppers, Provençal Sautéed Potatoes

6 salt anchovies, rinsed, filleted and chopped (see glossary)
⅔ cup (3 oz/100 g) black olives, pitted and halved
persillade made with 1 clove garlic (see glossary)
salt and freshly ground pepper
4 tablespoons (2 fl oz/60 ml) olive oil
semidried bread crumbs

▣ Grill, peel and seed the sweet peppers as directed for sweet pepper salad (recipe on page 32). Cut them lengthwise into narrow strips; collect and reserve the juices that result from the grilling.

▣ Preheat an oven to 350°F (180°C). In a gratin dish mix together the peppers and their juices, anchovies, olives, *persillade,* salt and pepper to taste and 2 tablespoons of the olive oil. Spread evenly over the bottom of the dish. Sprinkle with enough bread crumbs to cover the ingredients so they are no longer visible. Dribble the remaining 2 tablespoons olive oil over the top.
▣ Place in the oven and bake until the top is browned, about 30 minutes. Serve immediately.

SERVES 4

PETITS POIS À LA MÉNAGÈRE

Peas Braised with Onions and Lettuce

The peas should be tender enough to be eaten raw with pleasure.
Serve as a separate course.

1 small head leafy lettuce
1 fresh thyme sprig
bouquet of fresh flat-leaf (Italian) parsley sprigs
¼ lb (125 g) walnut-sized green (spring) onions,
    tops discarded
2 tablespoons water
4 lb (2 kg) small, young peas, shelled
¼ cup (2 oz/60 g) unsalted butter, chilled and diced
salt
pinch of sugar

▦ Remove the outer leaves from the head of lettuce. Wash, but do not dry, both the leaves and the heart. Enclose the thyme and parsley bouquet in the heart and tie as for a bouquet garni (see glossary). Place it in a small, flameproof earthenware casserole or heavy sauté pan. Scatter the onions around and add the water. Mix together the peas and butter and add to the pan. Sprinkle with salt to taste and the sugar and press the lettuce leaves over the surface.
▦ Cover the pan and sweat over very low heat until the peas are very tender, about 45 minutes. Remove the lettuce leaves and heart before serving.

SERVES 4

TIAN DE COURGETTES

Zucchini and Rice Gratin

Serve as a separate course, accompanied by tomato sauce, or
with a roast.

4 tablespoons (2 fl oz/60 ml) olive oil
1 large onion, finely chopped
1 lb (500 g) zucchini (courgettes), thinly sliced
salt and freshly ground pepper
2 cups (16 fl oz/500 ml) milk
1 cup (2 oz/60 g) fresh bread crumbs
3 eggs
large pinch of fresh marjoram flower buds and leaves,
    finely chopped
¾ cup (3 oz/100 g) freshly grated Parmesan cheese
½ cup (3 oz/90 g) long-grain white rice

▦ Preheat an oven to 350°F (180°C). Smear a 6-cup (48-fl oz/1.5-l) gratin dish with olive oil.
▦ Warm 2 tablespoons of the olive oil in a frying pan over low heat. Add the onion and cook gently until softened but not colored, about 10 minutes. Add the zucchini and salt and pepper to taste and sauté for a couple of minutes. Remove from the heat.
▦ In a mixing bowl, pour 1 cup (8 fl oz/250 ml) of the milk over the bread crumbs. Add the remaining 2 tablespoons olive oil, the eggs, marjoram, about two thirds of the cheese and salt and pepper to taste. Beat or whisk until smooth. Stir in the onion-zucchini mixture and the rice and pour into the gratin dish. Smooth the surface and pour the remaining 1 cup (8 fl oz/250 ml) milk evenly over the top.
▦ Sprinkle with the remaining cheese and place in the oven. Bake until golden, about 1 hour. Serve hot.

SERVES 4

POMMES DE TERRE AU GRATIN

Potato Gratin

2 lb (1 kg) potatoes, peeled and cut into slices ⅛ in (3 mm) thick
boiling broth or water as needed
salt, if needed

Clockwise from top: Peas Braised with Onions and Lettuce, Potato Gratin, Zucchini and Rice Gratin

½ cup (2 oz/60 g) freshly grated Gruyère or Parmesan cheese, or a mixture
½ cup (4 fl oz/125 ml) heavy whipping (double) cream
2 eggs
whole nutmeg

▨ Preheat an oven to 350°F (180°C). Put the potatoes in a saucepan and pour in just enough boiling broth or water to cover. Season with salt, if using water, cover and simmer until the potatoes are nearly done, about 15 minutes. Remove from the heat.

▨ Combine half of the cheese, the cream and eggs in a bowl. Scrape in a bit of the nutmeg and whisk together until well blended. Pour the mixture into the potatoes, swirl the contents of saucepan, and then pour into a gratin dish. Smooth the surface and sprinkle over the remaining cheese.
▨ Place in the oven and bake until the surface is golden and the potatoes are set in a light custard, about 20 minutes. Serve immediately.

SERVES 4

TRUFFES AU CHÂTEAUNEUF-DU-PAPE

Truffles in Red Wine

Fresh black truffles are in season in Provence during the months of December, January and February. They are best after the first of the year. In the truffle markets they are sold with soil adhering and must be brushed and washed before being used. Exported truffles are brushed and ready for use.

mirepoix (see glossary)
2 cups (16 fl oz/500 ml) dry red wine
8 tablespoons (4 oz/120 g) unsalted butter
1 tablespoon all-purpose (plain) flour
2 cups (16 fl oz/500 ml) broth, preferably *pot-au-feu* broth
½ lb (250 g) black truffles, brushed
salt and freshly ground pepper
1 tablespoon Cognac
8 slices baguette
1 garlic clove

◈ Combine the *mirepoix* and red wine in a saucepan and bring to a boil. Simmer, uncovered, until reduced to ¾ cup (6 fl oz/175 ml), about 45 minutes.
◈ Meanwhile, melt 1 tablespoon of the butter in a saucepan over medium-high heat. Stir in the flour until well blended, then slowly whisk in the broth and continue to whisk until a boil is reached. Reduce the heat and simmer gently for 30 minutes.
◈ Pour the red wine reduction through a fine-mesh sieve into the broth, pressing with the back of a spoon to extract all the liquid. Move the saucepan partially off the heat and adjust the heat to maintain a gentle boil on one side of the surface. Wait for 15 minutes, then remove the skin and fat from the still side by pulling it off with a spoon. Keep warm.
◈ Meanwhile, preheat an oven to 375°F (190°C). Butter a flameproof earthenware casserole or heavy sauté pan with 1 tablespoon of the butter.
◈ Peel the truffles and place the peels in a mortar. Pound to a purée; set aside. Cut the truffles into wedges and add them to the casserole. Salt lightly and grind over pepper generously. Sprinkle with Cognac, cover and place over the lowest possible heat for about 15 minutes—long enough to sweat only, not cook.
◈ Melt the remaining butter and brush it on both sides of the bread slices. Place them on a baking sheet, put them into the oven, and toast, turning once, until golden and crisp on the surfaces, just a few minutes. Stroke each slice once or twice on each side with the garlic clove. Stir the pounded truffle peels into the hot sauce, then pour the sauce over the truffles.
◈ To serve, place the bread slices on individual heated serving plates and spoon the truffles and sauce over the top.

SERVES 4

Truffles in Red Wine

Braised Belgian Endives

ENDIVES BRAISÉES

Braised Belgian Endives

Serve as a separate course or to accompany roasted or grilled veal or pork.

1½ lb (750 g) heads Belgian endive (chicory/witloof), bases trimmed and blemished leaves removed
salt
1 oz (30 g) raw ham such as prosciutto, cut into matchsticks
1 tablespoon unsalted butter, cut into small pieces
juice of ½ lemon
6 tablespoons (3 fl oz/90 ml) heavy whipping (double) cream

◉ Butter a flameproof earthenware casserole or heavy sauté pan of a size to just hold the endives. Arrange them in the casserole in a single layer. Sprinkle with salt to taste and scatter over the ham. Place the butter fragments on top of the endives. Cover tightly and place over very low heat to sweat, checking from time to time and turning them over, until very tender and colored on all sides, 50–60 minutes.

◉ Add the lemon juice and turn the endives around to coat them evenly. Pour the cream over the endives, rotate the pan to swirl the contents gently and serve.

SERVES 4

FENOUIL À LA NIÇOISE

Braised Fennel

The garlic is transformed, within its skin, into an irresistible purée, delicious spread on bread, on the fennel or on a slice of meat. Serve braised fennel on its own or as an accompaniment to any roast or grilled meat or fowl.

2 lb (1 kg) fennel bulbs
¼ cup (2 fl oz/60 ml) olive oil
1 head garlic, cloves separated and loose husk removed
   but unpeeled
salt
½ cup (4 fl oz/125 ml) dry white wine

◙ Remove and discard the outer blemished stalks from the fennel bulbs. Trim off the tubular stems, reserving the leaves, and split the bulbs in half lengthwise.

the fennel halves back onto their flat sides, cover and braise gently over very low heat for about 1 hour, adding a few drops of the remaining wine from time to time to keep the fennel from drying out. When finished, the fennel should be meltingly tender and the juices a rich brown color and slightly syrupy.

◉ Chop the reserved fennel leaves and sprinkle over the braised bulbs just before serving.

SERVES 4

Braised Fennel

◉ In a large, heavy sauté pan, warm the olive oil over medium-low heat. Place the fennel halves in the pan, cut sides down, and fill all the interstices with the garlic cloves. Sprinkle with salt to taste, cover and cook until the cut sides are a light golden brown. Turn the fennel halves, salt again, cover and lightly brown the other sides in the same way. It will take about 30 minutes to color the fennel.

◉ Uncover and pour about half of the wine over the fennel. Shake the pan gently until the liquid comes to a boil, turn

---

VAUCLUSE / BOUCHES · DU · RHÔNE

HARICOTS BLANCS À LA VILLAGEOISE

White Beans with Sausage and Salt Pork

When fresh white shell beans (cocos; see glossary) are available, substitute them for the dried large Great Northerns. Shell 4 pounds (2 kg) cocos and boil them, with the same aromatic elements, for about 20 minutes before joining them to the bacon and sausage. Save leftover cooking water for soup or broth. The sausage should be the best large, fresh pork sausage you can find that is suitable for poaching. The sausage meat described in the glossary could be stuffed into a fresh, natural casing and used for this dish.

2½ cups (1 lb/500 g) dried Great Northern beans
bouquet garni (see glossary)
1 onion stuck with 2 whole cloves
1 carrot, peeled and cut in half
3 cloves garlic, unpeeled
boiling water as needed
salt
1 slice lean salt pork (green bacon), about ¾ in (2 cm) thick
2 tablespoons olive oil
1 onion, chopped
1 fresh poaching sausage, about 10 oz (300 g), pricked on all sides with a sharp skewer or trussing needle

◉ Place the beans in a bowl; add water to cover and let stand for several hours or overnight. Drain the beans and place in a saucepan. Cover abundantly with cold water, bring to a boil and boil for 10 minutes. Drain, return the beans to the saucepan and add the bouquet garni, whole onion, carrot and garlic. Pour in boiling water to cover by a good inch (2.5 cm), cover and simmer for 45 minutes. Salt the water to taste and continue to simmer until the beans are not quite done, another 15 minutes or so, depending upon their quality and age.

◉ Meanwhile, place the salt pork in a saucepan, add water to cover and bring to a boil. Drain immediately and rinse in cold water. Set the pork aside.

◉ Warm the olive oil in a flameproof earthenware casserole or other heavy pot over low heat. Add the chopped onion and cook until softened, about 10 minutes. Place the salt pork and the sausage on top. Drain the beans, saving the liquid; discard the whole onion. Empty the beans over the meats. Add enough of the cooking liquid to cover barely, cover and simmer until tender, about 40 minutes, adding more liquid if necessary to keep the beans from drying out. When the beans are ready, they should have absorbed nearly all of the liquid.

◉ Discard the bouquet garni and carrot. Remove the meats; cut the salt pork into wedges and slice the sausage. Scatter the wedges and the slices over the beans and serve from the pan.

SERVES 4   *Photograph pages 164–165*

GRATIN DE CHOUFLEUR
Cauliflower Gratin

This is a Niçois gratin. Elsewhere in Provence, a cauliflower gratin often consists of parboiled florets covered with béchamel *sauce, sprinkled with cheese and baked until bubbling. The* béchamel *sauce can be enriched by whisking in a couple of egg yolks and a handful of grated cheese before pouring it over the cauliflower.*

1 unblemished white cauliflower, broken into florets and
    large florets split in half lengthwise
¼ cup (2 fl oz/60 ml) olive oil
salt and freshly ground pepper
whole nutmeg
½ cup (2 oz/60 g) freshly grated Parmesan cheese
handful of semidried bread crumbs

◻ Preheat an oven to 400°F (200°C). Fill a large saucepan with salted water and bring to a boil. Plunge the florets into the boiling water and cook until barely tender (when a knife tip still meets with slight resistance at the stem end of a floret), about 5 minutes. Drain well and toss the florets in a bowl with the olive oil.
◻ Spoon the florets into a gratin dish, arranging them snugly. Sprinkle lightly with salt, grind over some pepper, and scrape over a bit of nutmeg. Sprinkle with the Parmesan and then with the bread crumbs. Dribble over any olive oil remaining in the bowl.
◻ Place in the oven and bake until the surface is nicely colored, about 10 minutes. Serve hot.

SERVES 4

CAPOUNS NIÇOIS
Stuffed Cabbage Leaves

Swiss chard (silverbeet) leaves are often treated in the same way. Serve as a separate vegetable course or as a simple supper main course.

1 large savoy cabbage
FOR THE STUFFING:
1 large onion, finely chopped and cooked in 2 tablespoons
    olive oil until soft but not colored
½ cup (3½ oz/100 g) long-grain white rice, parboiled for
    15 minutes and drained
persillade made with 2 cloves garlic (see glossary)
5 oz (150 g) sausage meat (see glossary)
1 thick slice from shank end of raw ham such as prosciutto,
    chopped
½ cup (2 oz/60 g) freshly grated Parmesan cheese
pinch of Provençal mixed dried herbs (see glossary)
2 eggs
salt and freshly ground pepper
whole nutmeg

mirepoix (see glossary)
½ cup (4 fl oz/125 ml) tomato sauce (see glossary)
½ cup (4 fl oz/125 ml) dry white wine
broth as needed

◻ Discard any blemished outer leaves of the cabbage. Cut out a large cone at the base of the cabbage to remove the core and free the leaves. Carefully separate at least 8 perfect leaves, one by one, and trim the rib of each, slicing off excess thickness. Layer the leaves in a large saucepan, slowly pour over boiling water to cover, bring to a boil and, after a few seconds, carefully slip the contents of the saucepan into a large colander. Refresh the leaves under cold running water and lay them out, side by side, on cotton towels to drain.
◻ Split the heart of the cabbage lengthwise and cut out any remaining core; shred the halves coarsely and chop the shreds. Fill a saucepan with salted water and bring to a boil. Add the chopped cabbage and parboil for 5 minutes. Drain, refresh under cold running water and squeeze thoroughly dry. Place in a mixing bowl and add all the remaining stuffing ingredients, including salt and pepper to taste and a scrape of nutmeg. Using your hands mix thoroughly. Set aside.
◻ Preheat an oven to 325°F (165°C). Prepare the *mirepoix* in a large flameproof earthenware casserole or other heavy pot. Set aside off the heat.
◻ Place a handful of stuffing near the stem end on the inside surface of a cabbage leaf. Roll up the leaf a third of the way, fold the sides inward over the top and finish rolling. Place the package, seam side down, on the bed of *mirepoix*. Repeat with the remaining leaves and stuffing, arranging the packages snugly in the pan. Pour over the tomato sauce, the wine and enough broth to immerse the packages.
◻ Bring to a boil over medium heat, then cover and place in the oven. Bake until the cabbage packages are translucent, slightly wrinkled and are coated with the reduced sauce, about 1½ hours. Serve hot.

SERVES 4

AUBERGINES EN ÉVENTAIL
Eggplant Fans

Zucchini (courgettes) can be prepared in the same way, except that a dash of dry white wine should be added just after the seasonings and the cooking time should be shortened by 20 minutes. Both are as good as they are beautiful and provide perfect separate vegetable courses.

5 tablespoons (3 fl oz/80 ml) olive oil
2 large sweet white onions, cut in half lengthwise and
    thinly sliced
4 cloves firm, crisp garlic, sliced paper-thin
4 small, elongated eggplants (aubergines), about 5 oz
    (155 g) each
about 1½ lb (750 g) firm, garden-ripe tomatoes
small branches of fresh thyme and winter savory or a
    pinch of Provençal mixed dried herbs (see glossary)
3 bay leaves
pinch of coriander seeds
salt and freshly ground pepper

◻ Preheat an oven to 450°F (230°C). Smear a very large gratin dish (or use 2 dishes) with olive oil.
◻ Mix together the onions and garlic and spread half of the mixture in the bottom of the dish. Cut off the stem end and a sliver from the flower end of each eggplant. Cut each eggplant in half lengthwise symmetrically. Place the halves, cut side down, on a work surface. Beginning about ⅔ in (1.5 cm) from the stem end, cut each eggplant half lengthwise into slices ⅓ in (1 cm) thick. The uncut stem end will hold the slices together, creating intact fans.
◻ Slice the tomatoes in half lengthwise. Cut out the core at the stem end and place each half, cut side down, on a work surface. Cut into lengthwise slices ⅓ in (1 cm) thick. Slip 3 tomato slices in a row between each pair of eggplant slices and, each time an eggplant half is fully garnished, transfer it to the gratin dish using a wide spatula and holding the fan firmly together with your hand. Arrange the fans, packing gently, so that a minimum of space is lost. Scatter over the remaining onion-garlic mixture and tuck in the herbs here and there. Sprinkle over the coriander seeds and salt to taste

Clockwise from top: Eggplant Fans, Cauliflower Gratin, Stuffed Cabbage Leaves

and grind over some pepper. Dribble the olive oil evenly over all the fans. Cover with heavy-duty aluminum foil, pressing it firmly around the dish rim to keep it in place.

▨ Place in the oven and reduce the heat to 350°F (180°C). Cook until the eggplant is tender when pierced, about 1 hour.

Turn off the oven and leave the dish in the oven for 30 minutes before serving. If the oven is needed, remove the covered dish and place in a warm spot.

SERVES 4

CHICORÉE FRISÉE BRAISÉE

Braised Frisée

This preparation is specifically intended to accompany roast lamb. It is also good with roast veal or pork. Frisée is similar to chicory (curly endive) which can be used here as a substitute.

4 heads frisée, blemished leaves discarded and cored
handful of coarse salt
boiling water as needed
2 tablespoons olive oil
pinch of Provençal mixed dried herbs (see glossary)
persillade made with 1 clove garlic (see glossary)
1 tablespoon all-purpose (plain) flour
½ cup (4 fl oz/125 ml) broth, or as needed
deglazed roasting juices and carving juices

◼ Pack the frisée into a large saucepan, add the salt, and pour over boiling water to cover. Bring to a boil and boil for a couple of minutes. Drain, refresh under cold running water, squeeze as dry as possible and chop.
◼ Warm the olive oil in a heavy saucepan over medium heat. Add the frisée and cook, stirring with a wooden spoon, for a few minutes. Sprinkle with the herbs and *persillade* and cook a few minutes longer. Sprinkle with the flour and stir for 1 minute. Slowly stir in the ½ cup (4 fl oz/125 ml) broth. Reduce the heat to very low, cover and cook, stirring occasionally, about 1¼ hours. If the frisée begins to dry out, add a little boiling broth or water.
◼ Just before serving, stir in the roasting and carving juices.

SERVES 6

Spinach and Egg Gratin

ROUSSIN D'ÉPINARDS

Spinach and Egg Gratin

Serve this as a separate vegetable course or as a family supper main course.

4 tablespoons (3 fl oz/80 ml) olive oil
1 onion, finely chopped
2 lb (1 kg) spinach, parboiled, squeezed dry and chopped (see glossary)
salt
persillade made with 1 clove garlic (see glossary)
1 tablespoon all-purpose (plain) flour
2 cups (16 fl oz/500 ml) milk
freshly ground pepper
whole nutmeg
4 hard-cooked eggs, shelled and halved lengthwise
semidried bread crumbs

◼ Preheat an oven to 375°F (190°C).
◼ Warm 2 tablespoons of the olive oil in a sauté pan over low heat. Add the onion and cook until softened and lightly colored, about 10 minutes. Add the spinach and continue to cook, stirring regularly with a wooden spoon, until it exudes no more moisture and begins to stick to the pan, about 5–10 minutes. Season to taste with salt, add the *persillade* and sprinkle with the flour. Stir until the flour is no longer visible. Over the next 30 minutes, add the milk, a little at a time, stirring regularly.
◼ Smear a 6-cup (48-fl oz/1.5-l) gratin dish with olive oil. Grind some pepper and scrape some nutmeg over the spinach. Stir together and pour the mixture into the gratin dish. Push the half eggs into the spinach so that the cut surfaces are at the same level as the spinach mixture. Sprinkle the entire surface with bread crumbs and dribble over the remaining 2 tablespoons olive oil in a thread, forming a crisscross pattern.
◼ Place in the oven and bake until the surface is golden, about 30 minutes. Serve at once.

SERVES 4

TIAN D'ÉPINARDS À LA COMTADINE

Spinach Gratin

This rustic preparation, delicious with roast pork, is sometimes sprinkled with flour in place of the bread crumbs.

1½ lb (750 g) young, tender spinach leaves, stemmed and chopped
salt and freshly ground pepper
large handful of semidried bread crumbs
3 tablespoons (2 fl oz/60 ml) olive oil

◼ Preheat an oven to 450°F (230°C). Smear a large gratin dish with olive oil.
◼ In a mixing bowl, toss the spinach with salt and pepper to taste. Pack the spinach into the gratin dish, pressing it down firmly. Sprinkle a thick layer of bread crumbs over the spinach and then dribble on the olive oil in a thread, forming a crisscross pattern.
◼ Put the dish in the oven, turn the heat down to 325°F (165°C) and bake until the volume has reduced by more than half and the surface is browned, about 1 hour. Serve at once.

SERVES 4

Left to right: Braised Frisée, Spinach Gratin

TOMATES FARCIES
À L'ANTIBOISE

Antibes-Style Stuffed Tomatoes

Serve as a separate vegetable course.

8 firm, garden-ripe tomatoes
salt
4 tablespoons (2 fl oz/60 ml) olive oil
1 onion, finely chopped
pinch of coarse salt
freshly ground pepper

▦ Slice off the top quarter of each tomato. Scrape the flesh free from the skins of the top slices. With your little finger, loosen the seeds in the seed pockets and give the tomatoes an abrupt upside-down shake to empty them. Using a small, sharp-pointed knife, cut the walls of the seed pockets loose from the outside tomato walls and scoop out the centers of the tomatoes. Chop them, along with any flesh scraped from the top slices. Sprinkle the inside of the tomato shells with salt and turn upside down on a wire rack for 30 minutes to drain.

▦ Meanwhile, preheat an oven to 350°F (180°C). Smear a 6-cup (48-fl oz/1.5-l) gratin dish with olive oil.

▦ Warm 2 tablespoons of the olive oil in a small pan over low heat. Add the onion and cook until softened, about 10 minutes. Raise the heat to high, add the chopped tomato flesh and sauté briefly until it begins to fall apart. Remove from the heat.

▦ In a large mortar pound together the coarse salt, pepper, anchovies and basil to form a paste. Stir in 1 tablespoon of the remaining olive oil to loosen the mixture, then add the fresh bread crumbs. Mix well with the pestle and stir in the onion-tomato mixture and eggs.

▦ Stuff the tomato shells with the tomato-crumb mixture, mounding and molding the surfaces with an overturned spoon. Arrange the tomatoes in the gratin dish just large enough to accommodate them. Sprinkle with dried bread crumbs and dribble over the remaining 1 tablespoon olive oil.

▦ Place in the oven and bake until the tomatoes are tender and the tops are browned, about 30 minutes. Serve hot.

SERVES 4

Antibes-Style Stuffed Tomatoes

2 cloves garlic
2 salt anchovies, rinsed and filleted (see glossary)
small handful of fresh basil leaves
1 cup (2 oz/60 g) fresh bread crumbs
2 hard-cooked eggs, shelled and chopped
dried bread crumbs

P R O V E N C E

ARTICHAUTS À LA BARIGOULE

Braised Artichokes

Whether or not, as some people believe, artichauts à la barigoule *were originally simply grilled artichokes, today they are always braised, sometimes stuffed with a mushroom* duxelles, *the classic sauté of finely chopped mushrooms, onion and parsley with a hint of lemon juice. These artichokes are wonderful as a course on their own.*

mirepoix (see glossary)
bouquet garni (see glossary)
12 egg-sized artichokes, trimmed and left whole, or 6 medium-sized artichokes, trimmed, quartered and chokes removed if necessary (see glossary)
salt
¼ cup (2 fl oz/60 ml) olive oil
½ cup (4 fl oz/125 ml) dry white wine

▦ Prepare the *mirepoix* in a large flameproof earthenware casserole or nonreactive heavy sauté pan. Place the bouquet garni in the center and the artichokes all around, bottoms down if they are whole. Sprinkle with salt to taste, dribble the olive oil evenly all over the artichokes, and pour in the white wine.

▦ Cover and cook the artichokes very gently, turning them around and over two or three times and basting them, until they are tender and most of the liquid has evaporated, about 45 minutes. When serving, spoon the *mirepoix* and pan juices over the artichokes.

SERVES 4 *Photograph pages 164–165*

RAGOÛT D'ARTICHAUTS AUX PETITS POIS

Stew of Artichokes and Peas

In Nice this dish is known as petits pois à la niçoise. *Elsewhere in Provence it is called either* petits pois à la provençale *or the name given here. Similar preparations also exist in Italian cuisine.*

3 tablespoons olive oil
3 oz (100 g) salt pork (salt bacon), cut into ¼-in (6-mm) dice
12 egg-sized artichokes, trimmed and left whole, or 6 medium-sized artichokes, trimmed, quartered and chokes removed if necessary (see glossary)
½ lb (250 g) walnut-sized green (spring) onions, tops discarded
1 heart leafy lettuce enclosing a bouquet of fresh flat-leaf (Italian) parsley sprigs and 1 fresh thyme sprig, tied as for a bouquet garni (see glossary)
salt
4 lb (2 kg) small, young peas, shelled
¼ cup (2 fl oz/60 ml) water

▣ Warm the olive oil in a flameproof earthenware casserole or heavy sauté pan over medium-low heat. Add the salt pork, artichokes and onions, cover and cook, shaking the pan from time to time, until the contents are softened and just beginning to color, about 10 minutes.
▣ Add the lettuce bouquet, salt to taste, peas and water. Cover tightly and simmer over very low heat, shaking the pan occasionally, until the vegetables are tender, about 40 minutes. Serve immediately.

SERVES 4

TIAN DE COURGETTES AUX HERBES

Zucchini and Greens Gratin

There are countless variations on mixed-greens gratins in combination with other vegetables. Your imagination is the limit. They all escort roasts admirably and all can easily stand alone.

2 lb (1 kg) zucchini (courgettes)
salt
4 tablespoons (2 fl oz/60 ml) olive oil
3 oz (100 g) lean salt pork (salt bacon), cut into ¼-in (6-mm) dice
1 large sweet white onion, finely chopped
1 lb (500 g) Swiss chard (silverbeet) greens, parboiled, squeezed dry and chopped (see glossary)
large handful of sorrel leaves, stemmed, tightly rolled up and thinly sliced
persillade made with 3 cloves garlic (see glossary)
½ cup (2 oz/60 g) Parmesan cheese, grated
salt and freshly ground pepper
3 eggs

▣ Cut the zucchini into sections and shred them through a vegetable shredder fitted with the medium blade or in a food processor fitted with the shredding disk. Layer the zucchini on a plate, sprinkling salt between the layers, and let stand for 30 minutes. Squeeze dry and place in a mixing bowl.

▣ Meanwhile, preheat an oven to 350°F (175°C). Smear the bottom and sides of a 8-cup (64-fl oz/2-l) gratin dish with olive oil.
▣ In a small frying pan, warm 1 tablespoon of olive oil over very low heat. Add the salt pork and cook until lightly colored, about 10 minutes. Add the onion and cook, stirring with a wooden spoon, until soft and golden, about 15 minutes. Empty the salt pork and onion into the bowl holding the zucchini. Add the chard, sorrel, *persillade* and half of the Parmesan. Season to taste with salt and pepper and add the eggs. Using your hands mix thoroughly.
▣ Pack the mixture into the gratin dish. Smooth the surface and sprinkle the remaining cheese evenly over the top. Dribble on the remaining 3 tablespoons olive oil in a thread, forming a crisscross pattern. Place in the oven and bake until set and golden, about 40 minutes. Serve immediately.

SERVES 4

CHARLOTTE DE TOMATES

Gratin of Tomatoes and Potatoes

This rustic gratin is a perfect accompaniment to roast pork. A handful of pitted black olives can be scattered over the layer of potatoes.

1 lb (500 g) potatoes
4 tablespoons (2 fl oz/60 ml) olive oil
1 lb (500 g) onions, chopped
1 lb (500 g) firm, garden-ripe tomatoes, sliced
large pinch of fresh thyme leaves
1 teaspoon chopped fresh tarragon
salt and freshly ground pepper
whole nutmeg
dried bread crumbs

▣ Preheat an oven to 375°F (190°C).
▣ Fill a saucepan with salted water and bring to a boil. Add the unpeeled potatoes and boil until half-cooked, 15–20 minutes. Drain and, with your hand cradling the potato protected by a folded cotton towel, peel and then slice while still hot.
▣ Meanwhile, warm 2 tablespoons of the olive oil in a heavy pan over low heat. Add the onions, cover and cook, stirring occasionally with a wooden spoon, until soft, about 30 minutes.
▣ Smear the bottom and sides of a 6-cup (48-fl oz/1.5-l) gratin dish with olive oil. Line the gratin dish with half of the tomatoes. Sprinkle with a few thyme leaves, a pinch of tarragon, and salt and pepper to taste. Spread one third of the onions over the top. Layer the hot sliced potatoes on top, sprinkle with more thyme, tarragon, salt, and pepper and then scrape over a little nutmeg. Spread half of the remaining onions over the potatoes. Top with the remaining tomatoes, season with salt and pepper, and layer the remaining onions over them. Finally, sprinkle evenly with bread crumbs and dribble on the remaining 2 tablespoons olive oil in a thread, forming a crisscross pattern.
▣ Place in the oven and bake until golden and crisp, about 45 minutes. Serve hot.

SERVES 4

Top to bottom: Stew of Artichokes and Peas, Zucchini and Greens Gratin, Gratin of Tomatoes and Potatoes

Summer Rice

RIZOTTO D'ÉTÉ

Summer Rice

Parboiled little peas or rapidly sautéed sliced baby artichokes are also lovely added to this rizotto at the last minute. Round-grained Arborio rice from Piedmont is necessary for the success of this dish. Serve it as a separate course or, for a simple meal, as the main course.

mirepoix (see glossary)
2 cups (10 oz/300 g) Arborio rice
salt, if needed
about 5 cups (40 fl oz/1.2 l) broth or water, boiling
¼ lb (125 g) young, tender green beans, trimmed
¼ cup (2 oz/60 g) unsalted butter, chilled and diced
½ cup (2 oz/60 g) freshly grated Parmesan cheese

◉ Prepare the *mirepoix* in a heavy saucepan. Add the rice and stir with a wooden spoon over low heat until all the grains are coated with oil and opaque. Season with salt if you will be adding water.

◉ Over medium-low heat, add a ladleful of the boiling liquid and stir constantly until the rice is nearly dry. Continue adding the liquid in this manner, a ladleful at a time, until the rice is tender, 20–25 minutes.

◉ Meanwhile, gather the green beans together and slice crosswise into ¼-in (6-mm) lengths. Fill a saucepan with water and bring to a boil. Add the green beans, boil for 1 minute until barely tender and drain.

◉ Stir the green beans into the rice. The rice should be almost liquid but not quite pourable. It is usually necessary to add a little more liquid before removing it from the heat to achieve the correct consistency.

◉ Off the heat, stir in the butter and the cheese. Spoon onto hot plates to serve.

SERVES 4

POLENTE À LA NIÇOISE

Polenta Baked with Tomato Sauce

A memory of Nice's attachment to the kingdom of Piedmont. Serve as a first course, in place of a vegetable course, or as a main course.

4 cups (32 fl oz/1 l) water
salt
1½ cups (8 oz/250 g) coarse cornmeal
boiling water if needed
3 cups (24 fl oz/750 ml) tomato sauce, heated (see glossary)
¾ cup (3 oz/100 g) freshly grated Parmesan cheese

◉ In a saucepan bring the water to a boil and add salt to taste. Holding the cornmeal well above the saucepan, sprinkle it into the water in a slow stream while stirring constantly with a wooden spoon. Lower the heat to maintain a gentle boil and stir constantly until the cornmeal is thick and pulls away form the sides of the pan, at least 30 minutes. Add small amounts of boiling water if the cornmeal becomes too thick to stir before that time (if you have helpers, keep stirring for another 20 minutes).

◉ Lightly oil a marble slab or a large tray with olive oil and turn the polenta out onto it. Using a spatula moistened in cold water, quickly spread it out to a thickness of ½ in (12 mm) or less. Let cool completely, then cut into approximately 2-in (5-cm) squares.

◉ Preheat an oven to 350°F (180°C). Pour a little hot tomato sauce into the bottom of a 8-cup (64-fl oz/2-l) gratin dish to form a thin layer. Place half of the polenta squares on top of the sauce, slightly overlapping them. Cover with half of the remaining tomato sauce and sprinkle with half of the Parmesan cheese. Arrange the remaining polenta squares on top, pour on the remaining sauce and sprinkle with the remaining cheese.

◉ Place in the oven and bake until the sauce is bubbling and the cheese is lightly colored, about 30 minutes. Serve immediately.

SERVES 4–6

Polenta Baked with Tomato Sauce

PILAF DE RIZ
Rice Pilaf

In most of Provence this is called rizotto. *It is a perfect accompaniment to brochettes of mixed meats; grilled, peeled and seeded peppers; and most dishes in sauce, simple ragouts and* blanquettes *in particular. Depending upon the dish it escorts, it can often be enhanced by the addition of a pinch of saffron at the same time that the salt is added.*

2 teaspoons olive oil
1 onion, finely chopped, or, preferably, a handful of young
   green shallots, sliced
2 cups (10 oz/300 g) long-grain white rice
salt
4 cups (32 fl oz/1 l) broth or water, boiling
2 tablespoons unsalted butter, chilled and diced

❂ Warm the olive oil in a flameproof earthenware casserole or a heavy saucepan over low heat. Add the onion or shallots, cover, and sweat until softened, about 10 minutes. Add the rice and salt to taste and stir constantly until the rice is opaque. Add the boiling liquid, stir once, cover tightly and cook over very low heat until the grains are tender, about 20 minutes.
❂ Remove from the heat. Add the butter and toss the rice with 1 or 2 forks to incorporate the butter gently and to loosen the grains without damaging them. Serve immediately.

SERVES 4

POMMES PAYSANNE
Provençal Potato Casserole

Serve this as a supper main course.

5 oz (150 g) lean salt pork (green bacon), cut into lardoons
   (see glossary)
2 tablespoons olive oil
5 oz (150 g) small pickling onions
1 clove garlic, crushed
bouquet garni (see glossary)
2 tomatoes, peeled, seeded and coarsely chopped
1½ lb (750 g) small new potatoes, peeled, or larger potatoes,
   peeled and quartered
about 2 cups (16 fl oz/500 ml) broth or water, boiling
salt, if needed
1 tablespoon chopped fresh flat-leaf (Italian) parsley

❂ Preheat an oven to 350°F (180°C).
❂ Place the salt pork in a saucepan, add water to cover and bring to a boil. Drain and rinse in cold water. Pat dry with paper towels.
❂ Warm the olive oil in a flameproof casserole or Dutch oven over medium-low heat. Add the salt pork and when it begins to color lightly, add the onions. Shake the pan often until the onions are lightly colored, about 10 minutes. Add the garlic, bouquet garni and tomatoes and increase the heat. Stir until the tomatoes begin to break up, about 10 minutes.
❂ Add the potatoes, just enough boiling broth or water to cover them and salt if using water. Bring back to a boil, cover and place in the oven. Bake until the potatoes are tender, about 30 minutes.
❂ Remove from the oven, sprinkle with parsley and serve.

SERVES 4

Left to right: Rice Pilaf, Provençal Potato Casserole

TIAN DE COURGE

Squash Gratin

Serve as a separate vegetable course or to accompany veal, pork or rabbit, grilled or roasted.

4 tablespoons (2 fl oz/60 ml) olive oil
½ lb (250 g) leeks, including the tender green parts,
    thinly sliced
1½ lb (750 g) winter squash such as Hubbard or pumpkin,
    peeled and diced
salt
2 tablespoons water
½ cup (4 fl oz/125 ml) heavy whipping (double) cream
2 eggs
½ cup (2 oz/60 g) freshly grated Parmesan cheese
freshly ground pepper
whole nutmeg
semidried bread crumbs

◉ Heat 2 tablespoons of the olive oil in a flameproof earthenware casserole or heavy sauté pan over low heat. Add the leeks and cook gently until beginning to dissolve, 10–15 minutes. Add the squash, salt and water and cook, stirring often with a wooden spoon, until the squash has reduced almost to a purée, about 30 minutes. Remove from the heat.
◉ Meanwhile, preheat an oven to 375°F (190°C). Smear a 6-cup (48-fl oz/1.5-l) gratin dish with olive oil.
◉ In a small bowl, whisk together well the cream, eggs, half of the Parmesan cheese, pepper to taste and some scraped nutmeg. Stir the egg mixture into the squash, then empty the contents of the pan into the gratin dish. Sprinkle the surface evenly with the remaining cheese and then with a thin layer of bread crumbs. Dribble the remaining 2 tablespoons olive oil over the surface in a thread, forming a crisscross pattern.
◉ Place in the oven and bake until golden, about 30 minutes. Serve hot.

SERVES 4

HARICOTS VERTS À LA PROVENCALE

Provençal Green Beans

Small, tender green beans, 3–4 inches (7.5–10 cm) long, are best for sautéing. Larger beans should be snapped in two and parboiled before being sautéed. In place of the bread crumbs, add a couple of peeled, seeded and chopped tomatoes and sauté them until their liquid evaporates.

¼ cup (2 fl oz/60 ml) olive oil
4 cloves garlic, unpeeled, crushed
1 lb (500 g) small, tender green beans, trimmed
salt and freshly ground pepper
handful of semidried bread crumbs, prepared without crusts

◉ Warm the olive oil in a large frying pan over medium-high heat. Add the garlic cloves and, when they begin to sizzle and color, add the beans. Cook, tossing repeatedly, for 4–5 minutes. Season to taste with salt and grind over some pepper. Add the crumbs and toss or stir with a wooden spoon only until the crumbs are crisp and begin to color.
◉ Serve directly from the pan onto heated plates.

SERVES 4   *Photograph pages 164–165*

Squash Gratin

CHAMPIGNONS AU GRIL
Grilled Marinated Mushrooms

Saffron milk caps (Lactarius deliciosus), *called champignons des pins, safranés or lactaires délicieuses, flood the markets of Provence in late autumn. Healthy specimens about 2 inches (5 cm) in diameter are wonderful treated in this way. The stems must be removed to permit the mushrooms to lie flat on the grill; they can be reserved for other preparations. Cultivated mushrooms may be grilled in the same way.*

2 cloves garlic
pinch of coarse salt
freshly ground pepper
pinch of Provençal mixed dried herbs (see glossary)
1 tablespoon chopped fresh flat-leaf (Italian) parsley
2 tablespoons olive oil
juice of ½ lemon
1 lb (500 g) large, firm, unopened fresh mushrooms
   (see recipe introduction), stemmed

◈ In a mortar pound together the garlic, salt, pepper and dried herbs to form a paste. Stir in the parsley, olive oil and lemon juice and transfer to a large mixing bowl. Add the mushroom caps and mix with your hands, turning the mushroom caps around in the marinade until they are well coated on all sides. Leave to marinate for 30 minutes, turning them or tossing a couple of times.
◈ Meanwhile, prepare a fire in a charcoal grill. When the fire is ready, arrange the mushrooms on the grill rack over hot coals and grill, turning once, until nicely colored and visibly shrunken from their original size, 7–8 minutes on each side. Serve immediately.

SERVES 4

CHAMPIGNONS SAUTÉES À LA PROVENÇALE
Provençal Sautéed Mushrooms

Although this recipe is written for fresh cultivated mushrooms, chanterelles are a delicious alternative.

3 tablespoons olive oil
¾ lb (375 g) small fresh cultivated mushrooms, stem
   ends trimmed
salt and freshly ground pepper
persillade made with 1 clove garlic (see glossary)
1 lemon

◈ Warm the olive oil in a large frying pan over high heat. Add the mushrooms and sauté, tossing repeatedly in the air or stirring with a wooden spoon, for 3 or 4 minutes. Season to taste with salt and pepper and add the *persillade*. Continue to sauté for 1 minute or so, or until the scent of frying *persillade* fills the air.
◈ Squeeze over a few drops of lemon and serve.

SERVES 4

Provençal Sautéed Mushrooms

Grilled Marinated Mushrooms

AUBERGINES AU GRIL

Grilled Eggplant

*Even simpler than this preparation and equally delicious are
whole small eggplants (one per poerson) grilled over coals until
purée-tender and served with salt, pepper and olive oil at table.*

4 elongated eggplants (aubergines), about 2 lb (1 kg)
   total weight
salt
freshly ground pepper
olive oil

◉ Cut off the stem ends and split the eggplants in half
lengthwise. Using a small, sharp-pointed knife, cut a crisscross pattern in the flesh, taking care not to cut all the way
through to the skin. Salt the cut surfaces and leave for
30 minutes.

◉ Meanwhile, prepare a fire in a charcoal grill. When the
fire is ready, sponge the eggplant halves dry with paper
towels. Grind pepper over the cut surfaces and then sprinkle
with olive oil. Place cut side down on the grill rack over hot
coals and grill until marked with golden brown lines from
the grill. Turn skin side down and grill until the flesh is very
tender when tested near the stem end, about 15 minutes,
total cooking time.

SERVES 4

⊞ In a large frying pan with sharply slanted sides and rounded bottom edges, warm the olive oil over high heat. Add the zucchini and salt and pepper to taste and sauté for 3–4 minutes, shaking the pan constantly and tossing the zucchini into the air regularly (stir with a wooden spoon if you fear tossing, but the result is not the same).

⊞ Add the *persillade,* continue to toss for 1 minute and serve.

SERVES 4

PROVENCE

GRATIN DE NAVETS

Turnip Gratin

As an accompaniment to roast duck or pork, this gratin is especially good mingled with the roasting juices.

2 lb (1 kg) young, crisp turnips, peeled and cut into slices
    ¼ inch (6 mm) thick
3 tablespoons unsalted butter
thin slices semidry bread
salt and freshly ground pepper
½ cup (2 oz/60 g) freshly grated Parmesan cheese

⊞ Bring a saucepan filled with salted water to a boil. Add the turnip slices and boil until tender, 15–20 minutes.

⊞ Meanwhile, preheat an oven to 325°F (165°C). Butter a deep 6-cup (48-fl oz/1.5-l) gratin dish with 1 tablespoon of the butter and line it with bread slices.

⊞ Drain the turnip slices and spread a layer of them over the bread slices. Salt lightly, grind over some pepper and sprinkle with some of the Parmesan. Add another layer of bread slices, and then turnip slices, and again season and sprinkle with cheese. Repeat the layers until all ingredients are used, finishing with a layer of turnips seasoned with salt and pepper and sprinkled with Parmesan.

⊞ Cut the remaining 2 tablespoons of butter into small pieces and scatter over the top. Place in the oven and bake until golden and the turnips begin to melt, about 40 minutes. Serve immediately.

SERVES 4   *Photograph pages 8–9*

VAR

ÉTUVÉE DE POMMES DE TERRE AUX OLIVES

Potatoes with White Wine and Olives

Effortless and delicious, with grilled lamb chops, for instance.

1½ lb (750 g) potatoes, peeled and quartered or cut into
    large cubes
3 or 4 shallots, thinly sliced
2 cloves garlic, crushed
salt
3 tablespoons olive oil
½ cup (4 fl oz/125 ml) dry white wine
⅔ cup (3 oz/100 g) black olives, pitted if desired

⊞ Combine all of the ingredients in a flameproof earthenware casserole or heavy sauté pan. Cover and simmer over low heat until the potatoes are tender, about 40 minutes. Serve immediately.

SERVES 4

In a vineyard in Vaucluse, from left to right: Grilled Eggplant, Potatoes with White Wine and Olives, Provençal Sautéed Zucchini

PROVENCE

COURGETTES SAUTÉES À LA PROVENÇALE

Provençal Sautéed Zucchini

Serve this as a garnish to grilled or roasted meats. It is also very good tossed with pasta, grated cheese and butter.

¼ cup (2 fl oz/60 ml) olive oil
1 lb (500 g) zucchini (courgettes), thinly sliced
salt and freshly ground pepper
persillade made with 2 cloves garlic (see glossary)

SPAGHETTI AUX ANCHOIS

Spaghetti with Anchovies

The exhilarating, fresh flavor of this sauce depends on rapid execution. The larger the frying pan in which the tomatoes are sautéed, the more rapid will be the evaporation of their juices. The dish requires only about 10 minutes to prepare.

¾ lb (375 g) spaghetti
5 tablespoons (3 fl oz/80 ml) olive oil
6 salt anchovies, rinsed and filleted (see glossary)
4 cloves garlic
1 lb (500 g) tomatoes, peeled, seeded and coarsely chopped
salt
⅔ cup (3 oz/100 g) black olives, pitted

freshly ground pepper
handful of fresh basil leaves, torn into small fragments at the last minute
freshly grated Parmesan cheese and unsalted butter for serving

◉ Bring a large saucepan filled with salted water to a boil. Following the package directions, add the spaghetti so that it is ready just as the tomatoes are cooked.
◉ Pour 2 tablespoons of the olive oil into a large, flameproof earthenware casserole or heavy sauté pan. Lay out the anchovy fillets, side by side, in the oil and place the pan over the lowest possible heat. The anchovies will melt in the warm oil; they should not fry.
◉ Meanwhile, in a large frying pan, warm the remaining 3 tablespoons olive oil over high heat. Add the garlic cloves and, when they begin to sizzle but before browning, add the tomatoes and salt to taste. Toss the tomatoes until their liquid evaporates, about 5 minutes; the tomatoes should not cook to a purée. Add the olives and empty the frying pan into the pan with the anchovies. Grind over some pepper and stir in the basil.
◉ Drain the spaghetti and add to the anchovy sauce. Toss together with fork and spoon. Serve into heated pasta dishes or soup plates, accompanied with a dish of Parmesan and a dish of butter for diners to add as desired.

SERVES 4

TIAN D'ARTICHAUTS

Artichoke Gratin

Enclosed in a crisp golden sheath, these meltingly tender pale artichoke slices must be eaten as a separate course to be appreciated fully.

6 young, tender artichokes, trimmed, split in half lengthwise, chokes removed if necessary, and finely sliced lengthwise (see glossary)
6 tablespoons (3 fl oz/90 ml) olive oil
2½ cups (5 oz/150 g) fresh bread crumbs
3 oz (100 g) lean salt pork (green bacon), diced
persillade made with 2 cloves garlic (see glossary)
1 bunch tender green (spring) onions, including the tender green parts, finely sliced
salt and freshly ground pepper
2 eggs
½ cup (4 fl oz/125 ml) milk

◉ Preheat an oven to 400°F (200°C).
◉ Dry the sliced artichokes in a cotton towel or between paper towels and toss them in a bowl with 2 tablespoons of the olive oil.
◉ In a large bowl, combine the bread crumbs, salt pork, *persillade,* onions and salt and pepper to taste. In another, smaller bowl beat together the eggs, milk and 2 tablespoons of the olive oil until well blended. Add to the crumb mixture and stir together thoroughly.
◉ Smear the bottom and sides of a 6-cup (48-fl oz/1.5-l) gratin dish with olive oil. Spread half the crumb mixture in the bottom of the dish; spread the sliced artichokes evenly over the surface. Spread the remaining crumb mixture on top, smoothing the surface. Drizzle with the remaining 2 tablespoons olive oil.
◉ Place the dish in the oven and turn the heat down to 325°F (165°C).
◉ Bake until crisp and golden, about 1 hour. Serve hot.

SERVES 4

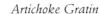

Artichoke Gratin

Spaghetti with Anchovies

COURGETTES AU GRATIN
Zucchini Gratin

Serve as a separate course.

3 tablespoons olive oil
1 onion, finely chopped
2 salt anchovies, rinsed, filleted and chopped (see glossary)
1½ lb (750 g) small, firm zucchini (courgettes), diced
salt and freshly ground pepper
persillade made with 1 clove garlic (see glossary)
⅔ cup (3 oz/100 g) black olives, pitted
3 hard-cooked eggs, shelled and chopped
dried bread crumbs

▦ Preheat an oven to 400°F (200°C). Smear a 6-cup (48-fl oz/1.5-l) gratin dish with olive oil.
▦ Warm 2 tablespoons of the olive oil in a frying pan over low heat. Add the onion and cook until softened, about 10 minutes. Add the anchovies and, as they begin to melt, add the zucchini. Cook over low heat, stirring regularly with a wooden spoon, until the zucchini are quite tender, about 15 minutes.
▦ Salt lightly and grind over pepper generously. Stir in the *persillade,* olives and eggs and spread in the gratin dish. Sprinkle bread crumbs over the top and dribble on the remaining 1 tablespoon olive oil.
▦ Place in the oven and bake until golden, about 20 minutes. Serve immediately.

SERVES 4

PAPETON D'AUBERGINES
Molded Eggplant Pudding

A quaint legend claims that one of the 14th-century Avignon popes, recently arrived from Rome, reproached the local cooks for their lack of finesse. To prove his worth, one Avignon cook created a divine eggplant dish in the form of a pope's tiara, which definitively converted the pope to la cuisine avignonnaise. *Serve as a separate course.*

3 lb (1.5 kg) elongated eggplants (aubergines)
salt
olive oil as needed
5 eggs
1 cup (8 fl oz/250 ml) milk
⅛ teaspoon powdered saffron dissolved in 1 tablespoon
    boiling water
boiling water as needed
3 cups (24 fl oz/750 ml) tomato sauce, heated (see glossary)

▦ Cut off the stem ends from the eggplants. Slice 2 or 3 lengthwise slices ⅓ in (8 mm) thick from the center of each eggplant. Using a sharp-pointed knife tip, crosshatch the leftover sides. Salt the slices and the sides and leave in a colander to drain for 30 minutes. Sponge dry with paper towels.
▦ Preheat an oven to 350°F (180°C). In a large frying pan, pour in olive oil to a depth of ¼ in (6 mm) and place over medium heat. Slip the eggplant slices, a few at a time, into the hot oil and fry, turning once, until golden on both sides, about 10 minutes. Add more oil as needed. Remove to paper towels to drain. Then fry the crosshatched sides in the same manner and drain on paper towels.
▦ Scrape all the flesh from the crosshatched sides into a bowl and mash to a purée with a fork. Add the eggs and a pinch of salt and whisk together. Then whisk in the milk and the

dissolved saffron until thoroughly incorporated. Set aside.
▦ Line a 6-cup (48-fl oz/1.5-l) savarin mold (circular mold with a well) or other round mold with the eggplant slices, overlapping them slightly and pressing firmly into place. The tips should extend beyond the outer rim and the central well. Pour in the custard mixture and fold the extending tips over the surface.
▦ Place the mold in a large oven pan and pour in boiling

Zucchini Gratin

water to reach halfway up the sides, to form a *bain-marie*. Place in the oven and bake until the surface of the custard is no longer liquid, about 40 minutes. Remove from the *bain-marie* and leave to settle for 10 minutes.

◉ To unmold, fold a kitchen towel lengthwise and place the mold on it. Place an overturned platter on top and grip the ridge of the mold, protected by the towel, using your finger-

nails. While holding the platter firmly in place with your thumbs, turn over the mold and platter together. Lift off the mold. Pour a ribbon of tomato sauce around the outside of the *papeton* and pour the remainder into a heated bowl to serve alongside.

SERVES 6

Photograph pages 206–207

AUBERGINES FARCIES À LA PROVENÇALE

Provençal Stuffed Eggplants

Delicious with roast lamb or as a separate course. Often chopped mushrooms are cooked with the onion and, for a supper main course, chopped leftover lamb can be incorporated into the stuffing.

4 elongated eggplants (aubergines), about 1½ lb (750 g)
   total weight
salt
olive oil as needed
1 onion, finely chopped

2 tomatoes, peeled, seeded and coarsely chopped
pinch of coarse salt
1 clove garlic
2 salt anchovies, rinsed and filleted (see glossary)
½ cup (1 oz/30 g) fresh bread crumbs
1 tablespoon chopped fresh flat-leaf (Italian) parsley
small pinch of Provençal mixed dried herbs (see glossary)
freshly ground pepper
1 egg
dried bread crumbs

Cut off the stem ends and split the eggplants in half lengthwise. Using a small, sharp-pointed knife, cut into the flesh all the way around each eggplant half. Cut at a slight bias, about ¼ inch (6 mm) from the edge, and be careful not to approach the skin. Using the knife tip, crosshatch the flesh within the border cut. Sprinkle the surfaces with salt and leave for

In a mortar pound together the coarse salt, garlic and anchovy fillets to form a paste. Add the fresh bread crumbs and mix well, wiping the mortar walls clean. Add the crumb mixture to the bowl, along with the parsley, herbs, pepper to taste and egg. Using your hands mix well. Taste for salt.

Arrange the eggplant shells in a large gratin dish, hollow sides up, and stuff them with the eggplant mixture. Smooth the surfaces with the back of a spoon, sprinkle with dried bread crumbs and dribble with olive oil. Bake until the surfaces are crisp and golden, 20–25 minutes. Serve immediately.

SERVES 4

V A R

Gratin d'Aubergines

Eggplant Custard Gratin

This can only stand alone, as a separate vegetable course;
it is exquisite.

3 elongated eggplants (aubergines), about 1½ lb (750 g) total
    weight, cut lengthwise into slices ½ in (12 mm) thick
salt
olive oil as needed
1 onion, finely chopped
2 cloves garlic, finely chopped
1 lb (500 g) tomatoes, peeled, seeded and coarsely chopped
¼ lb (125 g) *brousse* (see glossary) or ricotta cheese
2 eggs
½ cup (2 oz/60 g) freshly grated Parmesan cheese
½ cup (4 fl oz/125 ml) heavy whipping (double) cream
freshly ground pepper
fresh basil leaves

Sprinkle the eggplant slices on both sides with salt, spread them out on a tray and leave for 30 minutes. Sponge dry with paper towels.

In a large frying pan, pour in olive oil to a depth of ¼ in (6 mm) and place over medium heat. Fry the eggplant slices, in batches, in the hot oil until golden and tender at the stem ends, turning once, about 10 minutes. Add more oil to the pan as needed. Remove and drain on paper towels. Pour off any oil.

Preheat an oven to 450°F (230°C). In the same frying pan, warm 2 tablespoons olive oil over low heat. Add the onion and cook gently until softened, about 10 minutes. Add the garlic, tomatoes and salt to taste and increase the heat to high. Toss until the moisture from the tomatoes evaporates, about 15 minutes. Set aside.

In a mixing bowl break up the *brousse* or ricotta cheese and the eggs with a whisk. Add half of the grated cheese, cream, and salt and pepper to taste and whisk to the consistency of a pourable cream.

Line a 6-cup (48-fl oz/1.5-l) gratin dish with about half of the eggplant slices in a single layer, pressing them in place. Grind over some pepper. Tear basil leaves into fragments and scatter over the eggplant. Sprinkle lightly with half of the remaining grated cheese and then spread over the tomato mixture. Arrange the remaining eggplant slices on top in a single layer, pressing them firmly in place. If there are a few extra slices, press them on top. Pour over the cheese-egg mixture and smooth the top. Sprinkle with the remaining grated cheese.

Place in the oven and immediately reduce the heat to 350°F (180°C). Bake until the custard surface is swelled and golden with no depression in the middle, about 30 minutes. Serve hot.

SERVES 4

Clockwise from top: Provençal Stuffed Eggplants, Eggplant Daube,
Molded Eggplant Pudding, Eggplant Custard Gratin

30 minutes. Sponge dry with paper towels.

Preheat an oven to 375°F (190°C). In a large frying pan, pour in olive oil to a depth of ¼ in (6 mm) and place over medium heat. Slip the eggplant halves into the pan, cut sides down, and fry until lightly colored. Turn skin side down and fry, adjusting heat as necessary, until the flesh is tender enough to be easily scooped out with a teaspoon, about 15 minutes. Remove to paper towels to drain.

Pour off most of the oil from the frying pan. Reheat the oil remaining in the pan over low heat. Add the onion and cook gently until softened, about 10 minutes. Add the tomatoes and increase the heat to high. Toss until the moisture from the tomatoes evaporates, about 10 minutes. Empty the pan into a mixing bowl.

Scoop the flesh from the eggplant halves into the bowl, leaving the ¼-in (6-mm) border of flesh near the skin intact.

PURÉE BLANCHE

White Purée

Nothing accompanies braised lamb, especially stuffed shoulder (recipe on page 130), better than this magical purée. Do not discard the leftover cooking water; it is a wonderful soup base. Add a few allspice berries to the peppercorns in your mill.

1 lb (500 g) small, crisp turnips
½ cup (4 oz/125 g) unsalted butter
1 lb (500 g) celeriac (celery root), peeled and cut into
    large cubes
salt
1 lb (500 g) potatoes, peeled and quartered if large
1 lb (500 g) onions, peeled and quartered
1 head garlic, cloves separated and peeled
freshly ground pepper

◙ Peel the turnips and quarter them if large. Fill a saucepan with water and bring to a boil. Add the turnips and boil until half-cooked, about 15 minutes. Drain well.
◙ In a heavy pan, melt 2 tablespoons of the butter over very low heat. Add the turnips, cover and cook, shaking and tossing occasionally, until tender, 20–30 minutes.
◙ Meanwhile, bring a large saucepan filled with salted water to a boil. Add the celeriac and boil for 15 minutes. Add the potatoes, onions and garlic and cook at a gentle boil until all the vegetables are tender, about 30 minutes. Drain in a colander, saving the cooking water.
◙ Using a wooden pestle, pass the turnips and their cooking butter and the boiled vegetables into a purée. If it is very stiff, add a bit of the reserved cooking liquid.
◙ Reheat the purée in a heavy saucepan over medium heat, stirring and beating constantly with a wooden spoon to prevent sticking. When it is heated through, remove from the stove.
◙ Grind some pepper over the top. Dice the remaining butter into small pieces and stir it into the purée. Serve at once.

SERVES 6

CÔTES DE BLETTE À L'ANCHOIS

Chard Ribs with Anchovy Sauce

To arrive at 1 pound (500 g) of chard ribs, you will need at least 4 pounds (2 kg) chard. After cutting the ribs free from the green leaves, parboil the leaves, refresh them under cold running water and squeeze them dry (see glossary). Enclose the ball of squeezed leaves in plastic wrap and refrigerate it for up to 3 or 4 days. Use it in innumerable Provençal stuffings, soups, omelets or gratins.

FOR THE COURT BOUILLON:

8 cups (64 fl oz/2 l) water
1 large onion, finely sliced
1 bay leaf
1 large fresh thyme sprig
stems from a bouquet of fresh flat-leaf (Italian) parsley
1 small dried cayenne chili pepper or other dried small
    chili pepper
1 tablespoon vinegar
salt

1 lb (500 g) Swiss chard (silverbeet) ribs, strings removed
    and cut into pieces 4 in (10 cm) long by 1 in (2.5 cm) wide
freshly ground pepper

pinch of coarse salt
2 cloves garlic
2 salt anchovies, rinsed and filleted (see glossary)
2 tablespoons olive oil
2 tablespoons all-purpose (plain) flour

◙ Combine all the ingredients for the court bouillon in a large saucepan and bring to a boil. Cover and cook at a gentle boil for 45 minutes.
◙ Strain, return the liquid to the saucepan and add the chard ribs. Boil for 10 minutes, then drain, reserving the liquid. Spread the chard pieces in a gratin dish and grind over the pepper.
◙ Preheat an oven to 400°F (200°C). In a mortar, pound together the coarse salt, garlic cloves and anchovies to form a paste.
◙ Heat the olive oil in a saucepan over medium-high heat. Add the flour and stir for a minute or so. Stir in the anchovy paste and pour in 3 cups (24 fl oz/750 ml) of the reserved court bouillon, whisking at the same time. Continue to whisk until a boil is reached. Lower the heat and cook, uncovered, at a simmer or very gentle boil for 20 minutes. Taste for salt.
◙ Pour the anchovy sauce through a sieve over the chard ribs. Put the dish in the oven and bake until the sauce is bubbling and the surface is lightly colored, about 20 minutes. Serve at once.

SERVES 4

DAUBE D'AUBERGINES

Eggplant Daube

A sketchy version of this recipe was first published by René Jouveau in La cuisine provençale de tradition populaire, *1963. Its similarity to a traditional daube resides mainly in the choice of aromatic elements and, especially, in the presence of the dried orange rind.*

2 tablespoons olive oil
5 oz (150 g) lean salt pork (green bacon), cut into ⅓-in
    (8-mm) dice
2 large, sweet white onions, thinly sliced
5 oz (150 g) carrots, peeled and thickly sliced
1 lb (500 g) tomatoes, peeled, seeded and coarsely chopped
3 cloves garlic, crushed
bouquet garni including a strip of dried orange peel
    (see glossary)
2 lb (1 kg) firm, young eggplants (aubergines), cut into
    ¾-in (2-cm) cubes
½ cup (4 fl oz/125 ml) dry white wine
salt
freshly ground pepper
1 tablespoon chopped fresh flat-leaf (Italian) parsley

◙ Warm the olive oil in a flameproof earthenware casserole or other heavy pot over medium heat. Add the salt pork and fry gently, stirring occasionally with a wooden spoon. As the salt pork begins to color, add the onions and carrots. Cook over low heat until the onions are soft, about 15 minutes.
◙ Add the tomatoes, garlic and bouquet garni. Spread the eggplant cubes on top and pour in the white wine. Sprinkle with salt to taste and raise the heat so that the contents of the pan begins to bubble. Cover, reduce the heat to low and simmer gently until the eggplant is tender, about 1 hour.
◙ Drain off the liquid from the casserole into a small saucepan. Bring the liquid to a boil and reduce over medium-high heat to about ½ cup (4 fl oz/125 ml). Grind pepper over the eggplant and pour the reduced juices over the top. Swirl the contents of the pan to mix lightly, sprinkle with the parsley and serve.

SERVES 4   *Photograph pages 206–207*

Left to right: White Purée, Chard Ribs with Anchovy Sauce

Spring Vegetable Stew

ESTOUFFADE PRINTANIÈRE

Spring Vegetable Stew

*A lovely dish, served either on its own or as an accompaniment
to roast lamb. The broad beans should be freshly picked, about
thumbnail size, clear green when peeled and tender enough to
be eaten raw.*

several leaves tender, leafy lettuce
2 tablespoons olive oil
4 young, tender artichokes, trimmed, quartered and chokes
　　removed if necessary (see glossary)
½ lb (250 g) walnut-sized green (spring) onions,
　　tops discarded
12 cloves garlic, preferably new garlic, unpeeled
bouquet garni (see glossary)
salt
2 tablespoons water
4 lb (2 kg) young, tender broad (fava) beans, shelled and
　　each bean peeled

freshly ground pepper
2 tablespoons unsalted butter, chilled and diced
a few fresh savory leaves, finely chopped and mixed with a
　　pinch of chopped fresh flat-leaf (Italian) parsley

◉ Rinse the lettuce leaves but do not dry. Roll up the leaves
into a tight cylinder and thinly slice crosswise. Set aside.
◉ Warm the olive oil in a flameproof earthenware casserole
or heavy sauté pan over low heat. Add the artichokes,
onions, garlic and bouquet garni. Sprinkle with salt to taste
and spread the lettuce over the top. Cover tightly and cook
over very low heat, shaking the pan occasionally, until the
lettuce is "melting" and the artichokes are tender yet firm,
about 40 minutes.
◉ Add the water and the broad beans, cover and raise the heat
slightly to create steam. Shake to intermingle the contents
of the pan. When the broad beans are heated through, after
5 or 6 minutes, grind over some pepper and remove from
the heat.
◉ Swirl in the butter and sprinkle the savory-parsley mixture
over the top. Serve at once.

SERVES 4

BRANDADE DE HARICOTS
White Bean Brandade

The anchovies here replace poutargue—*salted tuna or mullet roe, pressed and dried—which is more traditional in this dish from Marseilles. Often served as a starter, these simmered white beans are also delicious as an accompaniment to roast lamb or pork.*

2½ cups (1 lb/500 g) dried Great Northern beans
1 cup (8 fl oz/250 ml) olive oil
about ½ cup (4 fl oz/125 ml) milk, heated
freshly ground pepper
6 salt anchovies, rinsed, filleted and chopped (see glossary)
juice of ½ lemon
salt
handful of small croutons, fried in olive oil until crisp
 and golden

◙ Prepare the dried beans as directed for white beans with sausage and salt pork (recipe on page 183) but simmer them with the bouquet garni, whole onion, carrot and garlic until tender enough to be puréed, about 1½ hours.

◙ Drain the hot beans, discard the aromatics and, using a wooden pestle, pass the beans through a fine-mesh sieve back into the saucepan. Place the saucepan over very low heat. Stir and beat the purée with a wooden spoon while adding the olive oil in a trickle (or ask someone else to trickle while you beat). Do not add all of the oil if the consistency of the purée is reasonably supple. Beat in only enough of the milk for the purée to remain very supple without being pourable. Grind over some pepper abundantly, then stir in the anchovies and lemon juice.

◙ Taste and adjust seasonings with salt and pepper. Empty the purée into a heated deep platter and scatter the croutons over the top. Serve immediately.

SERVES 4–6

FEUILLES DE CÉLERIS À LA MÉNAGÈRE
Celery Gratin Durand

Charles Durand, author of the first Provençal cookbook, suggests preparing purslane leaves in the same way as the celery in this recipe.

2 bunches celery
3 tablespoons olive oil
2 salt anchovies, rinsed, filleted and chopped (see glossary)
salt and freshly ground pepper
whole nutmeg
¼ lb (125 g) semidry bread, crusts removed
1½ cups (12 fl oz/375 ml) milk
3 egg yolks
¼ cup (1 oz/30 g) freshly grated Parmesan or Gruyère cheese
1 tablespoon unsalted butter, cut into small pieces

◙ Remove the tough outer stalks from the celery bunches and trim the root ends. Cut the bunches across, just below the leaf-branch joints. Remove the leaves and set aside. (Put the leaf branches and tough outer stalks aside for use in bouquets garnis.) Slice the stalk bunches crosswise into 3 or 4 sections.

◙ Fill a saucepan with salted water and bring to a boil. Add the sliced stalk bunches and the reserved leaves and parboil them for 10 minutes. Drain and, when cool enough to handle,

squeeze tightly in a towel to rid of excess moisture. Chop the leaves and stalks.

◙ Preheat an oven to 400°F (200°C). Heat 2 tablespoons of the olive oil in a sauté pan. Add the chopped celery and anchovies, season lightly with salt, grind over some pepper, and scrape over a bit of nutmeg. Cover and cook over very low heat, stirring occasionally with a wooden spoon, for 10 minutes.

◙ Meanwhile, break the bread into a small saucepan and pour in the milk. Bring to a boil and simmer over medium heat for 10 minutes. Pour the bread mixture into the sauté pan, stir well and simmer, stirring regularly, until the mixture is consistent but still quite loose, just a few minutes. Remove from the heat.

◙ Smear a 6-cup (48-fl oz/1.5-l) gratin dish with olive oil. In a small bowl, combine the egg yolks, the remaining 1 table-spoon olive oil and a couple tablespoons water. Using a fork beat together until blended. Then, using a wooden spoon, stir the egg mixture into the celery mixture. Pour into the gratin dish and smooth the surface. Sprinkle with the cheese and distribute butter fragments evenly over the top.

◙ Place in the oven and bake until the surface is slightly colored, about 10 minutes. Serve at once.

SERVES 4

Left to right: White Bean Brandade, Celery Gratin Durand

pompe à l'huile is transformed when broken and dipped into a glass of authentic, aged *vin cuit*.

Many simple sweet things are traditionally eaten on specific religious holidays. Village saints' days are celebrated with *oreillettes,* sweetened noodle dough rolled out into small ovals, slit, twisted into ear shapes and deep-fried. In Nice, fried ribbons of the same dough are called *ganses* and, in Arles, the ribbons are loosely tied and named *bugnes; ganses* and *bugnes* are both associated with carnival celebrations.

For Twelfth Night, January 6, bakers prepare crowns of sweet brioche, garnished with candied fruits and each enclosing a token, originally a dried broad (fava) bean. Friends gather to share a *gâteau des rois* and the recipient of the token is crowned king. For Candlemas, February 2, nearly everyone in Provence eats crêpes, but in Marseilles, Candlemas is celebrated with little boat-shaped sweet cookies called *navettes.* Sweet fritters are for Mardi Gras and Ash Wednesday, and *brassadeaux,* bracelets of sweetened egg dough, first poached and then baked like bagels, are reserved for Easter.

White cherry blossoms dot the valleys of Provence in the spring yeilding ripe, delicious fruit in the summer.

Because the Provençal meal usually ends with a simple fruit dessert, quality and freshness are essential.

OREILLETTES

Carnival Fritters

Oreillettes, *shaped like ears, are but one name for these fritters, which might also be called* ganses *("ribbons") and* bugnes *("knotted ribbons"). In fact, no matter what the shape, these fritters are called* bugnes *in Arles,* ganses *in Nice and* oreillettes *throughout Provence. They are sometimes simply small rectangles, about 1½ in (4 cm) by 3 in (4 cm), or larger rectangles with slits cut inside the borders.*

about 3 cups (12 oz/375 g) all-purpose (plain) flour
salt
2 tablespoons granulated sugar
2 eggs, beaten
¼ cup (2 oz/60 g) unsalted butter, at room temperature
¼ cup (2 fl oz/60 ml) dark rum
8 cups (64 fl oz/2 l) peanut oil or corn oil
confectioners' (icing) sugar

▨ In a mixing bowl stir together 2 cups (8 oz/250 g) of the flour, the salt and granulated sugar. Make a well in the center and add the eggs, butter and rum. Stir with a fork, working from the center outward to gather in all the flour progressively. Sprinkle over more of the flour as needed to create a supple dough. Knead the dough in the bowl, using your knuckles and sprinkling over a little more of the flour as needed to reduce stickiness. When the dough is smooth, form it into a ball in the bowl, cover the bowl with a towel and leave to rest for 1 hour.

▨ Line a baking sheet with a thin cotton towel and sprinkle with flour. To make "ears" pinch off apricot-sized pieces of dough and roll out into oval shapes ⅛ in (3 mm) thick. Alternatively, divide the dough in half and roll out each portion ⅛ in (3 mm) thick. Using a pastry cutter, cut out ovals about 4½ in (11 cm) long by 3 in (7.5 cm) wide. Cut 2 lengthwise slits within each oval, equidistant from the edges and from each other, to form 3 bands of attached dough. Lift the two outer bands up toward the center. Push one band through the far slit as you pull the other band in the opposite direction. Press the bands slightly to flatten them.

▨ To make knotted ribbons, divide the dough in half and roll out each portion into a long rectangle ⅛ in (3 mm) thick and about 8 in (20 cm) wide. Cut the rectangles into strips ¾ in (2 cm) wide and 8 in (20 cm) long. Loop each strip to form a loose knot in the middle, pulling gently at the ends to fix it.

▨ Following the directions for deep-frying in the glossary, heat the oil in a large pan. Working in small batches, slip the shapes into the hot oil; do not crowd the pan. After 1 minute turn the fritters in the oil. When they are uniformly golden, after about 2 minutes, lift them out with a slotted utensil and place on paper towels to drain briefly.

▨ Transfer to a large platter lined with a napkin. Sprinkle generously with confectioners' sugar. Serve hot.

SERVES 6

TIAN DE LAIT

Provençal Custard

This is the ancestor of all set custards. Serve it hot, tepid or cold, accompanied with little cookies (biscuits).

4 cups (32 fl oz/1 l) milk
1 cup (8 oz/250 g) sugar

4 whole eggs plus 6 egg yolks
¼ cup (2 fl oz/60 ml) dark rum

▨ Preheat an oven to 300°F (150°C).
▨ Pour the milk into a saucepan and warm over medium heat. Stir in the sugar and continue to stir until a boil is

Carnival Fritters

almost reached, then remove from the heat. Leave to cool for a few minutes.

▣ In a mixing bowl whisk together the whole eggs and egg yolks. Slowly add the milk, whisking constantly. Whisk in the rum. Pour into an earthenware oven dish. Place in the oven and bake until the custard is no longer liquid at the center—the timing depends upon the size of the dish and the depth of the custard—30–40 minutes. Test for doneness by touching the center with your fingertip; it should be firm.

SERVES 8   *Photograph pages 224–225*

Clockwise from top left: Provençal Pumpkin Pie; Sabayon with
Muscat de Beaumes-de-Venise (recipes page 226); Swiss Chard,
Apple and Raisin Pie; Provençal Custard (recipe page 222)

TOURTE DE BLETTES

Swiss Chard, Apple and Raisin Pie

The ingredients are surprising, but this sweet Niçois chard pie rarely fails to seduce. The original dough was bread dough, kneaded with sugar and egg. Some cooks add sliced bananas and others jellies or jams. A sweetened spinach tart is traditional in the Vaucluse; if chard is unavailable, substitute spinach.

Ingredient proportions vary for the pastry, which is called pâte sablée *and is the most commonly used pastry in Provence today for sweet tarts and pies. This recipe makes enough dough for one 9- or 10-in (23- or 25-cm) double-crust pie.*

FOR THE CRUMBLY PASTRY:

2 cups (8 oz/250 g) all-purpose (plain) flour
¼ cup (2 oz/60 g) sugar
pinch of salt
½ cup (4 oz/125 g) unsalted butter, at room temperature
2 eggs, beaten with a fork until just amalgamated

pinch of unsalted butter
2 eggs
1 tablespoon olive oil
½ cup (4 oz/125 g) granulated sugar
½ cup (2 oz/60 g) freshly grated Parmesan cheese
⅓ cup (2 oz/60 g) pine nuts
⅓ cup (2 oz/60 g) raisins soaked in ¼ cup (2 fl oz/60 ml) dark rum several hours or overnight
1 lb (500 g) Russet, pippin or Golden Delicious apples, quartered, cored, peeled and sliced or diced at last minute
1 teaspoon grated lemon zest
2 lb (1 kg) Swiss chard (silverbeet) greens, parboiled, squeezed dry and chopped (see glossary)
freshly ground pepper
whole nutmeg
confectioners' (icing) sugar

❋ To prepare the pastry, in a mixing bowl stir together the flour, sugar and salt. Make a well in the center and add the butter and eggs to the well. Stir, mix and mash rapidly with a fork to form a coherent mass. Turn out onto a floured work surface and knead briefly. Form the dough into a ball, enclose it in plastic wrap and refrigerate for 2 hours before rolling it out.

❋ Preheat an oven to 350°F (180°C). Use the butter to grease a 10-in (25-cm) deep pie plate. Divide the pastry dough into 2 portions, one portion slightly larger than the other.

❋ On a lightly floured work surface, roll out the larger dough portion into a round about ⅛ in (3 mm) thick. Drape the pastry around the rolling pin and transfer it to the prepared dish. Press the pastry lightly against the bottom and sides of the dish; leave the edges overhanging the rim.

❋ In a mixing bowl whisk together the eggs, olive oil, granulated sugar and cheese until well mixed. Add the pine nuts, raisins and any remaining liquid, apples, zest and chard. Grind over some pepper, scrape over some nutmeg and mix thoroughly. Empty the mixture into the pastry-lined plate, and smooth the surface.

❋ Roll out the remaining pastry and transfer it to the top of the pie. Trim the edges to overhang the rim of the dish by about ½ in (12 mm), then pinch the top and bottom layer together and roll them up onto the edge of the dish to form a rim. Crimp with a floured thumb or the back of the tines of a fork. Using the tips of pointed scissors held at an angle, snip the pastry's surface 4 or 5 times to create steam vents.

❋ Place in the oven and bake for 40 minutes, checking the color after 30 minutes. If very light, turn the oven up to 400°F (200°C) for the last 10 minutes.

❋ Remove from the oven and sprinkle generously with confectioners' sugar. Serve tepid, preferably, or at room temperature.

SERVES 6

SABAYON AU MUSCAT DE BEAUMES-DE-VENISE

Sabayon with Muscat de Beaumes-de-Venise

Nice claims sabayon *as its heritage from Piedmont. Made with* Muscat de Beaumes-de-Venise, *it belongs to the Vaucluse.*

½ cup (4 oz/125 g) sugar
4 egg yolks
¾ cup (6 fl oz/180 ml) Muscat de Beaumes-de-Venise

◙ Choose a small, heavy saucepan in which to make the *sabayon*. Place a tripod in a larger saucepan, pose the smaller pan on the tripod and pour water into the larger pan until the smaller pan is immersed by half. Remove the smaller pan and bring the water to a near boil. Adjust the heat to low. In the smaller pan whisk together the sugar and egg yolks until creamy. Whisk in the wine and set the saucepan on the tripod in the hot water. Whisk until the *sabayon* is thick, foamy and has more than doubled in volume, about 10 minutes. Raise the heat somewhat, if necessary, remembering that the water should not boil.

◙ Serve either directly from the saucepan or pour into small, individual serving dishes or sherbet glasses and cover and chill before serving.

SERVES 4   *Photograph pages 224–225*

TARTE DE POTIRON

Provençal Pumpkin Pie

In Provençal cuisine, squash is usually reserved for soups or savory gratins. This sweet tart is probably a fairly recent addition to the Provençal repertory, for there is no sign of it in cookbooks of the last century. Pumpkins and Hubbard squashes are generally larger than what is needed for this recipe; they are, however, sometimes sold by the piece in markets.

½ recipe crumbly pastry (recipe on page 225)
¼ cup (2 oz/60 g) plus pinch of unsalted butter
1½ lb (750 g) pumpkin or Hubbard squash, cut into pieces, seeds and fibers discarded, peeled and diced
2 tablespoons all-purpose (plain) flour
3 eggs
1 tablespoon orange blossom water
3 tablespoons dark rum
1 teaspoon grated lemon zest
1 teaspoon grated orange zest
½ cup (4 oz/125 g) granulated sugar
handful of toasted almonds, coarsely chopped
confectioners' (icing) sugar

◙ Make the pastry and chill for 2 hours.

◙ Melt the ¼ cup (2 oz/60 g) butter in a large, heavy sauté pan over very low heat. Add the squash, cover and cook, stirring often with a wooden spoon, until the pieces are falling into a purée, 40–45 minutes. Uncover and cook, stirring, for a few minutes longer to permit excess humidity to evaporate. Sprinkle with the flour and stir in well. Remove from the heat and let cool.

◙ Preheat an oven to 350°F (180°C). Use the pinch of butter to grease a 10-inch (25-cm) pie plate. On a lightly floured work surface, roll out the pastry dough into a round about ⅛ in (3 mm) thick. Drape the pastry round around the rolling pin and transfer it to the pie plate. Press the pastry lightly against the bottom and sides of the plate, then trim and crimp the edges.

◙ In a mixing bowl whisk together the eggs, orange blossom water, rum, grated zests and granulated sugar. Whisk in the pumpkin and stir in the almonds. Pour into the pastry-lined plate and smooth the surface.

◙ Place in the oven and bake until a toothpick inserted in the middle comes out dry, 45–50 minutes. Remove from the oven and sprinkle with confectioners' sugar. Serve tepid, preferably, or at room temperature.

SERVES 6   *Photograph pages 224–225*

NAVETTES DE LA CHANDELEUR

Marseilles Candlemas Cookies

These cookies (biscuits) are also called navettes de Saint-Victor *because they are traditionally sold in the square in front of the church of Saint-Victor in Marseilles on Candlemas day.*

1 teaspoon active dry yeast
2 tablespoons lukewarm water
about 4 cups (1 lb/500 g) all-purpose (plain) flour
pinch of salt
¼ cup (2 oz/60 g) unsalted butter, at room temperature
1 cup (8 oz/250 g) sugar
2 whole eggs
3 tablespoons orange blossom water
grated zest of 1 lemon
1 teaspoon olive oil
1 egg yolk beaten with 1 tablespoon water

◙ In a small bowl dissolve the yeast in the lukewarm water and let stand until creamy, about 10 minutes.

◙ Meanwhile, in a large mixing bowl stir together 3 cups (12 oz/375 g) of the flour and the salt. Make a well in the center. In another bowl mash together the butter and sugar until soft and crumbly. Beat in the whole eggs, dissolved yeast, orange blossom water and grated zest. Empty the egg mixture into the flour well and stir with a fork, working from the center outward to gather in all the flour progressively. Sprinkle over more of the flour as needed to create a firm but supple dough. Knead the dough in the bowl, using your knuckles and sprinkling over a little more of the flour as needed to reduce stickiness. When the dough is smooth and no longer sticky, form it into a ball in the bowl, cover with a towel and leave to rest in a warm place for at least 30 minutes or for up to 1 hour.

◙ Rub a large baking sheet with the olive oil. Turn the dough out onto a floured work surface and cut it into 3 equal portions. Using your hands, roll each portion into a log about 1 in (2.5 cm) thick. Cut each log crosswise into pieces about 2½–3 in (6–7.5 cm) long. You should have about 30 pieces in all. Roll each piece between your palms, tapering the ends, into a boat shape. Place the boats on the baking sheet, spacing them about 1½ in (4 cm) apart. Cover with a towel and leave in a warm place for 2 hours. They will rise somewhat in this time but will not have doubled.

◙ Meanwhile, preheat an oven to 375°F (190°C). Using a razor blade, make a slit the length of each boat and about one-third its depth. Using a pastry brush, paint the surface of each boat with the yolk-water mixture.

◙ Place in the oven and bake until light brown, about 25 minutes. Remove to a wire rack to cool.

MAKES ABOUT 30 COOKIES

Marseilles Candlemas Cookies

VAR

CLAFOUTIS
Cherry Pudding

Culinary historians will tell you that clafoutis *belongs to the Limousin. As far as the natives of the Gapeau river valley are concerned,* clafoutis *belongs to them. Until a few years ago, and for as long as anyone can remember, the Gapeau valley was famous for producing the first cherries in France. The whole-sale distribution center was Solliès-Pont. On the first of April, the entire valley lay beneath a blanket of white cherry blossoms, and, a month later, the small, black, sweet* cerises de Solliès *appeared in markets all over Europe. Today, the cherry orchards have been replaced by housing developments and prefabricated villas.*

2 tablespoons unsalted butter
1 lb (500 g) small black cherries, stemmed but not pitted
½ cup (4 oz/125 g) plus 2 tablespoons granulated sugar
4 eggs
small pinch of salt
½ cup (2 oz/60 g) all-purpose (plain) flour
1 cup (8 fl oz/250 ml) milk
¼ cup (2 fl oz/60 ml) kirsch
confectioners' (icing) sugar

▣ Preheat an oven to 400°F (200°C). Grease a shallow 10-in (25-cm) porcelain or earthenware oven dish with ¼ in (3 cm) sides with 1 tablespoon of the butter.

▣ Spread the cherries in a tight layer in the bottom of the dish. In a mixing bowl whisk together the ½ cup (4 oz/125 g) granulated sugar, the eggs and salt until well blended. Sift in the flour, stirring at the same time with the whisk. Whisk in the milk and kirsch. Pour the mixture over the cherries. Cut the remaining

1 tablespoon butter into shavings and scatter over the surface. Sprinkle with 2 tablespoons confectioners' sugar.

▣ Place in the oven and bake until the surface is golden, about 25 minutes. Remove from the oven and immediately sprinkle with additional confectioners' sugar. Serve lukewarm.

SERVES 6

VAR

FIGUES AU VIN ROUGE
Dried Figs in Thyme and Red Wine Syrup

This unusual melding of flavors recalls all the scents of the Provençal garrigue.

1 lb (500 g) dried figs
2 fresh thyme sprigs, tied in a piece of cheesecloth (muslin)
¼ cup (3 oz/90 g) honey
red wine as needed

▣ Put the figs in a saucepan and embed the cheesecloth package in their midst. Dribble the honey over the top and pour in red wine to cover generously. Bring to a boil, reduce the heat to low, cover and simmer for 1 hour.

▣ Using a slotted spoon, remove the figs to a serving dish. Discard the thyme package.

▣ Boil the liquid gently until reduced by half and syrupy, about 20 minutes. Pour the syrup over the figs.

▣ Serve tepid or cover tightly and chill before serving.

SERVES 4

Cherry Pudding

Dried Figs in Thyme and Red Wine Syrup in the kitchen of Domaine Tempier

Apple Tart

PROVENCE

TARTE AUX POMMES
Apple Tart

Provençal fruit tarts are always of an exemplary simplicity. Their goodness depends upon the quality of the fruit and the quality of the pastry. The subtle flavor of the honey produced around the lavender fields of the northern Var lends an attractive nuance to this tart.

½ recipe crumbly pastry (recipe on page 225)
pinch of unsalted butter
1 lb (500 g) Russet, pippin or Golden Delicious apples
½ cup (4 oz/125g) sugar
about ¼ cup (3 oz/90 g) Provençal lavender honey if available, or thyme or rosemary honey

▣ Make the pastry and chill for 2 hours.
▣ Preheat an oven to 350°F (180°C). Use the butter to grease a baking sheet. On a lightly floured work surface, roll out the pastry into a round about ⅛ in (3 mm) thick. Drape it around the rolling pin and transfer it to the prepared baking sheet. Roll up and crimp the edges to shape a free-form circular tart shell with a rim ⅛–¼ in (3–6 mm) high. Using a floured thumb or the back of the tines of a fork, to form an attractive rim.
▣ Split the apples lengthwise and cut out the cores. Peel the halves, then cut each half crosswise into slices about ⅛ in (3 mm) thick. Arrange the slices, starting just inside the pastry rim, in concentric circles with both the slices overlapping and the circles overlapping. Sprinkle with the sugar.
▣ Place in the oven and bake until both the pastry and the apples are beautifully golden, 50–60 minutes.
▣ Meanwhile, put the honey in a small bowl and immerse the base of the bowl in hot water for a couple of minutes to render the honey more fluid.
▣ Remove the tart from the oven. Using a pastry brush, paint the apples immediately with honey. Slip the tart onto a platter and serve warm.

SERVES 6

PROVENCE

TARTE AUX ABRICOTS
Apricot Tart

Apricots are one of the most important fruit crops of Provence. Small apricots with deep orange flesh and a distinct red blush on the skins are usually the most intensely flavored.

pinch of unsalted butter
½ recipe crumbly pastry (recipe on page 225)
1 lb (500 g) apricots, split in half and pitted
6 tablespoons (3 oz/90 g) sugar
6 tablespoons (4 oz/125 g) puréed apricot jam

▣ Preheat an oven to 375°F (190°C). Use the butter to grease a baking sheet.
▣ On a lightly floured work surface, roll out the pastry into a rectangle about ⅛ in (3 mm) thick. Drape it around the rolling pin and transfer it to the prepared baking sheet. Roll up and crimp the edges, to shape a free-form rectangular tart shell with a rim ⅛–¼ in (3–6 mm) high. Using a floured thumb or the back of the tines of a fork, form an attractive rim. Starting just inside the pastry rim, arrange the apricot halves, close together and skin sides down. Sprinkle with the sugar.
▣ Place in the oven and bake until both the pastry and the apricots are golden, about 40 minutes.
▣ Remove the tart from the oven and let stand for 15 minutes. In a pan, heat the apricot jam over low heat. Spoon the apricot jam thinly and evenly over the surface of the apricots. Serve the tart tepid or at room temperature.

SERVES 6   *Photograph pages 218–219*

VAUCLUSE

PÊCHES AU MUSCAT DE BEAUMES-DE-VENISE

Peaches in Muscat de Beaumes-de-Venise

The village of Beaumes-de-Venise lies in the heart of the Comtat Venaissin, papal territory until the Revolution and a stone's throw from the vines of Châteauneuf-du-Pape. In recent years the fame of its liquorous amber wine, which owes its intense, exotic perfume to the Muscat grape, has spread around the world.

1½ lb (750 g) ripe yellow peaches, peeled and sliced
¼ cup (2 oz/60 g) sugar
1 cup (8 fl oz/250 ml) Muscat de Beaumes-de-Venise

◉ Put the sliced peaches into a deep serving dish. Crystal is attractive for throwing into relief the warm colors of the peaches and the wine. Sprinkle with the sugar and pour over the wine over the top. Cover tightly with plastic wrap and chill well before serving.

SERVES 4

PROVENCE

COMPOTE D'ABRICOTS

Apricot Compote

The kernels of the apricot pits lend a delicate bitter almond flavor. Accompanied with a creamy custard, this is a sumptuous dessert.

1½ lb (750 g) ripe but firm apricots
1 cup (8 fl oz/250 ml) water
1 tablespoon fresh lemon juice
1 cup (8 oz/250 g) sugar

◉ Halve the apricots. Crack half the pits with a nutcracker or a hammer and tie them up in a piece of cheesecloth (muslin).
◉ Combine the water and lemon juice in a saucepan. Stir in the sugar and leave to melt. Bring to a boil, reduce the heat and simmer until the liquid is clear, 2–3 minutes. Add the apricot halves and the package of broken pits and return to a boil. Remove from the heat and leave to cool.
◉ Using a slotted spoon, remove the apricot halves to a serving dish. Discard the pits. Boil the liquid gently until reduced by half and syrupy, about 15 minutes. Pour the syrup over the apricots.
◉ Leave to cool, cover tightly with plastic wrap and chill before serving.

SERVES 4

PROVENCE

FIGUES AU FOUR

Baked Fresh Figs

Deep red–fleshed September figs are best for this dish. They should be picked at the moment cracks begin to appear on the skins.

1 lb (500 g) ripe figs
2 tablespoons green Chartreuse liqueur
¼ cup (3 oz/90 g) Provençal lavender honey, if available, or thyme or rosemary honey

◉ Preheat an oven to 450°F (230°C). Cut the figs in half lengthwise and arrange the halves closely in a gratin dish. Sprinkle the surfaces with the Chartreuse and dribble the honey over the top.
◉ Bake for about 7 minutes. Serve hot from the oven.

SERVES 4

In l'Isle-sur-la-Sorgue, clockwise from top: Peaches in Muscat de Beaumes-de-Venise, Baked Fresh Figs, Apricot Compote

POMPE DE NOËL

Sweet Christmas Bread

An alternative name for this bread is gibassier, *which is derived from the Provençal word* gibo, *meaning "bump." It refers to the bumps created by the slashes on the bread's surface. It is also known as* pompe à l'huile *because of the use of olive oil in the dough. In the Alpes-Maritimes,* pompes *are replaced by* fougassettes de Grasse, *smaller, oval breads made from a similar dough to which a pinch of saffron is often added.* Pompes de Noël *are traditionally broken and shared at the table.*

FOR THE SPONGE:

2 teaspoons active dry yeast
1 cup (8 fl oz/250 ml) lukewarm water
1 cup (4 oz/125 g) bread flour
about 4 cups (1 lb/500 g) bread flour

salt
6 tablespoons (3 oz/90 g) sugar
1 tablespoon grated orange zest
2 tablespoons orange blossom water
½ cup (4 fl oz/125 ml) olive oil

▨ To make the sponge, in a large bowl stir together the yeast and lukewarm water. Whisk in the flour to create an easily pourable batter. Cover the bowl tightly with plastic wrap and leave at room temperature for 24 hours.

▨ Put 3 cups (12 oz/375 g) of the flour into a large mixing bowl. Make a well in the center and add the salt, sugar, orange zest, orange blossom water, olive oil and the sponge. Stir with a fork, working from the center outward, until all the flour is incorporated. Thickly flour a work surface with the remaining flour. Turn the dough out onto the work surface and knead until elastic and no longer sticky, adding additional flour, a little at a time, if dough remains sticky. Form it into a ball, return to the mixing bowl, cover with a towel and let stand in a warm place until the dough has approximately doubled in volume, about 2 hours.

▨ Return the dough to the floured surface and punch it down. Knead hardly at all to avoid its becoming elastic and unworkable. Divide the dough into 3 equal portions. Flatten each portion as much as possible with the palm of your hand, turning it over repeatedly on the floured surface. Using a rolling pin, roll out each portion into a near round about ½ in (12 mm) thick.

▨ Transfer the dough rounds to 1 or more baking sheets. Using a razor blade, cut a circle about ¼ in (6 mm) deep (about half the thickness of the round) and ⅔ in (1.5 cm) in from the edge of the round. Then cut a checkerboard pattern within the circle, forming 1 in (2.5 cm) squares and again cutting about ¼ in (6 mm) deep. Cover with a towel and leave to rise in a warm place for 1 hour.

▨ Meanwhile, preheat an oven to 400°F (200°C). Place the loaves in the oven and bake until brown and crusty, 20–25 minutes. Remove to wire racks to cool.

MAKES 3 LOAVES 12 IN (30 CM) IN DIAMETER

TIAN DE PAIN AUX PÊCHES

Peach and Bread Pudding

Provence produces vast quantities of both white and yellow peaches. They are very different in flavor and texture, but either lends itself well to this preparation. If the peaches resist peeling, drop them into boiling water and drain immediately; the skins will then slip off effortlessly.

½ cup (4 oz/125 g) unsalted butter
¼ lb (4 oz/125 g) semidry bread, sliced and torn into pieces
handful of raisins, soaked in ½ cup (4 fl oz/125 ml) marc de Provence (see glossary) or Cognac for several hours or overnight
1½ lb (750 g) ripe peaches, peeled and sliced
3 eggs
½ cup (4 oz/125 g) sugar
3 cups (24 fl oz/750 ml) milk

Sweet Christmas Bread

◙ Preheat an oven to 350°F (180°C). Butter a 6-cup (48-fl oz/ 1.5-l) gratin dish.

◙ Melt ¼ cup (2 oz/60 g) of the butter in a sauté pan over low heat. Add the pieces of bread and cook gently, turning them around and over and adding more butter as necessary, until crisp and golden on all sides, 10–15 minutes.

◙ Empty the bread into the gratin dish. Drain the raisins, reserving the brandy, and scatter the raisins over the bread. Add the peaches and move them around to disperse the peaches, raisins and bread evenly.

◙ In a mixing bowl whisk together the eggs and sugar. Whisk in the milk and the reserved brandy. Pour the mixture evenly over the contents of the gratin dish.

◙ Place in the oven and bake until the custard is set and the surface is lightly colored, about 40 minutes. Serve warm or at room temperature.

SERVES 4 *Photograph pages 218–219*

POIRES AU VIN ROUGE

Pears in Red Wine Syrup

Peeled yellow peaches are also very good prepared this way, and a stunning sight if left whole and unpitted. Count half the cooking time.

6 slightly underripe Bartlett (Williams) pears, halved
    lengthwise, cored and peeled
strip of dried orange peel
piece of cinnamon stick
½ cup (4 oz/125 g) sugar
3 cups (24 fl oz/750 ml) red wine

◙ Arrange the pear halves in a large enameled ironware or stainless-steel pan. Tuck in the orange peel and cinnamon stick and sprinkle the sugar over the top. Pour in wine to cover and bring to a boil. Reduce the heat, cover and simmer for 1 hour.

◙ Using a perforated skimming spoon, remove the pear halves to a serving dish. Discard the orange peel and cinnamon. Boil the liquid gently until reduced by two thirds and syrupy, about 20 minutes. Pour the syrup over the pears.

◙ Leave to cool, cover tightly with plastic wrap and chill before serving.

SERVES 4

MACÉDOINE AU VIN DE BANDOL

Macédoine of Fruits in Bandol Wine

In late spring and early summer, this is a popular dessert on Provençal tables. If you prefer, the raspberries can be sieved and poured over the other fruits before adding the wine. The shells of green almonds are still unformed and can be removed by cutting into them with a knife. The skins are a tender white parchment that easily peel off. If green almonds are unavailable, a few slivered almonds can be scattered over the fruits, but not to the same effect.

½ lb (250 g) cherries, stemmed but not pitted
½ lb (250 g) small strawberries, stemmed
½ lb (250 g) raspberries
2 yellow or white ripe peaches, peeled and sliced
2 firm, ripe Bartlett (Williams) pears, quartered lengthwise,
    cored, peeled and cut into cubes
about ½ cup (3½ oz/100 g) sugar
about 30 green almonds, peeled
2 cups (16 fl oz/500 ml) young, deeply colored, tannic red
    wine

◙ Assemble all the fruits in a glass serving bowl. Sprinkle with the sugar and toss them gently together with splayed fingers. Leave to steep for 30 minutes.

◙ Toss in the almonds and pour the wine over the top. Cover tightly with plastic wrap and refrigerate for 2–3 hours before serving.

SERVES 6   *Photograph page 10*

Pears in Red Wine Syrup in a Vaucluse garden

CRÊPES

Crêpes are a favorite dessert in Provence. They are made in pans the size of dinner plates and receive no complicated treatments. A choice of jams (cherry and apricot are favorites), sugar, and, often, a bottle of génépi, a strong herbal liqueur, are placed at table. Each person flavors the crêpes to taste, spreading them with jam or sprinkling with sugar or génépi, or both, before rolling them up.

½ cup (2 oz/60 g) all-purpose (plain) flour
pinch of salt
4 eggs
1½ cups (12 fl oz/375 ml) milk
3 tablespoons unsalted butter
2 tablespoons marc de Provence (see glossary) or Cognac

▨ In a mixing bowl stir together the flour and the salt. Make a well in the center and add the eggs to the well. Whisk, working gradually from the center of the bowl outward, to incorporate the flour until no lumps remain. If the mixture begins to become pasty, add a little milk as you whisk. Slowly whisk in the milk, continuing to whisk until the batter is the consistency of light (single) cream. If the batter is not absolutely smooth, pass it through a sieve into another bowl. Melt the butter in a crêpe pan. A pan 9-in (23-cm) in diameter is traditional but any size will do. Pour the butter into the batter along with the brandy. Stir to mix.

▨ Using a cloth or a paper towel, wipe the crêpe pan to leave only a film of butter. Heat the pan over medium heat, then adjust the heat to medium-low. Give the batter a stir with a small ladle, lift the crêpe pan and pour in just enough batter to coat the bottom and edges of the pan, rotating the pan at the same time. The batter should sizzle on contact. Return the pan to the heat. When the surface of the crêpe is nearly dry and the edges turn golden and curl away from the pan (after 1–2 minutes), slip a round-tipped knife blade beneath the crêpe and flip it over. Or, using your fingertips, pick it up by the loosened edge and turn it over. A few seconds later, slip it onto a heated plate.

▨ Remove the pan from the heat for 2–3 seconds before adding batter for the succeeding crêpe. Give the batter a brief stir with the ladle each time before pouring. Do not butter the pan; the butter contained in the batter is sufficient lubrication. Stack the crêpes as they come out of the pan and serve while still warm.

SERVES 4

CRÈME AU CITRON

Creamy Lemon Custard

This custard is often flavored with orange blossom water, or locust (acacia) blossoms are infused in the hot milk. Lovely alone or as an accompaniment to fruits in red wine syrup, stewed apricots, and the like.

½ cup (4 oz/125 g) sugar
1 teaspoon cornstarch (corn flour)
6 egg yolks
3 thin strips lemon zest
2 cups (16 fl oz/500 ml) milk

▨ Prepare a large bowl of crushed ice, or of ice cubes with some water added. In a mixing bowl stir together the sugar and cornstarch. Place the egg yolks in another bowl.

▨ Fill a saucepan with cold water and empty it. Then add the lemon zest and milk to the pan, bring to a boil and remove from the heat.

▨ Add the egg yolks to the sugar mixture and whisk until pale yellow and the mixture falls in a lazy ribbon from the whisk, about 10 minutes. Remove the lemon zests from the milk and pour the milk slowly into the egg yolk mixture, whisking constantly at the same time.

Crêpes

■ Pour the egg-milk mixture into a heavy saucepan over low heat. Stir with a wooden spoon in a figure-eight pattern, reaching all corners, until the custard thickly coats the spoon but well before there is any suggestion of a boil. This should take about 15 minutes.

■ Remove from the heat, embed the saucepan in the bowl of ice and continue stirring until cooled. Pour the custard into 4 shallow bowls and chill before serving.

SERVES 4

Photograph page 10

POMMES AU MUSCAT DE BEAUMES-DE-VENISE

Apples Baked with Muscat de Beaumes-de-Venise

In Provence Russet apples (reinettes) are used for baking. Golden Delicious do not have as fine a flavor, but they share with Russets the virtue of holding together well during cooking.

¼ cup (2 oz/60 g) unsalted butter, at room temperature
⅓ cup (3 oz/90 g) plus 3 tablespoons sugar
1 teaspoon grated orange zest
4 large baking apples such as Russets, pippin or
    Golden Delicious
juice of ½ lemon
pinch of powdered saffron
½ cup (4 fl oz/125 ml) Muscat de Beaumes-de-Venise

◉ Preheat an oven to 325°F (165°C).
◉ Cream together the butter, ⅓ cup (3 oz/90 g) sugar and the zest. Core the apples, either with an apple corer or with a small, sharp-pointed paring knife, removing a ¾-in (2-cm) cylinder from stem end to flower end. Peel the top third of each apple and dip the peeled surfaces in lemon juice.
◉ Stuff the empty cylinders with the creamed mixture, spreading some on the peeled surfaces as well. Not all of it may be used at this point. Stand the apples up, side by side, in a porcelain or earthenware oven dish of a size to just hold them. Sprinkle a little saffron over the peeled surfaces and pour the wine into the bottom of the dish.
◉ Place in the oven and bake until tender when pierced, about 45 minutes, basting several times with the juices. As the filling empties out from the apples, add any leftover creamed mixture to the holes.

◉ Sprinkle the surfaces of the apples with 3 tablespoons sugar, raise the oven temperature to 450°F (230°C) and watch them closely. As soon as the sugar caramelizes, remove from the oven. Serve hot, tepid or at room temperature.

SERVES 4

GLACE AU MIEL

Honey Ice Cream

Honey lends a soft, seductive allure to ice cream, which may surprise those accustomed to sweetening with sugar.

2 cups (16 fl oz/500 ml) milk
5 egg yolks
½ cup (5 oz/155 g) herb honey such as lavender, thyme
    or rosemary
small pinch of salt
1 cup (8 fl oz/250 ml) heavy whipping (double) cream

◉ Prepare a large bowl of crushed ice, or ice cubes with some water added. Pour the milk into a saucepan and bring to a boil.
◉ Meanwhile, in a mixing bowl whisk together the egg yolks, honey and salt until the color lightens. Slowly pour in the hot milk, whisking constantly. Pour the mixture into a saucepan over low heat. Stir with a wooden spoon until the custard lightly coats the spoon, about 10 minutes.
◉ Remove from the heat, embed the saucepan in the bowl of ice and continue stirring until completely cooled. Stir in the cream and pass through a fine-mesh sieve into a bowl. Pour the custard into an ice cream freezer and freeze according to the manufacturer's instructions.

MAKES 1 QT (1 L); SERVES 4

Honey Ice Cream

Apples Baked with Muscat de Beaumes-de-Venise in
the kitchen of Château d'Ansouis

GLOSSARY

THE PROVENÇAL KITCHEN

Primordial to the Provençal kitchen is a marble mortar and a wooden pestle. The mortar should hold a minimum of four to five cups (32–48 fl oz/1–1.25 l) liquid; small apothecaries' mortars will not do. Ritual in the kitchen is as important to the cook as ritual at table is to the guests. Close to the heart of the Provençal cook is the simple gesture of smacking a garlic clove with the heel of one's hand, removing the loosened hull from the ruptured clove and, with abandon, tossing the garlic into a mortar. There it is pounded with a pinch of coarse sea salt, whose roughness helps reduce the garlic and salt, together, to a silken, liquid paste that no garlic press can approximate. A food processor can successfully replace a mortar and pestle in many instances, but an *aïoli* or a *pistou* made in a food processor is cottony and dry; the voluptuous texture and the fruit of the olive oil are destroyed.

The taste of Provence can never be complete without a bed of incandescent wood embers over which to grill foods. Even the *croûtes à l'ail*—slices of semidry bread, grilled, rubbed with garlic and dribbled with olive oil— so often served as an appetizer, along with olives and slices of raw-cured sausage *(saucisson sec),* are magical only when enhanced by the smoky caress of dying embers. A Provençal kitchen includes a table-height fireplace with a work-surface ledge in front. An outdoor barbecue for use in good weather is a welcome accessory, but a bonfire reduced to embers can serve as well. Heavy, welded cast-iron grills, preheated over the coals, are used for grilling meats, poultry and vegetables. Double-faced, heavy wire grills on legs, which can be turned over or upright, are used for fish whose fragile flesh easily sticks and tears if turned on a cast-iron grill; different sizes and forms exist, with swelled faces approximating the shape of sea bass or porgies (breams) and large, flat, double-faced grills designed to contain a dozen or two small fish—sardines or red mullets—that can be turned over with a single flip.

Much of the food of Provence is cooked in earthenware, which absorbs heat slowly and evenly and holds it for long; it also absorbs and holds flavors, which can subtly improve a dish on condition that its vessel always be used for similar types of preparations. The *poêlon,* an earthenware casserole shaped like a flattened sphere with a hollow handle, is constantly used (recipes begin, "Pour a *rasade* ["a large swallow"] of olive oil into a *poêlon,* smash a couple of cloves of garlic and throw them in . . ."). Gratins are prepared in a *tian,* a large, shallow earthenware dish, and boiled meats and poultry in a *pot-au-feu,* a large pot with bulging sides. Long-cooking stews go into a *daubière,* a potbellied vessel with a reduced evaporation surface; a daube prepared in anything else never tastes as good as a daube simmered for hours in a *daubière* in which, over the years, hundreds of daubes have simmered for thousands of hours. As in any kitchen, heavy sauce and sauté pans and good knives are essential. For chopping, the Provençal home cook uses a half-moon cutter, or *demi-lune,* the handle of which is held by both hands in order to rock the blade back and forth; the professional cook uses knives.

AÏOLI

The Provençaux often speak of *aïoli,* or garlic mayonnaise, as their "national" dish. The Marseillais believe that an *aïoli* should contain at least two cloves of garlic per person. In addition to the array of boiled and baked vegetables, poached salt cod and other preparations that compose the entire meal called *aïoli,* the mayonnaise is often served with room temperature or barely warm meats (roast leg of lamb or chicken, in particular), individual boiled vegetables, octopus stews and the like.

If possible, the garlic cloves should be fresh and crisp with no sign of a sprout or germ. If a tiny green sprout is visible, remove it from the heart of the clove before adding the clove to the mortar. The eggs and the olive oil should both be at room temperature and it is important always to add the oil—at first in a tiny trickle and then in a greater stream— interrupting the flow from time to time while continuing to turn the pestle. It is said the pestle should always be turned in the same direction (to know if this is true, one would have to break the rule, which makes no sense since it is easier to turn the pestle always in the same direction). If one person pours while another turns the pestle, the task is simplified.

To prepare *aïoli* for 6 persons, place a large pinch of coarse sea salt and 6–12 (fewer or more, to taste) firm, crisp garlic cloves in the mortar and pound to a paste. Add a large pinch (5 fingers) of fresh bread crumbs (without crusts, prepared in a blender or a processor) and pound and turn to a consistent paste. Then work in 2 egg yolks. Turn the mixture with the pestle for a minute or so before beginning to add 2 cups (16 fl oz/ 500 ml) olive oil. Pour it in at a slight trickle to the side of the mortar so that it is gradually incorporated into the mass by the movement of the pestle. As the sauce begins to thicken noticeably, the oil may be poured in a steadier flow, still to the side of the mortar. It should not become too stiff; after about half the oil has been added, add the juice of ½ lemon or 1 teaspoon water, continuing to turn the pestle. Keep adding oil and, if necessary, a bit of water until you have the desired quantity of sauce. You can add more or less oil.

To prepare a saffron *aïoli,* put a pinch of saffron threads into a small bowl, pour over 1 tablespoon boiling water, leave to cool and wipe out the bowl with the bread crumbs before adding them to the mortar.

To prepare a cold Provençal sauce *(sauce provençale froide),* rinse and fillet a couple of salt anchovies (q. v.)

and pound them to a paste with the garlic before adding the bread.

There is no reason for an *aïoli* to break up if it is prepared carefully; if the oil is too cool or added too rapidly this may happen. Pour the broken sauce into a bowl, clean out the mortar and start again with another egg yolk, adding the broken sauce slowly, a teaspoon at a time, to the side of the mortar, turning the pestle constantly.

ANCHOVIES see *salt anchovies.*

ARTICHOKES

An artichoke is a thistle-flower bud. It must be eaten at an undeveloped stage for, when it opens out into flower, it is the "choke" that becomes the purple blossom. Provençal recipes for artichokes are always for "young, tender artichokes," and the Provençal ideal is a violet artichoke the size of an egg in which the choke has not yet developed. The size of an artichoke, however, is not necessarily an indication of its age. The best artichokes are those that develop first at the summit of a stalk; if the whole length of the stalk is not cut, smaller artichokes of inferior quality spring from the lower leaf joints. Round globe artichokes, which in Provence are known as Brittany artichokes and which when mature are the size of a grapefruit, are wonderful if picked when the size of an orange, the choke still undeveloped. A young artichoke always has a stem that is thick in relation to the size of the artichoke itself (in Provence, the stems are peeled and cooked with the artichokes), and its contour, from the base of the leaves to their tips, describes a clean curve. Narrow, fibrous stems and an indented profile above the base are signs of advanced age.

The cut surfaces of artichokes discolor in contact with air and carbon steel. Keep at hand a bowl containing the juice of a lemon and use stainless-steel knives. Cut off the stem and remove the tough outer leaves, curving each backward and downward until it snaps free from the tender flesh at its base. Cut off the top third of the leaves of a young artichoke or about the top half from a fully developed artichoke. Hold the artichoke upside down and pare off the dark green surfaces, turning the artichoke in a spiraling fashion while keeping the knife more or less stationary. Turn it over and pare off the extremities of the outer leaves. Turn it around in the lemon juice and leave it in the bowl while preparing the others. Larger artichokes are often quartered for a stew or for deep-frying; the choke is then sliced free and the cut surface immediately rubbed with lemon. If the artichoke is to be sliced, it is first cut in half lengthwise, the choke cut out and the cut surface rubbed with lemon before each half is sliced and the slices tossed in the lemon juice.

BEEF MARROW

Beef marrow is taken from the thigh bone, or marrow bone, of beef. Ask your butcher to saw off the joint ends and to saw the bone into one- to two-inch (2.5–5-cm) lengths to facilitate prying the marrow out with a knife tip. Incorporated into stuffings, it lends a silken, velvety texture.

BOUQUET GARNI

A bouquet garni is a neatly tied bundle of herbs which, without disintegrating into the dish, imparts all of its flavors and is, at the same time, easily removed after cooking. The usual elements are thyme sprigs, bay leaf, parsley stems or, preferably, parsley root, and celery. Winter savory or dried orange peel is often included. For a large bouquet, a four- to five-inch (10–12-cm) section of leek green can be taken apart and reformed to enclose the package, sheathlike, before it is tied up, winding the string several times around and tying tightly.

BROUSSE

Except that this cheese is always made from sheep's milk, *brousse* is the same as Italian ricotta. Ricotta can always be substituted in recipes calling for *brousse.*

CAUL

In cooking, caul means pork caul. It is a fragile, transparent membrane, threaded with a pattern of veins of fat, that envelopes the intestines. Used as a protective and decorative covering for roasted or grilled meats, caul nourishes as the fat melts and is transformed into a golden brown, lacelike web.

COCOS

Cocos are fresh white shell beans. The beans are plump, almost round and, when cooked the texture is velvet smooth. Their green pods, or "shells," turn pale yellow when they mature. They appear on the Provençal market in July and persist until early November. Other fresh shell beans can be substituted. All shell beans are better fresh than dried—and more easily digested.

DEEP-FRYING

Olive oil cannot support the same high temperatures peanut or corn oil can, and, when used for deep-frying, it degrades rapidly; it is best reserved for shallow frying and used only once. For deep-frying, any relatively large kettle or saucepan will do. It should be tall enough so that it need not be more than half filled with oil and so that you can easily immerse the elements to be fried. If you are using a deep-fat fryer, the basket should be removed before frying batter-dipped foods. The most practical device for removing batter-dipped foods is a large, shallow wire spoon called a spider; next best is a shallow, slotted skimming spoon. Have ready a thick layer of newspapers with paper towels laid on top for draining the fried articles as they are removed from the oil. Also, preheat an oven to its lowest setting and have at hand a platter topped with a folded napkin in which the drained fried things will be placed and held in the warm oven while further batches are being cooked. Except in rare instances, 375°F (190°C) is, by common consensus, the correct frying temperature—the temperature is correct when a leaf of parsley crackles or a drop of batter sizzles at contact with the oil.

GAME BIRDS

In Provence hunters like to eat partridge *au bout du fusil,* that is, plucked, gutted and roasted the moment it is shot. As a general rule, game birds improve after hanging in their feathers for three or four days, either in a refrigerated room or, in winter, in an unheated room. They must be young to be tender; old birds are only good for braising. Supple beaks and breastbones, a pointed rather than rounded tip to the longest wing feather and delicate, thinly scaled feet are indications of youth.

Except for wild duck, game birds are barded for roasting by tying a thin sheet of pork back fat over the breast. They are roasted at high heat and kept underdone to be succulent. Those who complain that pheasant meat is dry and tasteless have always eaten it too fresh and overdone. A pheasant is roasted at 450°F (230°C) for 25 minutes; after 20 minutes, the bard is removed, the trussing strings clipped and the legs partially disjointed and opened out. Partridge and grouse are roasted for 18 minutes at the same temperature, and quail for 12 to 15 minutes.

Woodcock is not gutted, for the trail is clean; only the gizzard, because of its gravel sack, is not eaten. It is a self-trussing bird: After being plucked to the head, the skin is torn free of the neck and peeled from the head, taking the eyes with it. The heel joints of the legs are dislocated and crossed and locked yogalike. The head is drawn down to the side of the body and the drumsticks and body are transpierced by the long, needlelike beak near the thigh joint. The woodcock is barded and roasted for 15 minutes.

Because a duck's legs are so tightly wedged into the back of the body and because the breast meat of wild duck is best quite rare, the legs are still bloody when the breast is correctly cooked. After roasting, the legs of a wild duck are removed and grilled until the skin is crisp and the flesh no longer rare. The breast is carved thinly, served first, and the legs are served as a separate course, accompanied with a green salad. Count 15 to 20 minutes at 450°F (230°C) for mallard and 12 to 15 minutes for teal.

GREEN SHALLOTS see *shallots.*

HERBS

WILD: Provençal cooks divide the herb world into two categories, wild and cultivated. First, the wild herbs.

BAY (*laurier-sauce*) trees are, of course, planted, but they also reseed themselves and grow wild. Bay leaves are frequently used alone, to the exclusion of other herbs. Whereas recipes from other regions may call for a fraction of a bay leaf, Provençal recipes often call for two or three leaves. A bay leaf is always present in a bouquet garni. The fresh leaves are sometimes cut in two and strung on skewers between pieces of meat for grilling.

WILD FENNEL (*fenouil*) has a much stronger anise flavor than cultivated bulb fennel. It grows abundantly along roadsides or on other uncultivated lands, the stalks reaching a height of a yard and a half (1.5 m) or more before coming into flower in late summer. After the flowers have gone to seed, the stalks are cut and broken or bent to form bundles that are tied and used throughout the winter to flavor innumerable fish preparations. Fish merchants always keep a supply of dried fennel on hand and automatically stuff a bouquet into the body and head cavity of any large fish prepared for grilling or baking. In early spring the tender shoots and feathery leaves can be chopped and incorporated into a fish stuffing, and throughout the summer the green stalks and leaves are used to line fish grills or gratin dishes in which fish are to be baked.

WILD LAVENDER (*aspic*) is commonplace. A certain amount is often included in commercial mixtures of Provençal herbs (q. v.) destined for tourists; the flavor is too exotic for the Provençal palate.

OREGANO (*origan, marjolaine*), or wild marjoram, is known simply as *marjolaine*. It comes into flower in July when it is picked, tied into bundles and hung to dry; its perfume is improved by drying. Oregano enters into herb mixtures, but is so rarely used alone in traditional Provençal cuisine that it is commonly identified as "the pizza herb."

ROSEMARY (*romarin*) often grows so thickly as to form patches of tall, nearly impenetrable brush on the hillsides. It is a popular hedge in Provence, where it flowers year-round except for the hottest part of summer. In the Provençal air the scent is ravishing, but in cuisine it is overwhelming and hardly ever used. Rosemary thrown onto embers just before removing meats or poultry from the grill will flavor delicately and, if the rosemary is fresh, will not flame up.

THYME (*thym, farigoule, farigoulette*) covers the hillsides with its violet flowers in April, the best time to pick it for drying. For use in bouquets garnis, it is picked fresh as needed.

WINTER SAVORY (*sarriette de montagne, poivre d'âne, pebre d'ase, pebre d'aï*) flowers in July and August for picking and drying. The Provençaux have a special affection for savory, which nearly everyone knows as *pebre d'aï* ("garlic pepper"), a deformation of its real name, *pebre d'ase* or *poivre d'âne* ("ass's pepper"). Fresh sprigs of savory garnish the little Banon goat cheeses from the Alpes-de-Haute-Provence; tender early spring leaves are judged to be an indispensable presence with broad (fava) beans, and sprigs of savory often replace or accompany thyme in a bouquet garni.

CULTIVATED:

BASIL *(basilic)* comes in many forms—tiny leaf, large leaf, very large waffly leaf, purple flat leaf, purple frilly leaf. The purple basils are beautiful additions to salads. The large-leaf Italian basil has the most characteristic flavor and is the best for a *pistou.* In much of Provence, basil is used almost exclusively for *soupe au pistou;* Niçoise cooking finds other uses for it. It is good to have 8 or 10 plants in a kitchen garden. The budding flowers are as valuable as the leaves, but a basil plant should not be permitted to go to seed or it will die; when the budding flowers are too plentiful to be used, they should be pinched off and discarded.

CELERY, GARDEN *(céleri du potager)* is grown in all kitchen gardens. Its flavor is similar to but stronger than that of stalk celery; a single small branch with its leaf attached is all that is necessary for a bouquet garni. Those who have no kitchen garden ask their greengrocer for a stalk of celery; a bunch is always kept to the side, from which stalks are broken off to be offered to clients.

CHERVIL *(cerfeuil)* is always present in the salad mixture, *mesclun.* Its delicate, slight anise flavor is easily lost in most Provençal seasoning, however, and it is also difficult to grow in the meridional climate and soil.

CHIVES *(ciboulette)* are sometimes used in salads, but green (spring) onions and young green shallots (q. v.) are much more often used in the same way.

HYSSOP *(hysope)* is not widely used. The finely chopped leaves and the exquisite blue flowers have a slightly bitter, refreshing taste that can enhance many a salad.

LOVAGE *(livèche, ache de montagne)* is closely related to the celeries and its flavor is the same, but wilder. It can replace celery in a bouquet.

For certain Provençal preparations, a strip of DRIED ORANGE PEEL is required. Because most oranges now are treated to prevent their spoiling, rub them well under cold running water before removing the peel strip. Dry well in a towel and peel as thinly as possible to avoid taking any of the white, spongy part with the zest. Using a trussing needle—or darning needle—and some kitchen string, pass the peel strips onto the string and tie the two ends at two points to suspend the peels in the air without touching. A few days later, unstring them and store them for future use.

FLAT-LEAFED (ITALIAN) PARSLEY *(persil commun),* among the most common cultivated herbs, is the only parsley seen in the gardens and markets of Provence. Its flavor, on condition that it be freshly picked, is much finer than that of curly parsley (although the latter may be substituted if the flat-leaf variety cannot be found). Parsley is a biennial, but because it bolts and goes to seed in its second year, it must be planted every year.

It grows easily from seed if the seeds are first soaked in water overnight, well drained and mixed with dry sand to facilitate the planting. Bolted plants should not be torn up and discarded. The plant remains alive for the remainder of the season, and the root, pulled up when needed, scraped and washed, is a precious addition to a bouquet garni, replacing advantageously the parsley stems usually called for.

SAGE *(sauge)* is rustic and perennial; the long, flowering stems should be cut back after flowering. A sprig of fresh sage is usually an element in a garlic broth *(aïgo bouido)* and fresh leaves are tucked into slits in a pork roast or simply stuck to the surface of pork chops to be grilled.

SWEET MARJORAM *(marjolaine cultivée)* flowers throughout spring, summer and autumn; with mild winters, it is a perennial. The buds, before they break into flower, have the most delicate, sweetest flavor; finely chopped, along with the tender leaves closest to the buds, they do something very nice to eggs, either simply scrambled or in an omelet, alone or with zucchini (courgettes), onions or artichokes; marjoram and garlic do nothing for each other. The flower bud stems should be picked regularly to encourage others to grow; tie them in bundles and dry them—marjoram is a valuable element in a dried herb mixture.

TARRAGON *(estragon)* is used occasionally by a Niçois cook. Except for the other fines herbes—parsley, chervil and chives—it does not mix well with other herbs.

LARDOONS
Commonly cut from slices of lean salt pork (q. v.) or pork back fat, usually measuring ⅓–½ in (8–12 mm) wide, cut from pork slices of an equal thickness.

LENTILLES VERTES
These lentils, also known as *lentilles du Puy* for the city most famous for their production, are a small (less than half the size of the common blond or beige lentil) and a dark speckled brownish green. They hold their shape in cooking and their flavor is the finest of all lentils.

MARC DE PROVENCE
Marc is brandy made by distilling the grape pulp after the grapes have been pressed and the wine drawn off. Marc de Provence is usually aged in oak barrels for two or three years before being put into bottles.

MIREPOIX
A *mirepoix* is an aromatic base for many braised meat, fish or vegetable preparations. To prepare, warm 1 tablespoon olive oil in a saucepan over very low heat. Add 2 carrots, peeled and finely chopped; 1 large onion, finely chopped; 1 small celery stalk, finely chopped; pinch of Provençal mixed dried herbs and salt to taste. Cover and sweat, stirring occasionally, for 30 minutes.

MUSHROOMS see *wild mushrooms.*

MUSSELS
A simple bistro version of mussels *à la marinière*— mussels opened over heat with aromatics and white

wine—is used to prepare mussels for any number of dishes. They are also delicious served as they are: both the mussels in their shells and their liquid ladled into soup plates (in this case add 1 tablespoon unsalted butter and a generous grinding of pepper to the pan before placing it over the heat). To prepare, fill a large bowl or other vessel with cold water and add a handful of salt and the mussels. Let stand for 30 minutes. Discard any mussels with broken shells. Scrub, scrape or rub against the surfaces of the other mussels to remove loose adherences; barnacles, however, are harmless. Pull out the "beard," which is lodged near the hinge of the bivalve, and then press each mussel between a thumb and forefinger, to make certain it is alive. The resistance will be noticeable. Rinse well and place the mussels in a large, two-handled stew pot with a tight-fitting lid. Add 3 cloves garlic, crushed; 1 small onion, finely chopped; 1 bay leaf; 2 or 3 fresh thyme sprigs; 2 tablespoons chopped fresh flat-leaf (Italian) parsley; and ½ cup (4 fl oz/125 ml) dry white wine. Cover and place over high heat. As the wine approaches a boil (after 1 minute or less), begin shaking the pan, holding the lid and handles firmly together with a folded towel or kitchen gloves. After 2–3 minutes, remove the lid; if most of the mussels are gaping, remove the pot from the heat; if not, replace the lid and shake over high heat for a few seconds or as much as 1 minute longer. Pour the contents into a colander placed in a large bowl. Line a sieve with a dampened cloth or several layers of dampened cheesecloth (muslin) and filter the liquid through the sieve into another bowl. Remove the mussels from their shells, collecting them in a small bowl. Any mussels that are closed tightly should be discarded. Any mussels that are open only a crack can be opened fully by slipping a knife blade between the shells until it touches the muscle; these are often the fleshiest and juiciest mussels. Discard the shells and aromatic debris in the colander.

OLIVE OIL

The best olive oils are called "extra-virgin, first cold-pressing." The quality of a Provençal table depends very much upon the quality of the olive oil. Wine merchants often make a point of keeping superior olive oils in stock. The new year begins with wonderfully fruity, still cloudy new oil and it is first tasted poured over hot slices of semidry bread grilled over wood coals. It is also especially admired poured abundantly over hot chick-peas, seasoned at table with freshly ground pepper, vinegar, chopped shallots, garlic and parsley.

OLIVES

Dishes of olives are always present at the beginning of a Provençal midday meal. Black olives are puréed for the multipurpose *tapénade* (recipe on page 34), and olives, both black and green, garnish many a salad and sauce. By mid-October, the green olives are full size; they ripen irregularly on a single tree and from one tree and one variety to another. By mid-December, most are black. Black olives can be picked well into January.

The first home olive preparation of the season is called *olives cassées* ("broken olives") or, more correctly but more rarely, *olives écachées* ("crushed olives"): Between mid-October and mid-November, the green olives are picked, each is tapped lightly with a wooden mallet to break the skin and they are soaked in a large basin of water, changed at least once daily, for 9 or 10 days before being put into a stoneware jar and covered with an aromatic brine. To judge the necessary quantity of brine, drain off the olives' soaking water, put them into the stoneware jar and add enough water to immerse them generously. Put this quantity of water into a saucepan, add one tenth of its weight in coarse sea salt (⅓ cup/3 oz/100 g per 4 cups/32 fl oz/1 l) and, to each quart (l), a couple of segments of dried fennel stalk (or a large pinch of fennel seeds), a strip of dried orange peel, a large pinch of coriander seeds, and a couple of bay leaves. Bring to a boil, boil for 5 minutes, leave to cool and pour the cold brine through a sieve over the drained olives. Cover the jar with a plate. *Olives noires en saumur,* which are more often a mixture of green, half-ripened violet and black olives, are pricked with pins that have been pushed through a slice of cork, soaked in water for 10 days like the *olives cassées,* drained and put into the same cold brine. Both are ready to eat 5 or 6 days later and will keep well for a couple of months.

The traditional method of preparing *olives à la picholine* (and they certainly taste the best) is first to soak freshly picked green olives in a thick, but pourable paste of wood ashes for 5 or 6 days or until the bright green color turns olive green and, when cutting into one, the flesh of the olive can be felt to separate more easily from the pit. Hardwood ashes are the best (olive wood is wonderful); they burn more completely to a fine white ash, which should be passed through a sieve before being mixed with water. While soaking, the ashes slowly settle to the bottom of the basin and the olives settle in the water to the top; ashes and olives should be stirred gently together with a wooden spoon a couple of times daily. When they are removed from the paste of ashes, the olives should be thoroughly rinsed in several waters and put to soak in a basin of water like the others, with regular changes, for 9 or 10 days, after which they are put into exactly the same brine. They are less bitter and will hold longer than the others.

Best of all are the completely ripened, very black olives picked, preferably, after the first freeze. They will have lost much of their bitterness while ripening and are simply layered in a jar, heavily salted, tossed, drained and resalted daily for 5 or 6 days, then drained and transferred to a wicker basket placed on a platter, resalted and tossed several times daily until no more liquid drains from them—8 or 9 days in all, often less. Black olives that have begun to wither on the tree often drain hardly at all. If visible salt clings to the olives' surfaces, they can be briefly rinsed and well drained; if not, put them directly into an earthenware or stoneware container with a few bay leaves, a couple of sprigs of thyme, grind over pepper generously and pour over enough olive oil to keep them well coated, turning them around at least daily. Begin eating them 3 or 4 days later. Some varieties are sweeter or fleshier or have thinner skins than others; the preferred variety in the region of Toulon for this treatment is called, locally, *caillon* or *caillonne*. Note that, despite the abundance of salt with which they have been treated, black olives prepared in this way are never salty; the salt all runs off with the liquid it has drawn from the olives.

PARSLEY, GARLIC AND PERSILLADE

For information on parsley, see *herbs*. To chop parsley without making a mess, the leaves must be absolutely dry. To easily control the chopping, the leaves should remain attached to the stems. A parsley branch forks into three leaf stems of which the central stem is the longest: pinch off the central stem from each branch and form a tight bouquet at the base of the leaves, fold the outer leaves under, fixing the mass tightly against the chopping board with fingertips and slice the parsley into fine threads. Discard the stems (or save them for a bouquet garni) and chop through the threads if you want a finer cut.

To peel garlic without crushing it when whole cloves or fine slices are required, cut off the root-end tip, place the flat side of a large knife blade, sharp edge directed away from you, on the clove of garlic and tap it firmly but gently with the heel of your hand. The skin will be ruptured and will lift off easily; unless the tap carried too much force, the clove will remain intact. Cloves to be crushed, chopped or pounded can be smacked more vigorously, simply with the heel of your hand or using a knife blade. *Persillade*—flat-leaf (Italian) parsley and garlic, first chopped separately and, then, together—is a recurrent theme in Provençal cooking. Practically anything *"sauté à la provençale"* is first sautéed in olive oil, then sautéed for a minute or so with a *persillade* and, usually, finished with a few drops of lemon juice. The garlic for a persillade should be chopped very finely: First slice it paper-thin, then chop it repeatedly, gathering it together in a mound with the knife blade and chopping through it again before assembling it with the parsley and rechopping. A normal portion of *persillade* is 2 tablespoons of finely chopped flat-leaf (Italian) parsley chopped with 1 clove of finely chopped garlic.

PROVENÇAL HERB VINEGAR see *vinegar*.

PROVENÇAL MIXED DRIED HERBS

Commercial mixtures of dried Provençal herbs usually contain too many herbs, including rosemary, lavender and sage, and usually smell musty. If you are able to collect your own herbs and dry them, a good mixture is composed of thyme, oregano, savory and marjoram, in descending proportions. When the bundles are dry, store them in paper bags, stapled or covered over with other paper bags to protect them from dust without enclosing them in an airtight atmosphere, until autumn when all of the herbs have been picked and dried. Crumble the bunches between gloved hands, whirl the crumbles, small batches at a

time, in a food processor, pass the processed herbs through a sieve with the help of a gloved hand, put them into jars and store them. A wonderful seasoning for stuffings, marinades, sausage meat and pâtés, grilled meats and poultry, or to replace a bouquet garni if you are in a hurry or have no fresh herbs at hand.

SAFFRON

Saffron, the condiment, is the dried stigma—a mara thread—of the autumn-blooming purple saffron crocus. The stigmas of well over five thousand blossoms are said to be necessary to produce one ounce (30 g) of saffron. Its luminous color and captivating scent and taste are essential to many Provençal preparations. It is expensive, but a little goes a long way.

SALT ANCHOVIES

These prepared anchovies are a cornerstone of Provençal cuisine. They cannot be replaced by canned anchovies in oil, which have a harsh flavor and are always too salty. Freshly netted anchovies appear in abundance on the market in May, when they rise by the millions from the depths of the sea to the surface to spawn, and recur at intervals throughout the summer. To preserve them in salt, first spread a layer of coarse sea salt on a large tray. Split the abdomen of each anchovy with your finger or the tip of a small knife, then pinch off the head at the back and pull it forward, drawing out the guts at the same time. Discard the heads and guts. Layer the anchovies on the salt and sprinkle another layer of salt over them; leave them for 3 or 4 hours, then remove them to paper towels to sponge them dry. If you like, you can sprinkle them lightly with Provençal mixed dried herbs (q. v.) before beginning to pack them, in alternate layers, with coarse salt into a stoneware or wide-mouthed glass jar. Begin and end with a layer of salt. The layers of salt should be quite thick, about ½ in (12 mm), and the single layers of anchovies should be very closely packed in, side by side, head to tail, and curved to marry the inside surface of the jar. Place a weight made of nonreactive material—a water-filled, flat-bottomed bottle, for instance, whose circumference is slightly smaller than that of the jar—on the salt surface and keep in a cool place for several days. The salt will draw more liquid from the anchovies and partially dissolve to create a brine. Remove the weight and carefully skim off any traces of oil floating on the surface of the brine, then cover the jar and store in a cool place.

To prepare salt anchovies for use, they may or may not have to be soaked for some time to desalt them, depending upon the length of time they have been salted down. Anchovies that have been in salt for no more than a few months need only be carefully rinsed. Gently rub them under cold running water to remove clinging salt crystals and any remaining scales. Pry the fillets free from the spinal structure with fingertips; remove traces of fin bones from the edges, rinse again and lay out on paper towels with other towels pressed atop to sponge the fillets dry. The longer the anchovies remain in salt, the firmer, drier and saltier their flesh becomes. Those that have been in salt for a couple of years or more may have to be soaked in a bowl of cold water for a quarter of an hour, not only to desalt them partially, but also to render the flesh pliable enough to fillet them neatly. After being cleaned up and rinsed, they may need to be soaked again to get rid of salt—a taste will tell. Anchovies used during the first year after salting are the best. Salt anchovies are commonly available at Italian grocers and in fancy food shops. The recipes in this book simply specify "salt anchovies, rinsed and filleted;" the above message should alert you as to whether they must be soaked before and after. A recipe that calls for "2 salt anchovies, rinsed and filleted" means 4 fillets.

SALT COD

Called *morue* in French, fresh cod is roughly filleted, the spinal bone removed before and then the fillets are salted. Normally, if soaked for 24 hours, salt cod is ready to use. Depending upon its origin and the length of time it has been in salt, this can vary 12 to 36 hours. Check with your merchant about soaking time when buying salt cod. The best cod comes from the thickest part of the tail section, neither the abdomen nor the end of the tail. Cut it into sections and put it to soak in a colander immersed in a large basin of cold water, changing the water several times over the period of soaking; it will have whitened and doubled in bulk when it is ready to be cooked.

To poach soaked salt cod, put it into a large pan with a bay leaf and a sprig of fresh thyme, cover it abundantly with cold water, bring to a boil, cover the pan tightly and remove from the heat. Leave it in its poaching liquid for 10 minutes, or more if the piece or pieces are more than one inch (2.5 cm) thick.

SALT PORK

Called green bacon in Britain, salt pork is lean bacon that has been salted but not smoked.

SAUSAGE MEAT

Simply seasoned sausage meat is an important ingredient in pâtés, terrines and meat stuffings. Many commercial sausage meats contain more fat and filler than meat. To make your own basic sausage meat,

select 2 pounds (1 kg) pork without bones with a ratio of about two parts lean meat to one part fat. A side, belly, shoulder or blade cut is appropriate. Cut the pork into large sections and sprinkle on all sides with coarse salt. Place them in a nonmetallic container (tray or large gratin dish), cover with plastic wrap and let stand overnight. Discard the liquid, rinse the pieces well, drain them and dry in a cloth towel or with paper towels. Cut them up and pass them through the medium blade of a meat grinder into a bowl. Season generously with pepper, a few grains of freshly pounded or ground allspice and a hint of freshly scraped nutmeg. Sprinkle Provençal mixed dried herbs (q. v.) and ¼ cup (2 fl oz/60 ml) dry white wine over the top and mix thoroughly with your hands. Fry a small lump in a few drops of olive oil and salt to taste.

SHALLOTS

Milder in taste than the onion, shallots are members of the same family. The two most common types of shallot are pink and gray and they are usually about the size of a walnut. Young green shallots resemble green (spring) onions, except that the thin bulbs, which grow in clusters, are each covered with a brown husk. When the root tip is cut off and the husk removed, the white flesh and green leaves look very much like green onions. The flavor of green shallots is more complex and more intense but, if unavailable, green onions can be substituted.

SORREL

A green, leafy plant, sorrel has a distinctive acidity and flavor popular as a seasoning for Provençal dishes. It is easy to grow, perennial and should be picked regularly to encourage the formation of young leaves. Old leaves are dark in color and have an acrid taste; they should be rapidly parboiled and drained before use. Young leaves are a light, tender green and may be used raw, with discretion, in salads.

SPINACH AND SWISS CHARD (SILVERBEET)

Spinach or chard are first parboiled, refreshed, squeezed and chopped before adding to any number of Provençal stuffings, gratins or omelets. Except for the small tender leaves at the heart of the plant, spinach should be stemmed: with the stem pulled backward, fold the surface of the leaf upon itself, tearing out the central vein. Spinach needs abundant washing, usually at least three waters, before it is completely rid of clinging soil. After each washing, the leaves should be lifted loosely from the water to a colander, leaving the soil behind in the basin.

The variety of chard most common in the markets has large leaves, often 20 inches (50 cm) from stem end to tip and 10 inches (25 cm) wide, with fleshy white ribs that can be 3 in (7.5 cm) wide at the base. Each leaf is laid flat on a chopping board and the rib is cut away from the green parts before they are washed separately. The ribs are peeled, cut into sections, parboiled and treated like cardoon; only the green parts are treated like spinach. Small-leaf chard is stemmed in the same way as spinach.

To parboil spinach or chard, pack the leaves into a large saucepan, add a handful of coarse salt, place the saucepan over high heat and pour over boiling water (slowly, with the spout of the tea kettle close to the surface of the leaves, to avoid splashing) to cover. Using a wooden spoon immerse the leaves repeatedly in the water as it returns to a boil. Turn them around a couple of times in the boiling water and then pour into a colander. Run cold water over to cool, gather the leaves together in both hands and squeeze them several times, firmly, between cupped hands to form a well-drained, compact mass. To chop, place the ball on a chopping board, flatten it slightly, slice it thinly, give the mass a quarter of a turn and slice through it again.

SQUID

Available in various sizes, squid appear in a number of Provençal dishes, including stuffed with a variety of savory mixtures. To clean a squid, pull the head and clinging innards free from the body pouch. Pull out and discard the transparent quill-like cartilage from the pouch. Squeeze out the small beak from the mouth at the base of the tentacles and, using scissors, cut away the eyes. Using your fingers, clean out the pouch under cold running water. Discard everything except the tentacle-head portions and the body pouches with their attached wings. If you prefer, rub or peel off the brownish violet skin; it is harmless. Rinse all the squid parts well. Split the heads and tentacles into two parts. Cut the pouches as directed in individual recipes.

TOMATOES

Full-flavored, garden-ripe tomatoes are available in Provence from July through September. The rest of the year peeled canned tomatoes from Italy are the best choice. To peel fresh tomatoes, core them, removing a small cone from the stem end of each and, using a sharp knife tip, slit the skin in the form of a cross at the flower end. Slip the tomatoes, a few at a time into a large saucepan of boiling water and remove them immediately. Grasp each skin tip at the cross between thumb and knife blade and pull the skins toward the stem end. To seed them, cut each tomato in half horizontally, to expose cross sections of the seed packets. Loosen the seeds in each packet with your little finger and give the tomato half a good shake. To coarsely chop a tomato, place the halves, cut side down, on a chopping board, slice through each two or three times, give it a quarter turn and slice again to produce large dice.

TOMATO SAUCE (COULIS)

In culinary language, *coulis* means purée. A century ago, it meant a reduced meat sauce base. In America it is often believed to indicate specifically a purée of raspberries or other fruit. In Provence a *coulis* is a purée of tomatoes. Wonderful tomato sauce can be made from fresh tomatoes, garden ripened, only during the summer. Unless you put up your own tomatoes, peeled and chopped, canned plum (Roma) tomatoes from Italy *(polpa di pomodoro)* are the best out-of-season substitute. There is no need to peel fresh tomatoes since the peels will be left behind when the sauce is puréed. The reason for seeding them is to get rid of excess liquid and to shorten the cooking-reduction process; a fresh flavor depends on the sauce being reduced to the right consistency as rapidly as possible. The size of the pan is important; the larger the evaporation surface, the more rapid the reduction. The following proportions will produce 3–4 cups (24–32 fl oz/750 ml–1 l) of sauce.

Warm 3 tablespoons olive oil in a large, heavy saucepan or sauté pan. Add 1 onion, chopped, and cook over low heat until softened but not colored, about 10 minutes. Add 4–5 lb (2 kg) tomatoes, seeded and coarsely chopped; 3 garlic cloves, crushed; 1 bay leaf; 1 parsley root or a tied bundle of parsley stems; and salt to taste. Turn up the heat and stir and crush the tomatoes regularly with a wooden spoon until they are bathed in their liquid and beginning to boil. Reduce the heat to maintain a very light boil, cover with a lid ajar, and cook for about 40 minutes. Discard the bay leaf and parsley root or stems and pass the sauce through a food mill or through a sieve, pressing with a wooden pestle. If the sauce seems too thin, return it to its pan and reduce for a few minutes over medium heat, stirring all the while.

In small quantities, good tomato sauces can be made very rapidly and they are often the best: Join 2 or 3 tomatoes, cut up; 1 small onion, chopped; 1 clove garlic, crushed; 1 bay leaf; large pinch of salt; and 1 tablespoon water in a saucepan. Place over high heat, crush, stir and boil until reduced, about 15 minutes, then purée the sauce. Alternatively, in a large frying pan, heat 2 tablespoons olive oil and 1 clove garlic, crushed, over high heat. Before the garlic begins to brown, add 2 or 3 tomatoes, peeled, seeded and coarsely chopped; add salt and pepper to taste and sauté, tossing the tomatoes repeatedly in the air, for 3–4 minutes. Scatter over fresh basil leaves, torn into fragments, toss once or twice more and remove from heat. Do not purée.

For another simple yet excellent sauce, cut 2 or 3 tomatoes in half lengthwise. Cut a V at the stem end of each half to remove the core, place each half, cut side down, on a chopping board and slice very thinly (⅛ in/3 mm). Give the tomato half a quarter turn and slice thinly through the slices. In a large frying pan, heat 1 small onion, chopped, and 1 clove garlic, crushed, in 2 tablespoons olive oil over high heat. Before the onion and garlic begin to brown, add the tomatoes, pinch of Provençal mixed dried herbs and salt and pepper to taste and sauté over high heat, shaking the pan and tossing repeatedly, for a few minutes, or until the sauce has lost its liquid. The presence of tomato peel when the tomato is finely cut up is not troublesome.

TRUFFLES

The white Piedmont truffle doesn't exist in France. Black truffles, sometimes called *truffes du Périgord* (after the most important truffle-producing center in France), are seen in season from late November until late February. January and February truffles are usually the ripest and richest in flavor. The upper Vaucluse and the upper

Var are also known for their fine black truffles. Like mushrooms, truffles are parasitic fungus growths. They grow underground, usually near oak or hazelnut roots, and are searched out with trained dogs or pigs. Their penetrating, unique scent and flavor are the passion of all who taste them. Fresh truffles are flown to America. They are always expensive. If you can only find preserved truffles, purchase those sterilized with very little liquid, usually a bit of Cognac or Madeira, in glass jars. Truffles immersed in the water in which they have been boiled and packed in cans have very little flavor.

VINEGAR

The acetic bacteria that transform wine into vinegar are aerobic; they can live and propagate only in the presence of oxygen. They form a white veil, or flower, on the surface of the wine over which air should circulate freely, but which should never be disturbed for, if immersed, the bacteria are drowned and fall, inert, to the bottom of the wine vessel, or *vinaigrier*. A four-quart (4-l) ceramic or stoneware vinaigrier, with a hole at the base into which is fitted a cork-tipped wooden spigot, will provide enough vinegar for most kitchens. A bottle of good, unpasteurized wine vinegar should be poured in as a starter; then fill the *vinaigrier* three-quarters full with red wine, loosely cover and leave for several months at room temperature. It is a mistake to draw off small quantities of vinegar and to add wine frequently. Bottle ends of decanted or leftover wines and wine left in glasses at table should be saved in filled and corked bottles until the *vinaigrier* is partially emptied. It can then be refilled to the three-quarters mark by pouring in the wine through a long-necked funnel with the tip immersed in the remaining vinegar so as not to disturb the flower surface. The vinegar that has been drawn off can be turned into Provençal herb vinegar by macerating it for a month in a covered large stoneware jar containing bundles of thyme, oregano, winter savory and marjoram; a sprig each of rosemary and sage; several bay leaves and a few crushed, unpeeled cloves of garlic. Then strain it through a cheesecloth- (muslin-) lined funnel into bottles, cork them and lay them down. The vinegar will improve with bottle age.

A more serious *vinaigrier* can be fashioned from a small four-gallon (16-l) wine keg, first fitted with a wooden spigot and filled with water to soak for two or three days. When emptied, bore a hole for air circulation just beneath the top of the keg, diametrically opposite the spigot, and tack a piece of plastic screen over to keep out fruit flies. After filling the keg with starter and wine to the level of the air hole, cork the bunghole and keep it corked. Bore a hole in the bunghole cork and permanently fit it with a long-necked funnel that reaches to just below the spigot level. Except when filling the keg, keep the funnel covered with plastic wrap. This quantity of vinegar is best left undisturbed for some eight months before being drawn off to the spigot level. The loss by evaporation is quite dramatic; 14 three-cup (750-ml) wine bottles are required to fill the keg from spigot level to air-hole level and approximately eight bottles

of vinegar will be drawn off. The first batch of vinegar from a new *vinaigrier* is sometimes disappointing but, as the *vinaigrier* is broken in, the vinegar will progressively improve.

WILD MUSHROOMS

The mushroom most commonly encountered in the markets of Provence after the autumn rains (November is the richest month) are the saffron milk cap (*safrané, Lactarious delicious*); two varieties of chanterelle (*griolles, Canthorellus cibarious,* and *chanterelle, Canthorellus infundibuliformis*); the horn of plenty, also known as the trumpet of death (*trompette de la mort, Craterellus cornucopioides*) and the cèpes (*Boletus edulis*). Rare, but perhaps the most exquisite of all, is Caesar's mushroom (*orange, Amanita caesaria*). In May, both light and dark morels (*morille, Morchella*) appear, rarely in sufficient abundance to be seen in the market. There are many other edible mushrooms, but they are left to the collectors who, in theory, are supposed to check with a pharmacist for edibility before taking them home and sautéing them.

Saffron milk caps, chanterelles, horns of plenty and cèpes are usually sautéed in olive oil, seasoned with salt and pepper, finished with a *persillade* and, depending upon a personal taste, with a few drops of lemon juice, or, if the shape lends itself, marinated and grilled. Caesar's mushrooms are best simply anointed with olive oil, seasoned with salt and pepper and grilled. Morels are stewed gently in butter, seasoned and often finished with cream.

WINES OF PROVENCE

The wines and the food of a given region always seem to need each other for both to be thrown into perfect relief. The food of Provence is high-spirited, often with an edge of violence that, however joyous, can offend or destroy a delicate old Burgundy or an aristocratic Bordeaux. The native wines are exalted in its presence; their bouquets reflect the wild herbs and bramble of the hillsides and a rustic, solid structure refuses to be intimidated by the aggression of garlic, saffron or tomato. This is not to suggest that the most serious of Provençal wines will fail to evolve, to gain in complexity and elegance with age. A red Châteauneuf-du-Pape, Palette or Bandol will rise to unsuspected heights after 10, 15 or 20 years of bottle age, as the bouquets of wild herbs and fruits mellow into scents of undergrowth, humus, truffles and small game while retaining a suave fruit.

The best wines of France come from stony, arid soils, too poor to produce any other crop of value. Provence is no exception. In the Vaucluse, between Avignon and Orange, Châteauneuf-du-Pape, the most famous of Provençal wines and the largest single *Appellation d'Origine Contrôlée* (AOC) in France, with some eight thousand acres (3,200 hectares) of vines, produces an average of 13 million bottles of wine per year, nearly all red, about 75 percent of which are exported to all corners of the world. The landscape is unearthly: the vines rise from a sea of smooth, flattened, oval or round riverbed stones, varying in size from that of an egg to that of a human head, deposited there by prehistoric glaciers; no soil is visible. Until recently, red Châteauneuf-du-Pape could be made from any combination of 13 grape varieties, of which several are white. Because of its high sugar content and the intensity of its young fruit, some growers have leaned too heavily on Grenache, often to the exclusion of all the others. Pending legislation will limit the amount of Grenache that may be used and impose minimum percentages of Syrah, the Hermitage grape, and Mourvèdre, the dominant Bandol varietal.

Château de Beaucastel makes it a point of honor to use all 13 varieties. This property also produces an unusual and beautiful white Châteauneuf-du-Pape, principally from the Roussanne grape, which can age gracefully for 20 years or more. White Châteauneuf, steely structured, floral and honeyed, brings a new dimension to the local *caillettes* (pork crepinettes) and accompanies to perfection a *bourride,* a gratin of mussels and spinach or stuffed and braised squid. The black truffles from nearby Valréas and Richerenches are cooked in young red Châteauneuf and washed down with old Châteauneuf. Perhaps more than any other red wine, a Châteauneuf-du-Pape enjoys the assault of a blue cheese and it is an ideal companion to game in any form or to the richly aromatic daubes and *estouffades* of the region.

A neighboring appellation, Gigondas, produces a red wine from the same grape varieties, usually confined to Grenache, Syrah, Mourvèdre, Cinsault and Clairette, which, although similar in spirit, is rougher and more rustic and less apt to age; it is best when drunk at two, three or four years of age. From the same varietals, *Côtes du Rhône* and *Côtes du Rhône-*, hyphenated either with the word *Villages* or with a specific village name such as Cairanne, Valréas and so on—produce red, rosé and white wines of which the reds are usually the more interesting, often very good and reasonably priced. Rasteau produces a sweet apéritif or dessert wine from Grenache grapes, and Beaumes-de-Venise is known for its intensely perfumed, amber, sweet wine made from the Muscat grape, best served with a dessert or used in the confection of a dessert; sliced fresh peaches macerated in Muscat de Beaumes-de-Venise are delicious.

In the Bouches-du-Rhône, a few minutes drive from Aix-en-Provence, the tiny appellation Palette has long been recognized as one of the most distinguished of Provence. Almost the entire appellation is embraced by a single vineyard, Château Simone, whose proprietor, René Rougier, loyally vinifies his wines exactly as his father and grandfather did. The red, made from Cinsault, Grenache and Mourvèdre, is raised for two years in large oak tuns and passes its third year in barrels before being bottled; it profits immensely from being laid down for at least five or six years before being drunk. The rosé, made from the same grapes, is deep colored, the result of the grapes first macerating with the skins before being pressed and fermented, and is more muscular than most rosés; it lives in wood for a year before bottling. Two whites are made, mainly from Clairette; one, meant to be drunk young, is bottled six

months after the harvest to retain its fresh fruit, and the other is raised for two years in barrels, gaining in complexity and resistance to oxidation, and, like the red, it needs bottle age to open out fully. The Clairette, Ugni Blanc and Marsanne vines on the hillsides overlooking the fishing village of Cassis, 14 miles (23 km) east of Marseilles, produce a solid, stony, fruity white wine, the choice of the Marseillais for *bouillabaisse* or, for that matter, anything that comes from the sea. Cassis reds and rosés are less successful. From the Côteaux d'Aix-en-Provence, between Aix and Les Baux-de-Provence, the Domaine de Trévallon, with a microclimate too rude to plant traditional Provençal grape varieties, makes an astonishing red wine, big, rich and complex, from half Syrah and half Cabernet Sauvignon.

In the Var, the star is Bandol, an appellation encompassing eight villages whose hillsides, with the mountains behind, form a natural, protective amphitheater with the fishing village of Bandol at center stage. The grape varieties are Mourvèdre, Cinsault, Grenache, Syrah, Ugni Blanc and Clairette. Some white wine is made from the last two, but for the most part they go into the rosé, a pale, playful, spicy wine bottled in the spring following the harvest. For red Bandol—thanks mostly to the efforts of Lucien Peyraud, proprietor of the Domaine Tempier—legislation now imposes a minimum of 50 percent Mourvèdre, a late-ripening low producer, rich in tannins, intensely colored with exuberant flavors and antioxidant powers that ensure long life. Most bottlings at Domaine Tempier contain 70 to 80 percent Mourvèdre and one, from the old Cabassão vines on the lower half of the hillside rising to the village of Le Castellet, is 100 percent Mourvèdre and of a supreme elegance if given the chance to grow up. Red Bandol must pass a minimum of 18 months in wood before bottling; how much more depends on the natural evolution of the wine and on the discretion of the grower. At the apéritif hour, nothing is more at home with a *tapénade,* an *anchoïade* or with raw sea urchins than a Bandol rosé and a cool, young red Bandol served with *bouillabaisse* is a revelation; at 10 or 20 years of age, it will be happier with roasted or braised red meats or with a carefully selected cheese platter.

The Côtes de Provence appellation is scattered across all the Var. The rosé is a famous summer, seaside thirst quencher. Despite the inconsistency of soils and expositions, the rosés and the reds, because of more rigid disciplines than in the past, have greatly improved in recent years; many of the whites are innocuous, lacking in acidity.

Nice is proud of its Bellet, whose production is so limited that it is rarely encountered outside of the Alpes-Maritimes. In combination with traditional Provençal grape varieties, the specifically Niçoise Rolle (white), Folle and Braquet (both red) leave their mark on these light, tender, elegant wines. A *pissaladière* loves Bellet, red, rosé or white, drunk young and cool.

251

ACKNOWLEDGMENTS

Weldon Owen would like to thank the following people and organizations for their assistance in the preparation of this book:

Mme. Marie-Françoise Guichard, Patrick Benhamou, Wendely Harvey, Norman Kolpas, Tori Ritchie, Roger Smoothie, Richard Van Oosterhout, Fee-Ling Tan, Laurie Wertz, Dawn Low, Janique Poncelet, Jim Obata, Tara Brown, Sigrid Chase, Bruce Bailey, Pinnacle Publishing Services, Bob Firken.

The on-location photography team would like to thank the following for their contribution: Richard Olney; Jean Luc Villemot; Dixon Long and Ruthanne Dickerson; M. and Mme. François Peyraud and Mme. Lucie et M. Lucien Peyraud, Domaine Tempier;

Chateau d'Ansouis, residence of the De Sabran Ponteves family, M. Robert and Mme. Noelle Rocchi, Le Caveau de la Tour de L'Isle, L'Isle sur la Sorgue.

The photographer and stylist would like to thank the following for props provided for the studio photography in Sydney: Appley Hoare Antiques, Woollahra; The Bay Tree, Woollahra; Country Floors, Woollahra; Parterre Garden, Woollahra; Studio Haus, Double Bay; Les Olivades, Double Bay; In Residence, Paddington; John Normyle, Paddington; Gregory Ford, Paddington; The Art of Food and Wine, Woollahra; Alison Coates Flowers, Paddington; Country Furniture Antiques, Balmain; Accoutrement, Villeroy & Boch, Brookvale; Hale Imports for Pillivuyt, Brookvale; Sewita Marble, Silverwater.

ILLUSTRATION GUIDE

 This frieze was designed for the doors of the former priory of Notre-Dame-de-Salagon outside of Mane in Alpes-de-Haute-Provence. After falling to ruin when the monks abandoned it during the French Revolution, the church became a barn; its original artwork lay undiscovered for decades behind the bales of straw and farm equipment. Today the site is a center for study and research, with permanent exhibitions covering local history and botanical gardens.

The Aqueduc de Roquefavour in the Bouches-du-Rhône, was constructed from 1842 to 1847 by François 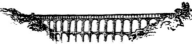 de Montricher to carry the waters of the Durance River to Marseilles. Built of hewn stones, it spans the Valley of the Arc and was designed to replicate the Roman Pont du Gard, an ancient aqueduct in Nîmes that has stood intact for almost two thousand years.

 Much of Provence is characterized by the way in which its *départements* celebrate water, from ancient Roman aqueducts, to innumerable sparkling fountains, recuperative spas and mineral-water baths that inspired the water worship of the early Gauls. Throughout Provence the sounds of trickling water lead to village squares where decoratively carved fountainheads provide a steady stream such as this one in Aspremont, Alpes-Maritimes.

The Carolingian antependium in Limans, Alpes-de-Haute-Provence, is an anonymous work of the early Middle Ages. Its monogram represents a combination of four Greek letters (chi, rho, alpha and omega) that form a cross signifying the beginning and end of all things in God. The letters, however, were used in the wrong order, leading to speculation that the artist did not understand their meaning.

 The famed Arc de Triomphe in Orange, Vaucluse, is the best preserved Roman arch in France. Built circa 20 B.C. to commemorate the campaigns of the II Legion, the monument is comprised of three archways and represents the force of Roman colonization. The decorative friezes and carvings depict Roman victories on land and sea and suggest Rome's triumph over ancient Gaul.

 Carved in the twelfth century, the figures on the doors of Saint-Trophime in Arles, Bouches-du-Rhône, depict Biblical lore and are characteristic of medieval Provençal sculpture. Perhaps the finest Romanesque church in Provence, it was built in dedication to Saint Trophime who was credited with having brought Christianity to France.

 This detail from a sarcophagus in the church of La Gayole in Brignoles, Var, was carved between A.D. 259 and 280 and is thought to be the most ancient funerary masterpiece in France. The stone sarcophagus, an example of early Roman Christian sculpture, was carved in Smyrna (the former name of Izmir, Turkey) and was brought to Brignoles in 1890.

INDEX